Unraveling the Crime-Development Nexus

Unraveling the Crime-Development Nexus

Jarrett Blaustein
Tom Chodor
Nathan W. Pino

ROWMAN & LITTLEFIELD
Lanham • Boulder • New York • London

Published by Rowman & Littlefield
An imprint of The Rowman & Littlefield Publishing Group, Inc.
4501 Forbes Boulevard, Suite 200, Lanham, Maryland 20706
www.rowman.com

86-90 Paul Street, London EC2A 4NE, United Kingdom

Copyright © 2022 by Jarrett Blaustein, Nathan W. Pino, and Tom Chodor

All rights reserved. No part of this book may be reproduced in any form or by any electronic or mechanical means, including information storage and retrieval systems, without written permission from the publisher, except by a reviewer who may quote passages in a review.

British Library Cataloguing in Publication Information Available

Library of Congress Cataloging-in-Publication Data

Names: Blaustein, Jarrett, author. | Chodor, Tom, author. | Pino, Nathan, author.
Title: Unraveling the crime-development nexus / Jarrett Blaustein, Tom Chodor, Nathan W. Pino.
Description: Lanham : Rowman & Littlefield, [2022] | Includes bibliographical references and index. | Summary: "Unraveling the Crime-Development Nexus offers the first criminological account of the relationship between international development, crime and security in nearly thirty-five years"— Provided by publisher.
Identifiers: LCCN 2022001245 (print) | LCCN 2022001246 (ebook) | ISBN 9781786611000 (cloth) | ISBN 9781786611017 (paperback) | ISBN 9781786611024 (epub)
Subjects: LCSH: Crime—Developing countries. | Developing countries—Social conditions. | Economic development.
Classification: LCC HN980 .B65 2022 (print) | LCC HN980 (ebook) | DDC 364.9172/4—dc23/eng/20220118
LC record available at https://lccn.loc.gov/2022001245
LC ebook record available at https://lccn.loc.gov/2022001246

Contents

List of Figures	vii
List of Abbreviations	ix
Acknowledgments	xi
Introduction	1
1 Is Crime a Development Issue?	25
2 Theorizing Global Crime Governance	49
3 Historicizing the Crime-Development Nexus	65
4 Development and Social Defense	83
5 International Crime in the Crisis Decades	105
6 Securing the Global Capitalist Economy	125
7 Reconstructing the Crime-Development Nexus	151
8 Global Crime Governance, Rule of Law, and the Sustainable Development Goals	175
Conclusion: Reimagining the Crime-Development Nexus	197
Notes	211
References	215
Index	245
About the Authors	261

Figures

Figure I.1	Organizational Structure of UNODC	16
Figure 6.1	Mentions of "Corruption" and "Crime" per Page in World Development Reports (1980–2019)	137
Figure 7.1	UNODC Pledges from Donors (1990–2020)	152

Abbreviations

AML	Anti–money laundering
ASEAN	Association of Southeast Asian Nations
CCP	Centre for Crime Prevention (United Nations)
CCPC	Committee on Crime Prevention and Control (United Nations)
CCPCJ	Commission on Crime Prevention and Criminal Justice
CICP	Centre for International Crime Prevention (United Nations)
CND	Commission on Narcotic Drugs (United Nations)
CPCJB	Crime Prevention and Criminal Justice Branch (United Nations)
CPCJS	Crime Prevention and Criminal Justice Section (United Nations)
CPTED	Crime prevention through environmental design
E4J	Education 4 Justice Programme (United Nations Office on Drugs and Crime)
EBRD	European Bank of Reconstruction and Development
ECOSOC	Economic and Social Council of the United Nations
EPTA	Extended Programme for Technical Assistance (United Nations)
EU	European Union
FATF	Financial Action Task Force (United States)
FCPA	Foreign Corrupt Practices Act (United States)
G77	Group of 77 (United Nations)
GBA	Global Business Alliance
GDP	Gross Domestic Product
GFC	Global Financial Crisis
GNP	Gross National Product
IADB	Inter-American Development Bank
ICVS	International Crime and Victim Survey
IFI	International financial institutions

IMF	International Monetary Fund
IPCC	International Penal and Penitentiary Commission
IR	International Relations
MDG	Millennium Development Goal
NGO	Non-governmental organization
NIEO	New International Economic Order
OECD	Organisation for Economic Co-operation and Development
OIOS	Office of Internal Oversight Services (United Nations)
OWG	Open Working Group (United Nations)
RBM	Results-based management
SAP	Structural adjustment programme
SAPRIN	Structural Adjustment Participatory Review International Network
SDG	Sustainable Development Goals
TI	Transparency International
TOCTA	Transnational Organized Crime Threat Assessment (United Nations Office of Drugs and Crime)
TST	Technical Support Team (United Nations)
UK	United Kingdom
UN	United Nations
UNCAC	United Nations Convention Against Corruption
UNDCP	United Nations Drug Control Programme
UNDESA	United Nations Department of Economic and Social Affairs
UNDPI	United Nations Department of Public Information
UNDPKO	United Nations Department of Peacekeeping Operations
UNDG	United Nations Development Group
UNDP	United Nations Development Programme
UNDPA	United Nations Department of Political Affairs
UNGA	United Nations General Assembly
UNIS	United Nations Information Service
UN-ODCCP	United Nations Office on Drug Control and Crime Prevention
UNODC	United Nations Office on Drugs and Crime
UNPBSO	United Nations Peacebuilding Support Office
UNSC	United Nations Security Council
UNSDRI	United Nations Social Defence Research Institute
UNTOC	United Nations Convention Against Transnational Organised Crime
US	United States
USD	United States Dollars
USAID	United States Agency for International Development

Acknowledgments

This book advances ideas developed in a series of papers about the history and architecture of the crime-development nexus. None of these papers are reproduced in this book but they have influenced our analysis and arguments. For example, a paper by Jarrett Blaustein and Nathan Pino (with Graham Ellison) which appeared in the *The Palgrave Handbook of Crime in the Global South* (Blaustein, Pino, & Ellison, 2018) provided a starting point for the narrative review of the criminological literature presented in chapter 1. Chapters 4 and 5 expand upon the historical narrative presented in our recent article in *Criminology & Criminal Justice* (Blaustein, Chodor, & Pino, 2021) and the analysis presented in chapters 7 and 8 builds upon that of our *British Journal of Criminology* article (Blaustein, Chodor, & Pino, 2020). Both papers also informed the development of our theoretical framework however, their focus was limited to constructivist and institutionalist perspectives whereas this book adopts a political economy framework to consider not only "how" crime became a sustainable development issue, but also "why." Some of the arguments presented in the book, specifically that crime should be governed as a *global* problem rather than a "Southern" problem, were developed by two of us in a separate article published in the *British Journal of Criminology* (Blaustein, Pino, Fitz-Gibbon, & White, 2018). We further explored this idea in sections of the *The Emerald Handbook of Crime, Justice and Sustainable Development* (Blaustein, Fitz-Gibbon, Pino, & White, 2020).

We are particularly grateful to current and former members of the United Nations (UN) and the wider international crime policy community who supported this research, particularly those who agreed to be interviewed. Their input was invaluable and their willingness to speak openly with us evidences their commitment to improving the work of the international crime policy community. The data presented in figure 7.1 have been provided by the United

Nations Office for Drugs and Crime (UNODC) and referenced with their permission.

The research for this book would not have been possible without the generous internal funding from the Faculty of Arts at Monash University. It is also unlikely that we ever would have found time to finish the manuscript had we not been permitted to take our sabbaticals at our respective universities due to the pandemic, which has had a significant impact on the higher education sector in both Australia and the United States. We are very fortunate to have been afforded this opportunity and grateful to our colleagues who have been a source of constant support and encouragement during what has at times been a difficult and isolating writing process. Several colleagues around the world have shaped our thinking around the issues presented in this manuscript but we are most directly indebted to Craig Murphy and Clifford Shearing for offering their advice and feedback on various sections of the manuscript. We would also like to thank Ariel Yap for helping us compile and catalogue relevant documents as a research assistant back in 2016.

We are grateful to the publisher, Rowman & Littlefield, for their patience and flexibility, particularly in relation to the word count. It appears that we had a lot more to say about this topic than originally anticipated!

Finally, we would like to thank our partners for their constant support and encouragement. Writing a book is a lonely and miserable process, particularly during a pandemic, so thank you for being there.

Introduction

In September 2015 the United Nations General Assembly (UNGA) adopted the Sustainable Development Goals (SDGs). SDG 16 calls upon members of the international community to "promote peaceful and inclusive societies for sustainable development, provide access to justice for all and build effective, accountable and inclusive institutions at all levels" (UNGA, 2015). Various other targets also touch upon a wide range of criminological problems. Consequently, the assumption that crime is an obstacle to sustainable development has become formally inscribed throughout the work of the UN development system and that of the wider international development community.

It is of course widely accepted that crime threatens the realization of economic and social development outcomes. In local communities around the world, crime and particularly violent crime generate instabilities that disrupt social order, interfere with commerce, and undermine social cohesion. At the national level, organized crime and corruption have also been identified as an obstacle to governance and human security, and thus impede human development and economic growth. Internationally, transnational organized crime and corruption have also gained increased recognition as threats to peace and security. Growing recognition of these problems since the 1990s has therefore prompted the creation of new normative instruments and institutional apparatuses that have been designed to enhance international cooperation and coordination in a global fight against crime (Findlay, 2008). It is also increasingly recognized that the harms arising from various forms of crime and corruption are not simply social or economic, but also environmental (White, 2013). Crime and corruption are therefore recognized as obstacles to *sustainable* development: "development that meets the needs of the present without compromising the ability of future generations to meet their own needs" (Brundtland Commission, 1987).

SDG TARGETS RELATED TO CRIME, JUSTICE, OR SECURITY

SDG 3.4: Strengthen the prevention and treatment of substance abuse, including narcotic drug abuse and harmful use of alcohol.

SDG 5.2: Eliminate all forms of violence against all women and girls in the public and private spheres, including trafficking and sexual and other exploitation.

SDG 5.3: Eliminate all harmful practices, such as child, early, and forced marriage and female genital mutilation.

SDG 8.7: Take immediate and effective measures to eradicate forced labour, end modern slavery and human trafficking, and secure the prohibition and elimination of the worst forms of child labour. [. . .]

SDG 8.8: Protect labour rights and promote safe and secure working environments for all workers, including migrant workers, in particular women migrants, and those in precarious employment.

SDG 10.5: Improve the regulation and monitoring of global financial markets and institutions and strengthen the implementation of such regulations.

SDG 10.7: Facilitate orderly, safe, regular, and responsible migration and mobility of people, including through the implementation of planned and managed migration policies.

SDG 11.4: Strengthen efforts to protect and safeguard the world's cultural and natural heritage.

SDG 11.8: By 2030, provide universal access to safe, inclusive, accessible, green and public spaces, in particular for women and children, older persons, and persons with disabilities

SDG 14.4: By 2020, effectively regulate harvesting and end overfishing; illegal, unreported, and unregulated fishing; and destructive fishing practices. [. . .]

SDG 15.7: Take urgent action to end poaching and trafficking of protected species of flora and fauna and address both demand and supply of illegal wildlife products.

SDG 16.1: Significantly reduce all forms of violence and related death rates everywhere.

SDG 16.2: End abuse, exploitation, trafficking, and all forms of violence against and torture of children.

SDG 16.3: Promote the rule of law at the national and international level and ensure equal access to justice for all.

SDG 16.4: By 2030, significantly reduce illicit financial and arms flows, strengthen the recovery and return of stolen assets and combat all forms of organised crime.

SDG 16.5: Substantially reduce corruption and bribery in all their forms.

SDG 16.6: Develop effective, accountable, and transparent institutions at all levels.

SDG 16.a: Strengthen relevant national institutions, including through international cooperation, for building capacity at all levels, in particular in developing countries, to prevent violence and combat terrorism and crime.

Source: United Nations General Assembly Resolution 70/1

These arguments are well rehearsed and appear outwardly credible, yet they are rarely interrogated. Scholars, international policy makers, and practitioners have therefore largely ignored the ideological, institutional, and material foundations of the *crime-development nexus* as a discursive assemblage that has come to shape both the international crime policy and development agenda. Accordingly, this book sets out to tell the story of how and why crime came to be recognized as a sustainable development issue by locating the historical construction of this idea in a wider analysis of the political economy of global crime and development governance. In adopting this approach, our assumption is that the construction of the crime-development nexus and its institutionalization within the SDG agenda cannot be reduced to the empirical realities of the issue linkage alone because the relationship between these phenomena is complex and historically and contextually contingent. Criminalized harms may therefore be theorized as an obstacle to, consequence of, precondition for, or perhaps even a model of development. And then there is the question, what is "development"?

The sustainable development paradigm conflates different theories and models of capitalist development (Carvalho, 2001), and a useful typology of these influences is provided by Murphy (2006). The ***development as growth*** model associates development with creating conditions that will boost the Gross National Product (GNP). It assumes that what is good for the economy is good for the individual. Economic liberalization and free market capitalism are therefore promoted to stimulate growth. Proponents assert that the expansion of the global economy will benefit wealthy and poorer countries alike, and this has been the preferred approach of the United States since the early decades of the 20th century. Since the 1970s, it has emerged as the dominant paradigm due to the rise and spread of neoliberalism.

The aspiration to promote economic growth is what links the first tradition to the ***development as efficiency*** model. With the latter, technical assistance is used to enable developing countries to build political and economic institutions so they can capitalize on their resources and participate in the international economy. Whereas the growth model theorizes the market as the key determinant of development, the efficiency model advocates development planning. The emphasis here is on transferring knowledge and expertise (but not necessarily resources) from North to South. Historically, this tradition has attracted criticism from dependency theorists, who associate it with neocolonialism.

Finally, the ***development as freedom*** model also advocates planning but seeks to create opportunities for citizens and local stakeholders to shape the development agenda and take ownership of its implementation. This is a progressive model of capitalist development that values human development outcomes—i.e., enhancing the circumstances and capabilities of individuals—over economic growth. This has been the preferred model of the UN Development Programme (UNDP) since the 1960s, and it is probably the most popular approach to promoting and measuring capitalist development today.

All three traditions shape work of the international development community that extends beyond the UN system. Within different institutional settings, they coexist in unique and creative ways. They are negotiated and reproduced through the work of development actors and their financiers, but this does not mean their aspirations and assumptions are necessarily compatible. Nor should it be assumed that "sustainable development" is rooted in a cohesive and coherent set of ideological or intellectual assumptions about what form the global capitalist order should take, or how this might be realized. Development, like crime, is a contested idea with its own politics. The traditions described above have distinct criminological implications, meaning there is little value in attempting to deconstruct and operationalize a concept like "sustainable development" for the purpose of examining its relationship with crime using traditional social scientific methods. The crime-development nexus must therefore be conceptualized and interrogated as a constellation of discourses.

We argue that the crime-development nexus has been shaped by a series of processes and events that can be traced back to the modern development of global capitalism and the establishment of a transnational legal order and institutions of global governance based on European (and later American) norms. This order has historically served to advance and legitimize the interests of Western, and later global, capital. Global governance institutions have in turn played an important role in maintaining this hegemonic order by placating, neutralizing, and, where necessary, pacifying dissidents, detractors, and deviants. Global crime governance has historically evolved as part of this project, albeit a relatively minor one, at least until recently. Accounting for how and why crime and corruption came to be recognized as sustainable development problems is therefore essential for advancing a more theoretically robust understanding of the crime-development nexus as a governmental phenomenon. This is particularly important at a time when inequality is growing, we are making our planet inhospitable for human and other life, and multilateralism and the liberal internationalist project appear to be in a state of crisis (Woods, 2010; Acharya, 2017). In light of these challenges, the conclusions and recommendations we present at the end of this book may appear quite radical, but the clock is ticking.

WHAT IS THE CRIME-DEVELOPMENT NEXUS?

A "nexus" denotes important linkages or connections, real or invented, between two or more issues or problems (Betts & Pilath, 2017). To characterize the relationship between multiple issues as a nexus is to suggest that one cannot be governed independently of the other. A prominent example is the "security-development nexus," which refers to the idea that "[w]ar retards development, but conversely, development retards war" (Collier et al., 2003, p. 1). This implies a coordinated approach is necessary for achieving holistic and sustainable solutions to these problems. This in turn necessitates partnership and collaboration between international actors with historically distinct mandates, interests, and areas of expertise. A nexus may therefore constitute both a site and an impetus for action.

With the security-development nexus, the emphasis on partnership and cooperation has enabled development actors like UNDP to get involved with issues relating to conflict and crime. The construction of this nexus has therefore created opportunities for UNDP to revise and expand its mandates, access new budgetary resources, and amplify its political influence throughout the UN system (Murphy, 2006). At the same time, critical scholars have argued that the rise of the security-development nexus has fueled a dynamic whereby self-interested sovereign donors from the Global North overwhelmingly allocate their aid budgets for development projects that narrowly align with national or regional security interests (Duffield, 2007). This has been described as a neo-colonial dynamic that fundamentally conflicts with the liberal aspirations of the development as a freedom model (Chandler, 2006).

Discursive elements of the crime-development nexus clearly mimic the security-development nexus. This is hardly coincidental, because the theoretical assumptions, structural changes, and ideological agendas that gave rise to the security-development nexus and the rule of law agenda in the 1990s influenced the construction of the crime-development nexus following the adoption of the Millennium Development Goals (MDGs). Similarly, the crime-development nexus overlaps with the so-called crime-conflict nexus (Shaw, 2001; Jesperson, 2016) and the "crime-terror nexus" (Hutchinson & O'Malley, 2007). A history of the crime-development nexus is also, in part, a history of the security-development nexus and vice versa. SDG 16 is a testament to this, but the crime-development nexus can also be studied as a semiautonomous field.

We note, for example, that the SDGs were the overarching focus of the 2021 UN Crime Congress in Kyoto, Japan; and prior to this, the issue linkage featured in the Doha Declaration adopted at the 2015 UN Crime Congress in Qatar (UN, 2015). Similar statements featured in UN promotional materials produced for this event. A riveting example is a YouTube video about "the nexus between crime and development" featuring evocative images and dramatic music:

> *The sound of heartbeats is accompanied by the image of a woman's face superimposed against a white background. Her eyes are closed. Tense music plays . . .*
> "CRIME UNDERMINES EDUCATION" *[photo of a school-aged child wearing a backpack and carrying books]*
> "CRIME INCREASES HUNGER" *[photo of the planet Earth next to a fork and a spoon]*
> "CRIME DEEPENS INEQUALITIES" *[photo of a homeless man with an urban skyline superimposed on his face]*
> "CRIME HINDERS THE ECONOMY" *[photo of a man in a business suit extending his hand with stock charts transposed on his suit]*
> "CRIME FINANCES TERRORISM" *[photo of an elderly woman crying into a tissue in what looks to be the aftermath of a terrorist attack superimposed on her face]*
> "CRIME SPREADS MISERY" *[photo of a sad child's face]*
> "CRIME DESTROYS HEALTH" *[photo of a man who appears to be in a hospital bed with pills in the background]*
> "CRIME WEAKENS TRUST" *[photo of a police officer in full riot gear with American dollars superimposed over him]*
> "CRIME DESTROYS WILDLIFE" *[photo of a pensive-looking woman]*
> "CRIME DIMINISHES PROSPERITY" *[photo of a woman in a veil with an urban landscape superimposed over her face]*
> "CRIME POLLUTES DRINKING WATER" *[photo of a woman and a rusty water pipe]*
> *The music fades to heartbeats. The woman with the closed eyes reappears, and her eyes suddenly open. The image fades to white. This is followed by the messages "CRIME AFFECTS US ALL" and "PREVENTING CRIME TO BUILD SUSTAINABLE DEVELOPMENT"* (UNIS, 2015)

The issue linkage also featured as a recurring theme of numerous statements and reports published by the United Nations Office on Drugs and Crime (UNODC) since the early 2000s. Prior to this, references also featured in documentation relating to the work of UNODC's predecessors, but before the 1980s, crime was primarily framed as a consequence of, rather than an obstacle to, development. The rise of economic globalization has also prompted other actors to take an interest in this issue since the 1980s. This includes other UN agencies, international financial institutions (IFIs), civil society actors (including business and industry), and, of course, states. All of these diverse influences have shaped the construction of the crime-development nexus as an element of the SDGs.

THEORETICAL FRAMEWORK

Theorizing the crime-development nexuses means "trac[ing] the erratic and discontinuous process[es]" (Garland, 2014, p. 372) that led to its construction. It is a genealogical exercise that necessitates an eclectic theoretical tool kit that allows us to consider how various forces have historically shaped the genesis, evolution, and institutionalization of this issue linkage. As a starting point then, we suggest that the institutional infrastructure of global crime governance was established and has evolved in response to the politicization of new and emerging problems by states and entrepreneurial non-state actors (sometimes referred to as "norm entrepreneurs" or "transnational moral entrepreneurs") through discourse (Andreas & Nadelmann, 2006). The same has been argued of the historical development of international police cooperation (Deflem, 2002), the transnational legal order (Halliday & Shaffer, 2015), and global policing (Bowling & Sheptycki, 2012). Adopting this constructivist lens does not imply a denial of the existence of actual criminological threats and problems. Rather, the factual merits of the speech acts used to amplify and frame these problems are difficult, if not impossible, to verify using traditional social scientific methods, and ignoring their politicization would reinforce and validate a reductionist, atheoretical, and ahistorical understanding of this issue linkage.

It is undeniable that constructivist approaches have gained popularity among international relations (IR) scholars and criminologists; and messaging associated with the crime-development nexus clearly resonates with what Buzan et al. (1998) have previously described as "securitizing moves," whereby "security actors" are said to discursively construct "something" as an "existential threat" to a "referent object" to legitimize or justify extraordinary or extralegal powers. If one accepts that the essence of the crime-development nexus is fundamentally about security, then the adoption of the Doha Declaration, the inclusion of SDG 16, and the UN General Assembly resolution quoted in the previous section might even be argued to signify the "securitization" of this issue. Similarly, one might attempt to interpret the construction of this issue linkage as an attempt to "govern through crime" (Simon, 2006). Indeed, the discursive emphasis on a multiform criminal threat with implications for different policy spheres fits with Simon's (2006, p. 4) observation that "crime has now become a significant strategic issue" and that "[a]cross all kinds of institutional settings, people are seen as acting legitimately when they act to prevent crimes or other troubling behaviors that can be closely analogized to crime." The fact that the United States played an instrumental role in amplifying the threat of transnational organized crime during the 1990s certainly resonates with this perspective and suggests it may hold relevance at the global level (Findlay, 2008).

However, the limitations of reducing this story to securitization or governing through crime narratives are twofold. First, any references to the crime-development nexus that feature in the SDGs coexist alongside other influential narratives relating to the nature of the global crime problem. Furthermore, the relative importance of SDG 16 and associated targets as a focus area of the SDGs is also debatable. In this respect, we reiterate that crime prevention and criminal justice have never been among the most significant priorities for the UN development community or developing countries. Second, constructivist approaches alone are insufficient for systematically exploring the deeper institutional and structural dynamics that contributed to the historical emergence of the crime-development nexus. The idea that crime is a threat to development was not simply invented by entrepreneurial actors in the lead-up to the SDGs. Rather, issues relating to social and economic development have long featured on the international crime policy agenda, meaning there are fundamental continuities and shifts between the UN's messaging today and earlier political framings and theorizations of the complex relationship between crime and development. This evolution has in turn been shaped by structural and ideological forces that have shaped development as a historical process rooted in the legacy of European imperialism. Accordingly, we set out to theorize the emergence of the crime-development nexus by grounding a constructivist analysis in institutionalist and materialist perspectives, which are discussed in chapter 2.

CONCEPTUALIZING GLOBAL CRIME GOVERNANCE

Global crime governance refers to "the attempt to govern crime not only via national regulations, but the successive establishment of worldwide regulations targeted at the criminalization, prosecution, and punishment of specific activities" (Jakobi, 2013, p. 3; Jakobi, 2020). The most significant institutional developments of the past thirty years have been the successful negotiation and adoption of the United Nations Convention Against Transnational Organized Crime (UNTOC) in 2003 and the United Nations Convention Against Corruption (UNCAC) in 2005. UNTOC and UNCAC, together with the three UN drug conventions[1] and various international treaties and resolutions relating to different aspects of terrorism, maritime piracy, and money laundering, supply a normative framework that contributes to the transnational ordering of criminal justice (Shaffer & Aaronson 2020). Their adoption and ongoing maintenance signifies that a formal consensus exists among nations that crime and corruption are global problems with transnational dimensions that must be addressed through international cooperation (Andreas & Nadelmann, 2006; Findlay, 2008; Aaronson & Shaffer, 2021).

Global crime governance is rooted in an enduring liberal internationalist belief that multilateralism is essential for collectively managing the various risks associated with crime as a threat to global and national security. Multilateralism describes an approach to global governance that involves "coordinat[ed] national policies in groups of three or more states . . . on the basis of certain principles of ordering relations among those states" (Ruggie, 1992, p. 567). In the post–Cold War international system, the "principles" in question have overwhelmingly aligned with a liberal ideology that has itself been shaped by the geopolitical and material interests of a global hegemon: the United States (Nye, 2003; Chandler, 2006). UNTOC and UNCAC represent important institutional mechanisms for managing the criminogenic consequences of neoliberal globalization; they also provide minimal scope or reason for state or non-state actors to overtly contest ideological or material dimensions of this global liberal order. By contrast, throughout the Cold War, the Economic and Social Council of the UN (ECOSOC) and the UN Secretariat, which served as the primary sites of international coordination and administration in the sphere of crime prevention and criminal justice, necessarily provided nations with greater scope for political discussion, contestation, and disagreement. This is explained by the divergent ideological positions of the world's major superpowers, the United States and the Soviet Union, and the influence of "Third Worldism," the Non-Aligned Movement, and the New International Economic Order (NIEO) as counter-hegemonic forces (Murphy, 1983).

By contrast, the post–Cold War liberal order signifies a consensus that transnational organized crime and corruption are collective security problems that necessitate a coordinated international response (Albanese, 2018; Findlay, 2008). It must be acknowledged, however, that the language of UNTOC and UNCAC is intentionally broad and vague so as to accommodate and sidestep specific points of disagreement between nations. This speaks to the criminological cliché that there is no ontological reality to crime, which in this case implies that there has never been, and never will be, universal agreement about what activities should be criminalized or how they should be regulated. What might be described as one of the few universal facts about crime is therefore intentionally ignored or de-emphasized because it draws attention to the inherently political nature of the international crime policy agenda, and the structural causes of issues like transnational organized crime and corruption. Most countries are seemingly content with this minimalist approach because they seek to preserve their sovereign right to determine what activities should be criminalized, and how these should be policed and punished.

Unsurprisingly, there has historically been resistance by some countries, developed and developing, to attempts to make international crime prevention a global policy priority. During the Cold War, resistance was largely rooted in ideological concerns about Western influence over the international crime policy agenda. Today, many governments perceive global crime governance as a potential threat to their political and cultural autonomy. The fact is that many countries that have adopted the Conventions and publicly support international cooperation have little interest in complying. In many cases, doing so would threaten the interests of political and economic elites that are intertwined with the problems the Conventions are designed to suppress. This highlights an important theme, which we revisit throughout the book: Illicit actors and economies are an integral part of the current global capitalist political economy, so maintaining a Manichaean emphasis on issues like crime and corruption as the "dark side" of capitalist development is actually crucial for generating and sustaining political and material support to address specific manifestations of these problems, which have been labeled a threat or a risk to the hegemonic order.[2] Constructing and sustaining this myth implies that the normative foundations of the international crime policy agenda are necessarily broad and flexible. As long as there is a fundamental consensus that there is a global crime problem and a need for cooperation, there will be space for the international crime policy community and institutions like UNODC to exist.

It would be misleading to suggest, however, that the international crime policy agenda is entirely responsive to the interest of states and international organizations. Rather, civil society, which includes "everything from non-governmental organizations to academia, private-sector and community groups," has played an important role in shaping this agenda, both directly and indirectly via their interactions with states and international organizations like the UN (Shaw et al., 2018). From this perspective, global crime governance is shaped by the work of a wider epistemic community that Haas (1992, p. 3) defines as a "network of professionals with recognized expertise and competence in a particular domain and an authoritative claim to policy relevant knowledge within that domain or issue-area." These actors share a collective interest in matters relating to crime and their activities often coalesce around institutional sites established to govern these problems. Ultimately, however, their concerns, motives, and modes of engagement are diverse, meaning that civil society cannot be theorized as an "integrated community . . . devoid of interests and internal power relations" (Betts & Pilath, 2017, p. 786). Crime is then governed globally "by a plurality of actors . . . forming more or less interconnected governance networks; a plurality of mechanisms (force, persuasion, economic pressure, norm creation and manipulation; and rapid adaptive change)" (Burris et al., 2005, pp. 31–32).

Within these networks, different nodes or "organizational sites (institutional settings that bring together and harness ways of thinking and acting) where attempts are made to intentionally shape the flow of events" (Wood & Shearing, 2007, p. 149) are established to facilitate coordinated responses and negotiate the governance of complex social phenomena. In this case, member states of the UN have nodes of global governance consisting of various organs of the UN, such as UNODC and its governing commissions, which are discussed below. Once established, nodes may convene or coalesce around preexisting problems or issues, such as those that feature in UNTOC and UNCAC. Alternatively, networks may develop or be extended in response to collective recognition of new and emerging problems and the interlinkages between criminal threats and other areas of global governance, such as conflict, human rights, and sustainable development. The point is that the nodal cartography of any governing network, together with the nature of the substantive issues it exists to address, is constantly in flux.

While a nodal governance approach is useful for *describing* the architecture of global crime governance, it ultimately tells us little about power relations or of the purpose and content of policy agendas developed within them. Accordingly, our theoretical approach to "unraveling" the nexus between crime and development also incorporates insights from neo-Gramscian theory, specifically the work of Robert Cox, who argues that the purpose of governance networks is to facilitate the expansion and management of global capitalism by developing a global consensus within which specific policies are framed (Cox, 1987, p. 254). As we show throughout this book, this has been the overriding logic of global governance networks that have sought to construct and reproduce a consensus about how crime should be governed and controlled so as to facilitate and manage the spread of global capitalism. Inevitably, the construction of this consensus is hierarchically structured.

Agendas, programs, activities, and projects of global crime governance, much like those of the international development agenda (Rist, 2009), are disproportionately shaped by those in a position of power. In the context of global crime governance, we refer to advanced capitalist countries from the Global North, particularly the United States and its European allies (Andreas & Nadelmann, 2006). At the same time these networks rarely resort to coercion and, in fact, lack the capacity to use force to implement their agendas. Instead, there is a consensual dimension to them. From a Coxian perspective, this implies that power is derived from material resources but maintained via the creation of political institutions and ideologies that are designed to legitimize and reproduce their hegemonic influence. Maintaining this influence is in turn predicated on the ability of powerful actors to continue to accumulate material resources, neutralize dissent, manage or prevent conflicts, and ultimately establish conditions of stability. It is here that the relevance of formal international organizations becomes apparent because they fulfill three functions: They embody and promote the rules that facilitate the expansion of global capitalism; ideologically legitimate the norms of the world order; and co-opt opposition and marginalize challenges to it (Cox, 1983, pp. 172–73).

The ability of international organizations to reproduce the interests of the powerful is at least partially dependent on their legitimacy as institutions in the eyes of the weak. In this regard, international organizations may constitute sites for counter-hegemony, where powerful actors make material and ideological concessions to secure consent from less-powerful actors to advance their agendas. Depending on the character of the international organization, these negotiations may in turn create opportunities for weaker state and non-state actors to pursue their own interests (Murphy, 1994, p. 32). The UN provides an excellent example of this during the 1960s and 1970s, as did the SDG negotiations that occurred in the wake of the 2008 Global Financial Crisis. Thus, even if international organizations like the UN remain materially and ideologically bound to a hegemonic order fundamentally grounded in the development as growth model, they represent a space where subordinate actors can articulate their own agendas and potentially challenge the consensus. By comparison, IFIs like the World Bank are by design less susceptible to political contestation, but even these were forced to make concessions to maintain their legitimacy by softening their commitments to the neoliberal development as growth model in the 1990s (see chapter 6).

A final point to consider is that while international organizations are established and predominantly financed by the most powerful capitalist states within the system, they often operate semi-autonomously. They feature their own cultures, values, and institutional goals, which are shaped by their mandates, history, and positionality within wider fields of governance. Staff at international organizations fundamentally believe that the work they do is important and that they are uniquely positioned to provide issue-leadership and engage in norm entrepreneurship (Barnett & Finnemore, 2004). The UN Secretariat, which includes UNODC and its predecessors, is an example of this, and our story highlights how this bureaucratic actor used its knowledge production and advocacy capabilities to amplify the visibility of its portfolio following its omission from the MDG.

Since the League of Nations' Secretariat was first established following the First World War, staff at international organizations have been overwhelmingly committed to the liberal internationalist project and the idea that multilateralism is essential for addressing global problems. In this regard, their interests as bureaucratic actors may deviate from those of their sovereign creators and benefactors, whose commitment to liberal internationalism has historically peaked and waned. Powerful countries, therefore, typically engage with international organizations and support their work (both politically and materially) when it suits their interests, and international organizations *may* act as an important normative counterbalance. Ultimately, however, material influence of powerful countries over international organizations cannot be ignored. Without funding, international bureaucrats cannot undertake activities that allow them to fulfill their mandate. Accordingly, they must consciously work to align their activities with what they recognize to be the interests or priorities of donors; this in turn provides powerful countries with a means of steering the work of international organizations from a distance. This dynamic is well documented in the international development context and is a recurring theme of our story, which focuses primarily on the contributions of the UN crime policy apparatus to the construction of the crime-development nexus.

THE UNITED NATIONS' CRIME POLICY APPARATUS

The UN Secretariat has historically supplied a bureaucratic infrastructure that supports and links nodal actors that collectively shape and implement the international crime policy agenda. The entity responsible for this is the UNODC, which was established in 1997 through a merger of the United Nations Drug Control Programme (UNDCP) and the Centre for Crime Prevention (CCP). Prior to this, UNODC's predecessors had historically operated with distinct policy mandates and organizational structures, despite the obvious overlaps that exist between these substantive issues. Today, UNODC has a three-pronged mandate that centers on technical assistance, research and advocacy, and normative work relating to the Conventions.

A diverse range of substantive issues fall within UNODC's portfolio. These include organized crime and trafficking, corruption, crime prevention and criminal justice reform, illicit drugs (treatment, demand reduction, and supply reduction), terrorism prevention, and, most recently, cybercrime. UNODC is also uniquely positioned to identify and draw attention to new and emerging threats or problems that align with this mandate thanks to various factors, including its active participation in seemingly every formal node of global crime governance; the technical expertise of its staff; its research capabilities; and the organization's use of advocacy and diplomacy (Redo & Platzer, 2013). All the issues that UNODC deals with either feature in the Conventions or have at least been acknowledged as international priorities by UNODC's two governing bodies: the Commission on Crime Prevention and

Criminal Justice (CCPCJ) and the Commission on Narcotic Drugs (CND). It is therefore important to acknowledge that UNODC's status as an semi-autonomous bureaucratic actor is constrained by its governance structure, at least compared to other UN agencies, so much of the work it does to shape the international crime policy agenda is informal.

The CCPCJ and the CND are composed of delegates from different countries and govern by consensus rather than a majority. All delegates must therefore agree on the exact wording of any resolutions, decisions, or statements before they are adopted. Of course countries do not always see eye to eye on these issues, so UNODC plays an important, albeit rarely discussed, role in brokering agreements and maintaining the consensus behind the scenes. It also plays a role in drawing attention to new and emerging issues and advocating for a normative mandate to address them in ways that are universally palatable. UNODC must do this carefully because it cannot be seen to act as a political actor or policy making body. UNODC must always present itself as apolitical and value-neutral. To this effect, it has a vested institutional interest in maintaining the Manichaean myth described above, because doing so is integral to maintaining the fragile consensus and, by extension, its mandate. As discussed in chapters 7 and 8, de-politicizing the international crime policy agenda means framing crime as an issue that can be addressed through technical cooperation. This in turn has implications for how the problem of crime is theorized at the global level.

For reasons described above, UNODC's organizational worldview is quite conservative, and it has historically struggled to present its portfolio in a positive or progressive light. Those sections of UNODC that are engaged in more progressive activities have also historically faced significant constraints by the entity's leadership, which does not wish to upset the Commissions. This has complicated UNODC's ability to define its role and establish an coherent identity for itself in a UN system that is comparatively progressive. We note for example that "human rights" represents one of the three pillars of the UN system, yet this is an issue that many governments are keen to avoid in relation to crime control and criminal justice. UNODC might therefore be described as a black sheep of the UN system, and this has historically made developing effective partnerships with other UN entities rather difficult. There are multiple interrelated reasons for this.

For starters, the entity was established with a mandate to lead "the United Nations fight against *uncivil society*; i.e., those elements that take advantage of the benefits of globalization by trafficking human beings and illegal drugs, laundering money and engaging in terrorism" (Redo, 2012, p. 153; original emphasis) rather than support the attainment of a positive outcome such as peace, justice, or security. As discussed in chapter 7, the ability of UNODC to promote recognition of the relevance of its portfolio to the SDGs and MDGs was directly linked with its ability to reframe its contributions in a positive light. This has certainly enhanced its foundation for partnership and collaboration, particularly at the regional and country levels.

What further complicates the governance of UNODC and the international crime policy agenda is that these are simultaneously responsive to resolutions or declarations that have been adopted by the Commissions in Vienna and the UNGA/ECOSOC in New York. This is important, because the UNGA adopts decisions by majority rather than consensus, meaning it is typically much more progressive than the Commissions. For this reason, the resolution that eventually led to the adoption of UNTOC was introduced in New York rather than Vienna, where it was thought a consensus would not be achieved.

UNODC's work, specifically that of its Division of Operations but also increasingly its Division of Treaty Affairs (see figure 1.1 below), is heavily influenced by the interests of sovereign donors. Put simply, UNODC, like any UN entity, needs money to operate and sustain its operations, and the decline in the UN's General Purpose Fund since the 1990s has rendered the organization increasingly dependent on voluntary contributions from donors. These are benchmarked for specific project activities or programs that fall within the scope of the Conventions, but this does not mean they align with the immediate needs or interests of recipient countries in the Global South. Rather, donor countries from the Global North typically provide financial support for programs and projects in developing countries that will benefit them either strategically or reputationally.

UNODC as a multilateral entity may be contracted to oversee the implementation of such projects and programs for a variety of reasons, including the organization's diplomatic and political connections; its international network of regional and national advisors; the technical expertise of its staff; and, perhaps most significantly, the legitimacy it bestows upon such interventions. In this regard, UNODC frequently functions as an intermediary when it comes to administering international development aid that has been allocated for crime prevention or security sector reform projects, and in such cases the challenge becomes balancing the interests of donors with the needs of recipients. The dynamic is not unique to the sphere of international crime prevention (Murphy, 2006; Blaustein, 2015), and much like the wider UN development system, UNODC has become increasingly beholden to donor interests. This model, which emphasizes Northern funding to address Southern problems, also signifies the enduring influence of the development as efficiency model within UNODC and the wider UN development system. At the same time, our research highlights that over the past decade, UNODC has developed alternative funding models that have seemingly helped it address these issues

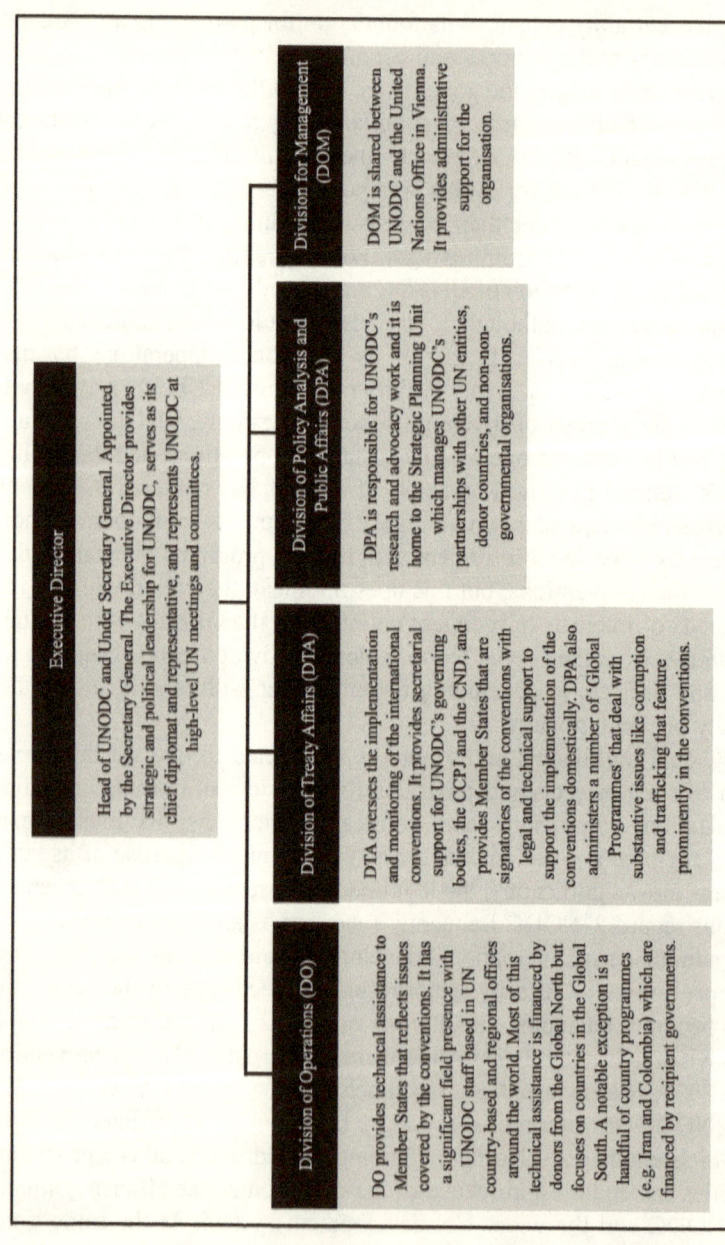

Figure I.1. Organizational Structure of UNODC
Source: Author created, adapted from UNODC website and interview data

(see chapter 8). Once again, this signifies that international organizations have agentive qualities and should be studied as actors in their own right.

UNODC provides a logical focal point for our research, but we make an effort to acknowledge the contributions of other actors (state and non-state) throughout this book. UNODC and its predecessors are, however, unique because this entity has consistently served as a coordinating node for the international crime policy agenda since the late 1940s. It thus represents a site of institutional continuity and a source of narrative coherence for our story. Members of the UN crime program have seemingly participated in and shaped every deliberation concerning the relationship between crime and development that has occurred in the UN system, and these contributions are well documented. By comparison, other UN entities like UNDP have shaped the wider international development agenda and the "security-development nexus," but crime has never been their primary concern. For the UN crime program, governing the crime-development nexus has always been an integral part of its work, and this entity has long produced and disseminated knowledge that has directly shaped the discursive construction of the crime-development nexus. In doing so, the UN crime program, together with its governing and advisory bodies, has functioned as a conduit through which changing ideas about crime together with ideological, institutional, and material shifts have indirectly shaped the international crime policy agenda.

ABOUT OUR STUDY

This book draws on years of desk-based research, supplemented with qualitative interviews with 28 current and retired members of the UN crime program.[3] In the first instance, we accessed an abundance of documentary material that has been digitized by the UN and compiled this into a digital archive. In total, we analyzed more than 200 primary documents published between 1916 and 2020. These included official transcripts and summaries of UN/League of Nations meetings, debates, and assemblies; UN yearbooks; preparatory material for the quinquennial UN Conferences on the Prevention and Criminal Justice; UN Secretariat reports and working papers; reports by World Bank and other international financial institutions; and documentation relating to the creation of the UNODC, UNTOC, UNCAC, and the SDG negotiations. We read these documents chronologically to develop a preliminary timeline then undertook a more careful analysis of relevant documents to try and make sense of when and how key shifts in the framing of the relationship between crime and development occurred. This provided a strong sense of the official history of the UN's crime policy apparatus, but only limited insight into what occurred behind the scenes (and also beyond) within the UN system. In other words, details relating to the actual contributions of the UN crime program and its staff that are necessary for undertaking an institutionalist analysis were rarely included in official UN documents. Rather, many of the official documents were written by the Secretariat so as to portray Member States as the primary architects and drivers of global crime governance. The reason for this goes back to our earlier point about how the Secretariat cannot be seen to make or influence the policy agenda. Writing a history of the crime-development nexus that drew solely on official UN documents would therefore reduce global governance to sovereign interests and official deliberations and negotiations, which would be theoretically limiting.

We knew from the theoretical literature and informal conversations with UN crime policy insiders that research and advocacy work of staff employed by the UN crime program has always been important for generating support for key initiatives among Member States. We therefore set out to explore the agentive qualities of the UN crime program and its staff by referring to published "insider" accounts, which are referenced throughout the book. Drawing inspiration from Murphy's (2006) history of UNDP and previous historical studies of crime policy development, we then conducted interviews with 28 international crime policy insiders who were actively involved with the UN crime program at various times and in different capacities between the late 1960s and 2018. These semi-structured interviews supplied us with otherwise inaccessible insight into the work of UNODC and its predecessors.

Understanding how behind-the-scenes activities shaped the construction of the crime-development nexus over a period spanning more than five decades allowed us to contextualize and link various milestones. It also enabled us to consider how and why key documents, including working papers, research reports, advocacy statements, and resolutions were produced, along with their empirical and theoretical significance. The interviews further afforded us insight into the organizational politics of the UN crime program, its relationship with its governing bodies, and the transformation of the wider UN system over a period that spanned more than five decades.

Many of our participants occupied senior or mid-level roles in the organization and directly contributed to or observed the events described in this book. The "old-timers" were asked to reflect at length about their history of the organization over the course of their careers, including key transformations and shifts, which we identified from our preliminary desktop review. Specific questions were also tailored to each participant based on publicly available biographical details, including their roles and postings. For example, a participant who was involved with authoring a working paper or report would be asked to reflect on the process and describe the significance of the document or its content. In some instances, participants drew our attention to documents and events we had initially overlooked. Less senior members of the UNODC, who we approached with permission from the entity, were asked to discuss how their work was being impacted by the SDGs.

Most participants spoke candidly and expressed opinions that were often critical. The old-timers were particularly open about their experiences and views, while current employees were understandably much more careful about what they said. In recognition of the professional risks our participants face, we do not provide any identifying information about them in this book. Some of the interview quotes we draw upon to illustrate and support our analysis have also been edited, albeit in such a way as to preserve the substance and emphasis of their original words. For example, accents and biographical details have been removed or altered. In some cases, the first-person may be changed to third-person to obscure the precise nature of the participant's involvement with events they are describing.

Approximately half the interviews were conducted via Skype/Zoom and the remainder in person in August/September 2018. The interviews lasted between 45 minutes and 2 hours, and all except four were audio recorded with participants' consent. Interview transcripts and notes were initially analyzed using open-coding techniques to identify themes that appeared to be relevant and interesting in relation to our overarching research question: How and why did crime come to be recognized as a sustainable development issue? This initial coding also enabled us to refine our reading of primary documents and revise our timeline of events. This served as the basis for constructing the narrative presented in this book. While preparing this manuscript, we then revisited our interview data to consider how the three elements of Coxian analysis (ideological, institutional, and material) shaped the construction of the crime-development nexus. Additional primary and secondary source material was also consulted and used to develop our historical and theoretical analysis and fill in any gaps.

The interviews confirmed that UNODC had actively worked to put crime on the UN's development agenda following the adoption of the MDGs, and in the lead-up to the SDG negotiations. This was reassuring but hardly a significant revelation. More significantly, the data enabled us to make sense of how and why this occurred. As is often the case with elite interviews with a policy focus, our participants sometimes differed in their interpretation of different factors, events, and individuals (particularly UNODC's executive directors). We have attempted to reconcile these differences through our analysis and our engagement with primary and secondary source material. We also privilege the perspectives of those participants with direct knowledge of a contested issue or event yet consider these in relation to what we know about their professional biographies and viewpoints. Those with inside knowledge of UNODC and the events described in this book may take issue with some of our claims, but this is unavoidable. We hope those who have worked for the UN and spent time in Vienna will at least appreciate that a text that pleases everyone probably says and accomplishes nothing.

We hope that readers will find the empirical and, by extension, theoretical contributions of this book to be both unique and valuable for making sense of both the history of global crime governance and the politics of the crime-development nexus today. At the same time, we feel it is important to acknowledge that our decision to examine the origins of this nexus primarily from the perspective of the UN's crime policy apparatus inevitably downplays the important contributions of other influential international development actors such as the UNDP and international financial institutions like the World Bank when it came to shaping the contours of this nexus. In our story, UNDP and the World Bank feature as a supporting cast of institutional characters whose ideas and influence were conducive to UNODC's success insofar as their interests in achieving formal recognition of SDG 16 more or less aligned. An alternative telling of the history of SDG 16 might therefore locate the institutional origins of this goal with UNDP's interest in human security or the World Bank's enthusiasm for the rule of law, both of which are considered. Accordingly, we do not set out to present the definitive history of UNODC or the crime-development nexus, but rather a theoretically informed, historical inquiry into its ideological, institutional, and geopolitical origins.

Finally, we feel it is necessary to acknowledge that the analysis presented in this book has two significant blind spots. First, there is very little discussion of gender. This is not so much an oversight on our part, but rather a reflection of the fact that most of the UN's work on crime has been gender-blind and that white men have long had a disproportionate influence on the international crime policy agenda. The second blind spot relates to the actual implementation of the international crime policy agenda at the national and local levels. Implementation is to varying degrees influenced by international policy agendas, but we know that these are selectively adopted and translated into concrete policies and practices by national and subnational actors (Blaustein, 2015; Hameiri & Jones, 2015). There is invariably a gap between what an international organization thinks it does and what happens on the ground. Analyzing this disconnect and the translational processes used to bridge it can therefore offer a more complete picture of global governance as a collection of multiscalar and polycentric activities, but this is beyond the scope of our book.

STRUCTURE AND ARGUMENT

In chapter 1 we consider how the empirical relationship between crime and development has been theorized in the criminological literature. We approach this from a historical perspective by considering how the scholarly literature on development and crime has evolved since the early decades of the 20th century and trace this to more recent discussions of neoliberal globalization and crime. While there is certainly a sophisticated body of theory and evidence that highlights potentially interesting and important links between crime and development, our analysis suggests that it is meaningless to reduce their relationship to a simple narrative such as "modernization causes crime" or "crime is an obstacle to development." This prompts us to ask how and why the issue linkage came to exist.

In chapter 2 we provide a more detailed overview of our theoretical framework. We begin by outlining the key theoretical approaches to understanding global crime governance (functionalism, realism, institutionalism, constructivism) and proceed to discuss the importance of situating these perspectives in an overarching political economy framework. We therefore turn to the work of Robert Cox to account for how global crime governance can be theorized as an interplay of material, institutional, and ideological forces that are inextricably linked with the history of capitalist development.

Chapter 3 sets out to historicize the development of the crime-development nexus by examining the origins of global crime governance, which we trace back to the age of European imperialism in the 19th century. We reflect on early attempts to develop multilateral regimes to manage collective security threats in the metropole and consider how colonialism contributed to the transposition of European norms and institutions throughout what is today known as the Global South. Both systems of governance were integral to the maintenance and expansion of this capitalist order and directly influenced the work of the League of Nations. The remainder of the chapter thus reflects on how crime and development featured in the League of Nations' work program and notes that the period coincided with the beginning of an important transformation of the global capitalist order that would subsequently lead to decolonization and the birth of the liberal development paradigm.

Chapter 4 picks up with the establishment of the UN when the focus of the international crime policy agenda shifted from international problems (which had been a key focus of the interwar period) to addressing crime as a social development issue. This was particularly important in relation to the anticipated instabilities generated by the modernization of recently decolonized, or soon-to-be decolonized, nations. The concern was that the rapid integration of former colonies into a global capitalist economy would generate social instabilities comparable to those previously experienced by industrialized nations of the developed West. Unsurprisingly then, the aforementioned criminological paradigm of sociological positivism with its emphasis on social disorganization sat at the heart of the UN's Social Defence Section, which attempted to manage these instabilities through technical assistance throughout the 1950s and 1960s. This was consistent with the development as efficiency model described by Murphy (2006) and thus an extension of the "benevolent imperialist" mentality (Pedersen, 2015) that evolved as a fixture of liberal internationalism through the League of Nations' Mandate System. At the same time, these activities and the wider international crime policy agenda were also shaped by Cold War politics, which we reflect on in this chapter. Accordingly, we argue that social defense represented an element of a wider program for advancing Western hegemony through development, albeit one that was largely inconsequential at the time.

By the late 1960s, concerns about the financial viability of the Social Defence Section and the changing composition of the UN's political bodies contributed to significant shifts in the UN crime policy agenda. These transformations and the conditions that contributed to them are the focus of chapter 5, which examines the internationalization and diversification of the UN's crime policy agenda throughout the 1970s and 1980s. It is in relation to these changes that we see the discursive emphasis shift from "crime as a consequence of modernization" to "crime as an obstacle to economic development." Various factors contributed to this, including the rising influence of the NIEO, which rendered the UN a site of counter-hegemony in the 1970s; Western divestment from the UN as a consequence of this; growing disillusionment with "social defense" among various academic advisors to the UN; heightened awareness among UN crime policy insiders and Member States of new and emerging criminal threats that were thought to necessitate greater international cooperation in the sphere of international crime prevention; and the rise of neoliberal globalization, the collapse of NIEO, and America's foreign policy agenda in the 1980s.

Chapter 6 picks up with the collapse of the Soviet Union in 1991, when the international community embraced free market democracy as a one-size-fits-all recipe for building a thriving international community. One former member of the UN crime program described this as the "Golden Era of international cooperation," and it was against this backdrop that issues of transnational organized crime and corruption gained greater visibility within and beyond the UN system. This reflected widespread awareness of the growing reality of neoliberal globalization during this time, which enabled criminal organizations to emulate their legitimate counterparts and "go global." This gave rise to an illicit global economy across which all sorts of illegal goods and services were traded, from drugs to humans to arms. Money from these activities were in turn laundered through legitimate businesses and financial institutions. It was against this backdrop that UNTOC and later UNCAC were negotiated, UNODC was established, and a Manichaean narrative about transnational organized crime and corruption as the "dark side of globalization" would emerge as the focal point of the international crime policy agenda. Concurrently, other international actors began to take an interest in related issues. These included IFIs, which embraced the "good governance agenda" amid growing criticism of their neoliberal structural adjustment policies, and UNDP, which introduced the concepts of "human development" and "human security" into the international policy lexicon.

Chapters 7 and 8 detail the construction of the crime-development nexus following the adoption of the MDGs in 2000. At first glance, this is a story about one troubled entity's successful attempt to amplify the visibility of its portfolio within the wider UN system, which had become increasingly development-oriented by the late 1990s. From an institutional perspective, our analysis clearly shows that UNODC's advocacy of this issue linkage was driven by material and bureaucratic considerations. However, our Coxian perspective also prompts deeper consideration of the institutional, ideological, and material forces that shaped its attempts to generate and disseminate evidence in support of its argument that the rule of law (a concept it had by this point come to embrace) represented was a prerequisite for sustainable development but was threatened by problems relating to transnational organized crime and corruption.

The analysis presented in chapter 7 is particularly interesting from a Coxian perspective because it evidences that the unconventional leadership of UNODC's second executive director, Antonio Maria Costa, temporarily rendered UNODC a site of resistance to the Manichaean narrative, which emphasized the distinction between licit and illicit economies at a time when the global capitalist order was experiencing its most significant crisis since the Great Depression. The example is particularly interesting because it signified an attempt to reframe transnational organized crime and corruption as global, as opposed to Southern, problems. In this regard, it threatened to shift the onus of responsibility for addressing the root causes of these problems from Southern elites to their Northern counterparts. From this perspective, crime was not a threat to capitalist development but an integral component of it.

Chapter 8 reflects on the legacy of Costa and that legacy's impact on UNODC and the SDG negotiations. The first part of the chapter reflects on the significance of a task force created to promote cooperation between UN entities to address transnational organized crime and corruption, and mainstream these activities throughout the wider development system. The impact of these developments is evidenced in relation to the expansion of UNODC's regional programs and a significant increase in voluntary contributions from Northern, and increasingly Southern, donors during this period. Part two of the chapter then considers how the mainstreaming of UNODC's portfolio contributed to the institutionalization of the crime-development nexus as part of the SDGs. We reflect on the negotiations that led to the adoption of the SDGs and draw attention to the conflict surrounding the inclusion of SDG 16, which was advocated by Northern donors but opposed by some countries from the Global South.

Finally, the conclusion considers how and why the international crime policy community must reorient itself toward promoting a more equitable and sustainable global order. To this effect, we draw on the work of critical criminologists and political economists to sketch out the contours of a radical agenda for shifting the focus of the international crime policy agenda from *crime and development* to *harm and sustainability*. We conclude that this shift is not only necessary but inevitable in light of the structural, geopolitical, and ecological challenges we face in the decades ahead.

Chapter One

Is Crime a Development Issue?

This chapter considers how the relationship between "crime" and "development" has been theorized by criminologists and scholars from aligned fields. By situating these understandings in broader intellectual traditions and thought paradigms, it accounts for how influential theorizations of the criminogenic consequences of development and the impact of crime on development have been shaped by historical conditions. We specifically consider how these understandings have evolved since the early decades of the 20th century, when the ideas of Emile Durkheim that gave birth to the Modernization Thesis and the Chicago School of Sociology supplied the early intellectual foundations of the crime-development nexus. This particular brand of sociological positivism came to underpin much of the criminological research on the relationship between crime and development in the "Third World" during the 1950s and 1960s. Despite important conceptual and methodological limitations of modernization theory and the dependency critique, these thought-paradigms provide important starting points for critically theorizing the domestic criminological consequences of development. This, together with research that theorizes the impact of neoliberal globalization on crime and cross-national studies shed light on interesting and important relationships between crime and development. Ultimately, however, our review in this chapter suggests that we must adopt a more critical stance toward universalizing and reductionist claims about the relationship between these phenomena, including those that sit at the heart of Sustainable Development Goal (SDG) 16.

MODERNIZATION, DEPENDENCY, AND CRIME

Development is rarely an explicit focus of Northern criminological scholarship today. In the early 20th century however, the destabilizing effects of economic development, exemplified by rapid industrialization and urbanization, was the dominant focus—and instigator—of research on the social ecology of crime in the United States. What was known as the Chicago School gave rise to influential ideas such as "social disorganization theory" (Park, 1921) and "cultural transmission" (Shaw & McKay, 1942) that subsequently shaped how criminologists and policy experts understood and worked to address the criminogenic consequences of modernization throughout the decolonized world.

As DiCristina (2016) notes, Durkheim (1893/1964) produced multiple conceptions of anomie that influenced the early American sociological literature on modernization and crime. Most significantly, Durkheim argued that rapid transition to an industrial economy from an agrarian one leads to a weakening of social regulation, antiquating the rules and relationships that make order possible. This conception of anomie resonates closely with the argument that social disorganization inhibits the development of effective modes of social control (Park, 1921) in transitional neighborhoods characterized by economic deprivation, large immigrant populations, and high population turnover (Park, Burgess, & McKenzie, 1925). Durkheim's arguments that anomie weakens the collective consciousness of society and erodes moral solidarity also resonate with certain formulations of social disorganization theory and its emphasis on cultural transmission (Shaw & McKay, 1942). Similarly, Durkheim's argument that family relations are negatively affected by the destabilizing impacts of modern economic activity is reflected in Shaw and McKay's revised formulation of social disorganization theory, which emphasized that "family organizations in high-crime areas are affected in different ways by the divergent systems of values encountered" (Shaw & McKay, 1969, p. 183; quoted in Wardyns & Pauwels, 2017, p. 130). More distinctly, Durkheim's arguments also directly influenced Mertonian strain theory, which associated criminality with the inability of individuals to achieve material success through legitimate channels (Merton, 1938).

This body of work advanced criminological theory at a time when biological and psychological positivism remained dominant. However, there were seemingly few opportunities for sociological positivists to draw upon these ideas to influence the international crime policy agenda during the interwar period. Nor is it clear that there would have been much inclination by American criminologists to engage in international, comparative research, because America's rapid economic development during its Gilded Age rendered its urban centers ideal laboratories for developing and refining these ideas. Further to this point, America during the interwar period embraced isolationist and protectionist policies, so it was not actively involved with the League of Nations. It was therefore only after World War II that American criminologists seemingly worked to promote these ideas internationally.

As discussed in chapter 3, the international appetite for this knowledge after World War II was linked with reconstruction and the decolonization project. Specifically, the concern was that the failure to manage the social instabilities associated with capitalist development might amplify the potential appeal of communism. Insofar as modernization theory emerged as the dominant capitalist development model in the 1950s and 1960s, it was only logical that Durkheimian approaches to studying crime would attract interest. But to what extent could these American theories actually explain and predict the criminological impacts of modernization in the developing world?

A significant study published in 1973 by American criminologists Marshall Clinard and Daniel Abbott offers some relevant insight into this question. Their research involved a mixed-methods empirical case study of Kampala, Uganda, during the late 1960s when the country, which had gained its independence in 1962, was experiencing rapid economic growth and a near threefold increase in crime rates (Clinard & Abbott, 1973). Clinard and Abbott thus wanted to examine how economic growth—together with cultural and social factors—contributed to rising crime rates. In line with Durkheim, they adopted the view that increases in crime in the developing world were a natural result of modernization and articulated three specific explanations for why this was occurring in Kampala.

First, recent rural-to-urban migrants did not have friends or family to help them get settled, so they struggled to adapt to their urban environments. The rapidly expanding city had residents, many of them recent arrivals, who were strangers to one another, and this was associated with low levels of informal social control (Clinard & Abbott, 1973). In Durkheimian terms, this was interpreted as a shift from mechanical to organic solidarity.

Second, Clinard and Abbott focused on the spatial distribution of crime and found that crime in Kampala was concentrated in the informal settlements. Crime rates were not uniform across informal settlements, however, but rather varied based on the levels of cultural heterogeneity and residential mobility. As social disorganization theory might predict, informal social control was found to be weaker in areas of higher cultural heterogeneity and higher residential mobility.

The third explanation focused on differential opportunity, an integrated theory developed by Cloward and Ohlin (1961) that drew on Merton's (1938) strain theory, Albert Cohen's (1955) subcultural theory, and Edwin

Sutherland's (1939) differential association theory. Drawing on interviews with convicted offenders, Clinard and Abbott (1973) found that many participants became involved with criminality for material reasons, because illegitimate opportunities presented themselves in the absence of legitimate ones. This was in turn attributed to a labor surplus in Kampala, which was compounded by a skills gap between urban and rural areas, meaning many rural-to-urban migrants lacked the skills or education required to actually transition into industrialized work.

Clinard and Abbott's study seemingly evidenced the applicability of Western theories to developing countries that were thought to be following in the footsteps of their economically and socially developed peers. There were of course nuances, contextual and cultural differences, which they openly acknowledged, but their study seemingly supported the generalizability of the Durkheimian approach. While this was perhaps the most famous comparative study of modernization and crime, it was not, however, the first attempt to examine this phenomenon in the developing world. Indeed, several of Clinard and Abbott's arguments were consistent with the findings of previous studies that had been commissioned by the UN in the late 1950s. We discuss these in chapter 4, but the point to emphasize here is that by the time Clinard and Abbott's book was published in 1973, the influence of the Chicago School as a criminological paradigm was already on the decline. Within a matter of years, the focus of sociological criminologists would shift to inequality, while those with an interest in crime prevention embraced the neoclassical traditional, with its emphasis on deterrence and prevention. It is also important to stress that even in the 1960s, the dominant tradition of sociological positivism was not universally accepted by criminologists in the West.

It is beyond the scope of this book to review the history of Marxist criminology, but one study by influential critical criminologist William Chambliss (1975) is worth reflecting on because it directly challenged Durkheimian assumptions about the nature of crime and the function of the law and criminal justice institutions through a focused comparison of urban centers in developed and developing countries. Drawing on ethnographic case studies, Chambliss analyzed the political economy of crime in Ibadan, Nigeria, and Seattle, Washington (United States), and concluded that law-enforcement systems "are organized to *manage* crime by cooperating with the most criminal groups and enforcing laws against those whose crimes are a minimal threat to society" (Chambliss, 1975, p. 177, original emphasis). This argument is significant because it challenges the belief that stable and cohesive communities commit less crime than those undergoing transition, characterized by ethnic/cultural diversity and high population turnover. Rather, Chambliss suggested that unstable or heterogeneous societies were typically associated with higher levels of criminality because of over-policing. This was attributed to their lack of social capital and political influence, which encouraged police and other state regulatory institutions to turn a blind eye to the illegal activities in more affluent and homogenous communities. By extension, Chambliss argued that police themselves had a vested interest in reproducing the "myth of [homogenous and established] communities as 'no crime' sections of the city," despite the fact their visible presence in economically deprived neighborhoods where vices were geographically concentrated "helped to assure the 'respectable' citizen that he [sic] could partake of his prurient interests without fear of being the victim of a robbery or of any violence" (p. 177).

Consequently, Chambliss (1975, p. 168) argued that crime statistics and other empirical measures utilized by sociological positivists were "notoriously unreliable" and, in fact, served to reproduce the Durkheimian assumption that "the lower classes are more likely to be arrested because they commit more crimes." Chambliss's analysis is important because it challenges the deterministic assumption that certain populations or areas are inherently more criminogenic than others. This is not to suggest that factors such as poverty and social disorganization are irrelevant, but rather that the criminogenic influence of these macrostructural factors is potentially amplified and exaggerated by societal attempts to control crime. The selective manner in which this occurs is therefore said to reflect and reproduce inequality. This argument has since become a fixture of critical criminology.

The Durkheimian assumption that "socialist and capitalist societies should have the same amount of crime where they have comparable rates of industrialization and bureaucratization" also warrants critical attention (quoting Chambliss, 1975, p. 169). Marx and his followers challenged these assumptions in arguing that crime was not inevitable but rather a product of the economic inequality and social instabilities generated by *capitalist* development specifically (Lynch, 2017). Thus, it was hypothesized from a Marxist perspective that a socialist development model that centered on planning, state ownership, and distribution of wealth, and achieved full employment, would be less criminogenic than its laissez-faire, capitalist counterpart. Contrasting these positions highlights a second important question about the relationship between development and crime that had significant ideological and geopolitical implications during the Cold War: Is modernization or capitalism criminogenic?

Soviet criminologists argued that capitalism rather than modernization was the problem, and they constructed a research tradition that attempted to evidence this, along with the superiority of the Soviet model (Grygier, 1951). As noted in chapter 4, their ideologically-driven approach to theorizing crime meant that this body of work was generally ignored by Western social scientists, who dismissed it as propaganda. The only significant social scientific study that attempted to examine this question empirically was therefore Louise Shelley's *Crime and Modernization*, published in 1981.

Shelley (1981) used a historical analysis of cross-national statistics to compare the criminological consequences of industrialization and urbanization in 19th century Europe with those in developing countries of "Third World" and Eastern Bloc countries. Her analysis revealed some notable similarities, which she interpreted through a Durkheimian lens and argued that "both the process of development and the achievement of development are conducive to criminality" (Shelley, 1981, p. 137). Regarding the distinction between capitalist and socialist countries, Shelley argued the latter typically have lower crime rates due to increased levels of state control and communal/ ideological values and structures, which help to mitigate the disruptive effects of industrialization and urbanization. At the same time she observed that some socialist countries, including the USSR, had seemingly bucked this trend and continued to exhibit unusually high levels of violent crime because they remained economically underdeveloped. This implied that the potential advantage of the Soviet model was not its economic system or ideology, which attached less significance to personal property, but rather to the system's ability to control and regulate its citizens (albeit at the expense of their individual freedoms and liberties). In other words, there were cracks in what Soviet criminologists presented as a utopian system.

Crime and Modernization was a significant work of its time, but its conceptual and methodological limitations illustrate the futility of making macro-theoretical generalizations about the relationship between development and crime. These were discussed by multiple reviewers who suggested, for example, that the study design utilized an imprecise definition of "modernization" rooted in Durkheimian assumptions about the historical relationship between industrialization and urbanization that could not readily be operationalized for comparative purposes (Huggins, 1983; Jones, 1984). Shelley's use of "traditional" American criminological theories to interpret her findings was also described as "ethnocentric" by Huggins (1983), specifically with reference to her discussion of the criminogenic effects of social disorganization in Third World cities, which was inconsistent with the wider anthropological literature on the unique social organization of slums. The study was also limited by the poor quality of available statistical data, which Shelley (1981) herself acknowledged, particularly for socialist societies. Her conclusions about the similarities between socialist and capitalist countries are therefore questionable, while Huggins (1983) also described her analysis of crime in developing countries as "ahistorical" because it did not consider how colonization and later modernization shaped the economic and social development trajectories of recently decolonized nations.

The ethnocentric and ahistorical limitations of the "traditional criminology-modernization approach" (Huggins, 1983, p. 105) were also the focus of an edited volume by Colin Sumner (1982), which was influenced by dependency theorists and radical criminologists. Like Chambliss (1975) and other radical criminologists, Sumner (1982) saw crime as a social and political construct and argued that political elites uphold their privilege and interests by defining crimes and establishing criminal justice responses to them. In his introductory chapter, he argued that modern criminal justice systems "are not universal, inevitable, or 'natural,' but legitimated practices of moral-political control which develop in response to conflicts spawned by the class relationships of exploitation and domination constituting the capitalist mode of production" (Sumner, 1982, p. 10). From this perspective, the criminal law and criminal justice systems throughout the Global South must be studied as vestiges of colonialism that deepen inequality and class-based oppression. This perspective was accorded further credence by historical studies that later examined the development and application of criminal law in Third World countries (for example, Huggins, 1985).

Sumner (1982) further emphasized that former dependencies do not develop similarly to developed countries of the West due to enduring neocolonial relations. Accordingly, Sumner (1982, p. 5) called upon criminologists to consider the unique structural characteristics of underdeveloped countries, including their "lack of internal capital, the capital intensiveness of industry, the preservation of backward rural sectors, minimal urban employment changes, and military government[s]." In addition, he argued that because crimes of the poor—especially those that threaten the interests of the powerful—are more likely to be policed and punished, criminologists must not fail to focus on crimes of the powerful, which he accused Clinard and Abbott (1973) of overlooking. Finally, Sumner (1982) argued that increased government spending on crime control in the Third World would not reduce crime but rather intensify the over-policing and marginalization of the urban poor. Thus, echoing Chambliss (1975), he argued that police deviance and misconduct is rampant in many underdeveloped countries, and Western approaches to crime control that emphasized enhancing formal control were inappropriate.

The issues raised by Sumner (1982) highlight some additional deficiencies of the traditional criminology-modernization perspective, but the generalizability of a dependency critique is also questionable. As Rogers (1989, p. 326) would later argue, development, law-making, and crime are complex and contextually specific phenomena that cannot be reduced to either a Durkheimian/Modernization or a Marxist/Dependency perspective. Meaningful commonalities certainly exist between the former dependencies, namely that the ideologies, institutions, and material interests of "Southern" elites have been influenced historically by the legacy of the dual-revolution (Hobsbawm, 1962), colonization, and imperialism (Prashad, 2012; Hobsbawm, 1989). But is it really possible to compare the historical development of Uganda, which gained its independence from the British in 1962, with Latin American countries like Uruguay that became independent in the 19th century? And then what about the fact that since the Second World War, decolonized countries have adopted different capitalist development models, with varying degrees of success? Is a low-crime, high-income country like Singapore, which experienced significant economic growth through a program that centered on state planning, comparable to Chile, another low-crime country, which was an early adopter of neoliberal reform? And reflecting on these "economic miracles," how might we think about the criminological implications of development as they relate to state crimes, human rights violations, and corruption? What about developing countries that were denied the opportunity to capitalize on their immense natural resources due to neocolonial practices of the 1950s and 1960s? What about those low-income, high-crime countries like El Salvador or Honduras, whose economic and political development were driven not by the invisible hand of the market but American foreign policy interests during the Cold War? We raise these questions simply to highlight the limitations of adopting a universalizing, ahistorical approach to studying the nexus between crime and development.

NEOLIBERAL DEVELOPMENT AND CRIME

With the advent of neoliberalism in the late 1970s to early 1980s to contend with the global debt crisis, the Washington Consensus prescribed the same standardized macroeconomic reforms for countries in the Global South, regardless of their circumstances. These took the form of structural adjustment programs (SAPs) and economic shock therapies managed by the World Bank and International Monetary Fund (IMF) (Williamson, 1990). These reforms were meant to increase economic growth for countries in the Global South and standardize rules for private transactions and the functioning of markets that severely limited state intervention (Krever, 2011). Neoliberal activities include the privatization of state enterprises and essential services such as education, utilities, and health care; marketization and liberalization; deregulation; and various other policies that shift responsibility for governance from the public to the private sphere (Harvey, 2005).

We have also seen in the neoliberal era a reconfiguration of not only states but also of North-South interdependencies, social cleavages, and inequalities. The damaging effects of structural adjustment are well known, and these policies are widely acknowledged to have put more wealth into the hands of the already wealthy, collapse domestic manufacturing sectors, increase unemployment, price out small agricultural producers and local mining companies, and reduce government services to contend with increases in poverty and unemployment, all of which increased inequality and reduced economic growth (SAPRIN, 2004). Today, some original architects of the neoliberal shock doctrine, including Jeffrey Sachs, acknowledge its failure and regard their once dogmatic commitment to the "development as growth" model as misguided, a significant driver of inequality, and a threat to environmental sustainability (see Wilson, 2014).

Research suggests that structural reforms associated with neoliberal development have contributed to increased levels of violence in several ways. Studies based in the Global South tend to focus on the effects of SAPs. For example, the inequality generated by SAPs can exacerbate existing social conflicts between different ethnic and religious communities (Adekanye, 1995; Kaiser, 1996). SAPs have also been associated with heightened levels of street crime thanks in part to the increases in poverty and unemployment they generate (Romo, 2002; Sanchez, 2006). Increases in crime in the neoliberal era are not limited to the Global South, however. It is important to stress that neoliberal reforms have also had a significant impact on economic and social governance in Western countries, along with those of the former Soviet Union. Criminologists in the Anglophone North have therefore come to associate deregulation, privatization, and deindustrialization with the destruction of livelihoods and the creation of what right-realists described as an "underclass," which is perceived as a criminal problem group superfluous to the needs of the current capitalist order, and governed as such (Wacquant, 2009). Concurrently, mass consumption as a defining feature of the neoliberal order has created new opportunities and incentives for criminality, which state and private actors have attempted to control through a combination of preventative technologies and punitive policies that are oriented toward incapacitation. Various scholars have come to associate the impact of these changes on the governance of crime in the Anglophone North with the "decline of the rehabilitative ideal" (Allen, 1981); the dismantling of the welfare state (Garland, 2001); a preventative turn (Edwards & Hughes, 2009); governments shifting responsibility for the implementation of crime control to private actors, including corporations, communities, and individuals (Crawford, 1999; Garland, 2001; O'Malley, 1992); and the rise of regressive, populist, punitive policies (Pratt, 2004; Garland, 2001; Simon, 2006) that are dismissive of the social causes of crime (e.g., Wilson, 1975) and indifferent to scientific evidence about "what works" (Loader, 2006). At the same time, the most widely debated criminological phenomena in many Western countries since the onset of neoliberalism has been declining levels of recorded crime (see Sharkey, 2018; Weatherburn & Rahman, 2021; Zimring, 2008).

The Anglo-American literature has had a significant impact on how criminologists globally have come to theorize the consequences of neoliberalism. This is in part attributable to the globalized effects of neoliberalism, which have coincided with (and stimulated) the development of criminology as a truly international, albeit geographically imbalanced, field of scholarship (Carrington et al., 2015). Thus, much like the aforementioned critiques of modernization and dependency approaches, the generalizability and relevance of Western experiences and concepts to interpreting the criminogenic and penological effects of neoliberalism throughout the Global South have been questioned (Steinberg, 2016). Nevertheless, several criminologists have persisted in their efforts to examine the impact of economic development on crime using traditional social scientific methods, namely cross-national studies.

CROSS-NATIONAL STUDIES

By nature of their design and purpose, cross-national studies have rarely or only superficially engaged with the complex methodological and conceptual issues detailed in the previous section, so their value for theorizing the crime-development nexus is perhaps questionable. Nevertheless, this body of research has highlighted some interesting empirical findings. It is worth reviewing, if for no other reason than to illustrate how the empirical study of crime and development has evolved since the publication of Clinard and Abbott's (1973) and Shelley's (1981) studies.

One of the more theoretically sophisticated studies of neoliberalization and crime was conducted by Elliott Currie (1997). Currie's study highlights some common mechanisms through which neoliberal globalization appears to contribute to increased rates of violence in both the Global North and South. These include (1) the progressive destruction of livelihoods; (2) growth of economic inequality and material deprivation; (3) the withdrawal of public services and supports, particularly for families and children; (4) the erosion of informal and communal networks of mutual support, supervision, and care; (5) the spread of a materialistic, neglectful, and "hard" culture; (6) the unregulated marketing of the technology of violence; and (7) the weakening of political and social alternatives (p. 154). Currie (1997) posited that there would be rapid increases in crime in the Global South, owing to the exacerbation of harms committed against populations from structural adjustment and other austerity policies. He predicted that crime rate hikes in the Global North, on the other hand, would be more gradual, owing to established social welfare policies that could buffer some of the social harms caused by neoliberal economic policies. Nevertheless, he argued that the structural effects of neoliberal reforms in market societies would contribute to heightened perceptions of insecurity and stimulate demand for more punitive crime control policies. Almost 20 years later, Currie (2015) extended this argument by suggesting that violence in both the Global North and South would continue to rise thanks to the increasing availability of firearms and the counterproductive effects of bloated criminal justice systems.

Few other scholars have attempted to explicitly test the relationship between economic development and crime in the Global North. This is perhaps attributable to the fact that criminologists uncritically assume that countries like the United States are already developed, so the relationship is unimportant. In this regard, those researchers who have examined the relationship between economic development (typically measured by growth) and crime in this context have adopted an ahistorical approach to operationalizing development and failed to appreciate its multifaceted nature, or the fact that even from a liberal standpoint, development does not have an end point. To this effect, these studies remain wedded to the modernization paradigm and are of limited relevance to our discussion here (see Koeppel, Rhineberger-Dunn & Mack, 2015; LaFree, Curtis & McDowall, 2015). One of the few exceptions however is Bjørnskov's (2015) panel study of different US states, which found no direct relationship between neoliberalism and homicide but that nonviolent offending had an inverse relationship with public spending.

More relevant is a body of cross-national research on economic development and crime. With regard to crime in general, Kick and LaFree (1985) found that economic development contributes to increases in property crime but reductions in violent crime. Braithwaite (1989) later claimed that in both developing and developed societies, crime is more likely to be committed by males, the young (15–25 years old), the unmarried, those experiencing high residential mobility, those less attached to school and who do more poorly in school, those who have criminal friends, those with less attachment to their parents, and those from the lower class. Bennett (1991) later found that development level and growth rate do not affect homicide rates but that development affects rates of theft, while the economic growth rate does not. Accordingly, he concluded that while development and crime are not directly related, they might be indirectly related, with cultural differences mediating this relationship. Soares (2004), by contrast, found that crime and inequality were related, and that crime reporting was positively related with modernization and rising incomes.

Many quantitative studies have focused narrowly on the relationship between social structure (or economic and human development) and homicide rates, since homicide rates are seen as a relatively reliable measure of crime that can gauge a country's general criminal violence rate (Howard, Newman, & Pridemore, 2000). For example, Trent and Pridemore (2012) provided an excellent comprehensive review of the entire known cross-national research literature on homicide, and Nivette (2011) conducted a meta-analysis of studies from 1960 to 2010. Koeppel, Rhinenberg-Dunn, and Mack (2013) conducted a review similar to Trent and Pridemore (2012), but only for the 50 studies that had been published from 1997 to 2011, comparing them to an older review by LaFree (1999) of studies published up until 1996. All of these reviews concluded that findings were not consistent across studies. The theories tested in these articles varied widely, but the variables were typically rooted in similar concepts. Concepts that are theoretically related to homicide rates in the criminological literature include age structure, economic development/productivity, labor conditions, educational attainment, and inequality, among others (Chamlin & Cochran, 2006, 2005, 2004; Levchak, 2016; McLean et al., 2019; Messner, 1986; Pare & Felson, 2014; Pridemore, 2011; Trent & Pridemore, 2012; Tuttle, McCall & Land, 2018). In her meta-analysis of the cross-national literature on homicide, Nivette (2011) concluded that variables associated with social integration and stability are important in explaining homicide, but that other variables involving population density, economic development, and deterrence show little to no impact.

One of the concepts used in the vast majority of studies was economic development, or "modernization," which was usually measured as GNP/GDP or as a development index (Koeppel et al., 2013; Trent & Pridemore, 2012). GDP (gross domestic product), a measure of economic output that can be used to see if economic growth is occurring over time, is by itself a very poor measure of socioeconomic development, in part because it does not take inequality into account (McMichael, 2017). Nevertheless, many criminologists continue to conflate growth with progress, regardless of who is or is not benefitting from it. When it comes to GNP/GDP and homicide rates, the results are mixed (Koeppel et al., 2013; Trent & Pridemore, 2012) and a majority of studies found a negative relationship between GNP/GDP and homicide rates, but several found a positive or null association.

We are aware of only one recent cross-national study that has explicitly tested the theoretical relationship between neoliberalism and crime. McLean et al. (2019) operationalized neoliberalism using variables derived from two indexes: the Economic Freedom World Index and the Index of Economic

Freedom. Neoliberal policies regarding government spending, government size, and tax burden were associated with increased inequality (Gini index), which was in turn associated with increased homicide rates. Neoliberal government spending and tax burden were also linked to poverty (as measured by infant mortality), which was also associated with increased homicide rates. McLean et al. (2019) concluded that general pronouncements that neoliberalism increases homicide rates are not accurate, but that certain neoliberal policies create conditions that are conducive to higher homicide rates.

The Gini index is the most used measure of economic deprivation or inequality in cross-national studies on homicide rates, and the majority find that the Gini index is positively related to homicide, making it the most consistent predictor across studies, even though the data sources and the years for which data were collected varied (Koeppel et al., 2013; Trent & Pridemore, 2012). More recent studies, however, have found that when absolute deprivation is included, it is positively associated with homicide and inequality is no longer significant (Pare & Felson, 2010). Findings from studies that examined unemployment generated mixed results, while studies examining ethnic heterogeneity found a positive relationship between heterogeneity and homicide (Koeppel et al., 2015).

In some of the studies reviewed by Trent and Pridemore (2012), population structure was treated as an independent variable. Koeppel et al. (2015) found that the youth population (up to age 30) was often either negatively associated or not at all, with only a few studies finding a positive relationship. Delving into more detail, Trent and Pridemore (2012) found that the youth population was actually positively associated with homicide rates, except in studies with lower sample sizes or those focusing on Russia and Eastern Europe, where homicide offenders and victims tend to be older. A small number of studies included divorce rates and most found that homicide and divorce rates were positively correlated (Trent & Pridemore, 2012).

Urbanization and population size are key independent variables, though they are measured in numerous ways. In addition to the modernization and dependency theories discussed above, social control, structuralist, and subcultural theories contend that increases in population size are associated with increases in crime (Chamlin & Cochran, 2004). Respectively, urbanization and population growth can weaken informal social control, increase the likelihood that individuals come into contact with criminal individuals, and increase the expansion of deviant subcultures (Chamlin & Cochran, 2004). As with GNP/GDP, however, the results are not definitive. Some studies used population growth, size, or density to measure urbanization. In studies where population growth was significantly related to homicide, there was a positive association, but in studies where population size was significantly related to homicide, there was usually a negative association (Trent & Pridemore, 2012). Most studies testing population density found no significant association with homicide (Koeppel et al., 2015). When it comes to the proportion of the population residing in urban areas, the results were mixed (Koeppel et al., 2013; Trent & Pridemore, 2012).

Koeppel et al. (2015) found that the more recent articles they reviewed were examining new variables or concepts to see if they correlated with homicide. One of these concepts was "social support," measured for example by the percentage of GDP spent on education or health care, or by using the commodification index. Most studies examining social support found a negative relationship with homicide, unless it was used as an interaction term, in which case the results were mixed (Koeppel et al., 2015). Other variables examined in the more recent studies included sex ratio (number of males per 100 females), and alcohol- and gun-related variables. As expected, gun ownership and alcohol use were positively associated with homicide rates, while the sex ratio was unexpectedly negatively related (Koeppel et al., 2015).

Cross-national studies such as those noted above highlight important lines of inquiry, but they have been plagued with numerous methodological and theoretical problems. While Koeppel et al. (2015) noted that the more recent studies they reviewed engaged in more multivariate instead of bivariate analyses, and incorporated more sophisticated statistical techniques in some cases, Trent and Pridemore (2012, p. 132) argued that "too often" the quantitative studies they reviewed suffered from serious limitations. These include under-theorization; the downloading of data with little regard for data integrity; how the data were collected or what they represent; or the comparability of data collected from different sources for various purposes, using whatever data are available to obtain the largest sample size. Nivette (2011) also notes that most cross-national study designs are cross-sectional, even though longitudinal analyses are needed to test theories explaining homicide adequately. Data integrity is obviously a crucial issue as well, but the validity of independent variables used in these studies, largely consisting of development statistics, has been questioned. The process for producing development statistics on measures such as per capita income and GDP, for example, differs by country and can be an arbitrary process, producing unreliable data with the appearance of accuracy, particularly in countries where resources are scarce (Jerven, 2013).

With regard to theory, earlier studies focused most on modernization, social disorganization, and economic stress perspectives, whereas more recent studies focus on inequality, poverty, stress, and deprivation (Koeppel et al., 2015). The variables used to test these theories often overlap, however, and even though situational and ecological theories are not often mentioned, variables often associated with those theories are regularly tested. Variables used, therefore, are often "theoretically vague, with considerable overlap and no agreement on operationalization" (Nivette, 2011, p. 123). Chamlin and Cochran (2005) suggest, for example, that the inequality-homicide relationship has been poorly theorized, relying on reductionist, social-psychological theories to explain macro-social phenomena that cannot be extended logically to homicide. To contend with this issue, they proposed a macro-social approach, suggesting that variations in homicide rates across countries are best explained by high levels of ascribed, rather than achieved, economic inequality, because ascribed inequalities lead to the undermining of the legitimacy of the social order.

A final methodological consideration is sample size. Nivette (2011) found that cross-national studies on homicide had small, biased samples, with only about one-fifth of countries covered, primarily from the developed, industrialized world. Variables in cross-national data sets, especially longitudinal ones, have incomplete coverage with missing values. Therefore, when handling missing data, the analytic techniques used in the studies cited by Trent and Pridemore (2012) and in more recent work (e.g., LaFree et al., 2015; Levchak, 2016) typically rely on list-wise deletion. Analyses therefore only include waves for which there is complete coverage for all variables in the model, leaving researchers with less information used for model estimation (see Clement et al., 2019). Consequently, countries in the Global South, and even some Organization for Economic Cooperation and Development (OECD) countries, are excluded from analyses. This is important because we cannot measure the effects of globalization or modernization on homicide and other forms of crime while excluding the Global South, which is obviously an integral part of the globalization process (Clement et al., 2019).

Cross-national studies published in the past 10 years have gone in new directions. Some have attempted to test whether there has been a global homicide decline and whether national crime rates follow supranational trends, but these studies found weak trends or none at all, instead finding heterogeneity in regional crime patterns (Baumer & Wolff, 2014; LaFree, Curtis & McDowall, 2015; Rogers & Pridemore, 2018, p. 718). Other contemporary cross-national and local-level studies specifically examining urbanization and homicide have revealed that it might be best to treat urbanization as a multidimensional concept in order to capture both the overall urban proportion in a country but also the proportion of those living in the largest urban centers (Chang et al., 2019; Clement, Pino & Blaustein, 2019; Levchak, 2016; Sahasranaman & Bettencourt, 2019). The commonly used basic measure of urbanization (percent of the population living in urban areas) establishes a lower threshold for identifying rural versus urban areas, failing to distinguish mega-cities from smaller-sized cities (UN, 2005). Clement et al. (2019) pointed out, for example, that according to the World Bank's urbanization measure, Greenland, with a population of around 20,000 inhabitants, is 86% urban. What Clement et al. (2019) did, then, was include two variables capturing urbanization in their models using cross-national longitudinal data: the basic measure of urbanization (proportion of the population that is urban) and proportion of the population living in cities of at least one million or more inhabitants (both from World Bank data). What they found was that while the basic urbanization measure was significantly and positively related to homicide rates (as expected), contrary to expectations, the proportion living in large cities was significantly and negatively related to homicide (Clement et al., 2019). This suggests a protective effect in terms of homicide as a larger proportion of a country's population resides in bigger cities. City-level studies in the United States and India found this pattern as well, with larger cities having lower violent and property crime rates (Chang et al., 2019; Sahasranaman & Bettencourt, 2019).

There is another important tradition of cross-national research worth acknowledging here. This research draws on data from the International Crime and Victim Survey (ICVS), which was developed in the late 1980s to "produce estimates of victimization that can be used for international comparison" (ICVS, n.d.) rather than official statistics. The advantage is that self-reported victimization data are better suited for assessing and comparing a more diverse array of offence categories that are often underrepresented (or misrepresented) in official statistics.[1] Thus, drawing on ICVS data, Zvekic and Alvazzi del Fate (1995) attempted to group developing countries based on region and observed that urban areas (Beijing, Bombay, Jakarta, and Manila) in Asian countries had the lowest victimization rates, while those in Sub-Saharan Africa (Kampala, Dar es Salaam, and Johannesburg) had the highest rates. Sub-Saharan African and Latin American cities were found to have the highest rates of violence, respectively, including sexual violence reported by women. These findings indicated that people in peripheral countries are more frequently victims of virtually all types of crime (including sexual violence against women, fraud, and corruption) than those in countries considered developed (industrialized).

ICVS data has also been used for comparative research that examines the links between transnational organized crime, corruption, and development. A seminal study was undertaken by one of the creators of the ICVS, Jan van Dijk (2007), who worked for the UN crime program at the time that the Millennium Development Goals were being negotiated. We do not have space to provide a detailed overview of van Dijk's analysis, but two significant points are worth noting here. First, van Dijk drew attention to the changing nature of crime as an international phenomenon as a consequence of globalization. Second, the analysis supplied scientific evidence of a global crime problem and its impacts on victims around the world (see also van Dijk, Nieuwbeerta & Joudo Larsen, 2021). The latter point is particularly important here because it directly feeds into the narrative that crime is a global phenomenon that must be addressed through cooperation.

CRITICAL PERSPECTIVES

There have been numerous critiques leveled at Western/Northern-centric approaches to theorizing and researching crime in the Global South. Historically, there have been relatively few in-depth empirical studies of Southern countries or regions, and much of this scholarship is dominated by Northern authors (Salahub, de Boer, & Gottsbacher, 2018). For example, Northern criminological scholarship on crime and the crime-development relationship has been characterized as ethnocentric and rooted in Orientalism and Occidentalism (Cain, 2000, p. 239; also Agozino, 2003). Cain (2000) contends that these tendencies are mutually reinforcing and contribute to myopic and misguided analyses. Somewhat similarly, Rogers (1989) has argued that both mainstream and critical approaches to studying the relationship between development and crime are based on essentialist and universalizing assertions. Karstedt (2018) also notes that "big picture criminology" studies have been criticized for overgeneralizing while understating differences, limiting their policy relevance.

Cain (2000) cautioned criminologists undertaking comparative research to be sensitive to local meaning and context. For example, seemingly straightforward concepts like "community" or "age" are often understood differently throughout the Global South. This can obviously have important implications for the applicability of Northern criminological theories to the Global South. Relatedly, Liu (2004) noted that the destabilizing effects of modernization can be experienced differently in different contexts. His analysis of the development of market institutions in China found that modernization did not weaken traditional social institutions, but rather "institutional disorganization" weakened social controls in China due to "the loss of coordination among traditional social control institutions under the rapidly developing demands of market institutions" (Liu, 2004, p. 135).

To overcome these issues, Rogers (1989) has advocated for using detailed, qualitative case studies to account for the distinctive features of the crime-development relationship in specific historical contexts. He illustrated the value of this approach by examining the different historical origins of cattle theft, rioting, and homicide in Sri Lanka and concluded that attempts to control these behaviors were driven by the government's insecurity rather than its desire to affect relations of production. Similarly, Huhn and Warnecke-Berger (2017, p. 9) suggest "qualitative, historical, ethnological, or field-research-based micro-perspective studies are indispensable to really understand the phenomenon of the social meaning of violence in Central America." Arthur and Marenin (1995) have also advocated case study approaches, albeit as a means of linking macro- and micro-level approaches to studying the relationship between development and crime in specific contexts.

Another important point is that crime in the Global South must be understood as a product of historical and enduring North-South relations rather than simply as a uniquely "Southern" or "local" phenomenon. For example, Bennett and Lynch (1996, p. 12) argued that the Caribbean has developed differently from Western countries because the former "must contend with developed nations while those which developed in the past did not." Caribbean countries are also more reliant on tourism and, thanks to their geographic location, are an important transit region for narcotics trafficking and are therefore both heavily impacted by drug-related crimes and a major background from the US-led war on drugs (Bennett & Lynch, 1996; Bowling, 2010). This example highlights the transnational character of development as a historical process.

Studies by Southern scholars, including criminologists, also "directly challenge Northern-led theory, and show the futility of trying to apply it in a cookie-cutter fashion to places with very different dynamics of poverty, inequality, and violence" (Salahub, de Boer, & Gottsbacher, 2018, p. 9). This body of work highlights that harms deemed criminal by Anglo-European standards are not the only forms of violence that people in Southern cities experience. Salahub et al. (2018, p. 1) note, for example, that there are "structural, infrastructural, physical, and exclusionary forms of violence that reflect the complexity of the phenomenon." Living in overcrowded, dilapidated conditions and being unable to afford already inadequate utilities and other services while facing interpersonal violence, violent evictions, and the like can therefore contribute to heightened levels of criminalized, interpersonal violence in over-policed, informal settlements such as the *favelas* in Brazil. These and other forms of social, economic, and political exclusion are important factors when it comes to explaining violence in the Global South, and why some poor countries and communities have higher crime rates than others.

Other scholars have also drawn attention to the complex, cumulative, and overlapping factors that contribute to urban violence. Ambraseys and Bilham (2011) argue that these include not only political, social, and economic factors but also, increasingly, environmental risks. Environmental risks lead to mass migrations and therefore new residency patterns that disrupt social cohesion and informal social control, and fear of crime can reduce school attendance and increase the proliferation of vigilante groups (de Boer & Gottsbacher, 2019). In areas where violence is rampant, trust in one's neighbors and institutions tend to be very low as well, necessitating the need to build social cohesion and trust within and between neighborhood areas, particularly in impoverished parts of cities (de Boer & Gottsbacher, 2019; Salahub & Zaaroura, 2018).

Latin America has been a region of particular interest to scholars and international policy makers. This is attributable to a combination of factors, including elevated levels of violent crime and the region's turbulent political and economic history. An important focus of this debate relates to whether the region's problems can be attributed to a common historical experience linked with its distinct trajectory of colonialism, modernization, and, perhaps most significantly, neoliberalism. The evidence is mixed.

There are certainly common structural forces that have shaped the region and generated instabilities (Sanchez, 2006), but these have had a varied and complex impact across countries and even individual communities (Iturralde, 2015; Hilgers & Macdonald, 2017; Perlman, 2010). Kruijt (2012) echoes this assessment and notes violence against the internal enemies of the Latin American dictatorships and civil-military governments has been a key contributing factor to the problem of urban violence and, specifically, gangs. Non-state actor violence has also increased in Latin America over time, and Kruijt (2012) attributes this to poverty stemming from structural adjustment policies; the shrinking of the middle class; the disruption of family structures leading to larger numbers of female-headed households; social exclusion; and the development of informal, transnational economies, including the drug trade.

Others have argued that urban violence in Latin America cannot be reduced to the impact of neoliberal reforms and note that these have been adapted and, in some cases, resisted by governments throughout the region. Structural adjustment policies may have therefore exacerbated inequalities and instabilities throughout the region, but governments have attempted to manage these in different ways (Iturralde, 2015). It must also be acknowledged that neoliberalism is not the only model of capitalist development that has historically contributed to these conditions. For example, Davis (2014) argues that modernist urban planning practices established the geographic and social fault lines that underpin the uneven distribution of poverty, urban violence, and repressive state control in Latin American cities today. And of course prior to this, the history of settler colonialism, European migration, and the economic development of politically independent Latin American countries since the 19th century generated inequalities that extended and reproduced racial ideologies (Quijano, 2007).

Even Central America, widely regarded as the most dangerous region in the world (UNODC, 2019), defies generalization and demonstrates the limits of reductionist theories (Martinez, 2017). For one thing, this violence is unevenly distributed, with Guatemala, El Salvador, and Honduras experiencing very high rates of violence, while their Southern neighbors (Panama, Costa Rica, and Nicaragua) have much lower rates, though still higher than those seen in Western countries (Huhn & Warnecke-Berger, 2017). The three more violent countries thus account for 87% of all homicides in Central America and the most commonly cited explanations for violence in the literature cannot explain why some Central American countries are more violent than others (Zinecker, 2017). For example, one cannot pin the blame squarely on the region's violent civil-war past because (1) homicide rates were high prior to the outbreak of civil wars; (2) current levels of violence are even higher than they were during these conflicts; and (3) among the three most violent countries, only two (El Salvador and Guatemala) suffered from civil wars, although Honduras was affected by US intervention via the Contras. Nicaragua is also an intriguing case because the country has relatively low levels of violence despite a history similar to countries like El Salvador and Honduras, including a civil war (Zinecker 2017).

Furthermore, with few exceptions, many criminologists who undertake comparative research on crime and development have failed to consider gender. While there is clearly growing criminological interest in gender-based violence in the Global South (see Amin, Watson, & Girard, 2020; Fitz-Gibbon & Walklate, 2020), the gender-specific consequences of historical development policies or projects on the nature and distribution of crime and victimization are rarely considered. Other disciplines, therefore, contain most of the existing scholarship on the political economy of gender-based violence in the Global South (see Wies & Haldane, 2011; True, 2012). Criminologists and scholars in public health (Heise, Ellsber, & Gottmoeller, 2002) are therefore typically (and perhaps justifiably) more concerned with preventing violence against women than understanding its complex and historically rooted causes.

A key theoretical contribution of the growing literature on gender-based violence is that it has started to change how women in the Global South are characterized. It has increased not only the visibility of the harms they experience but also their agency. For example, recent scholarship has highlighted how women assert their agency by initiating and participating in community-based crime prevention initiatives around the world (Salahub, de Boer, & Gottsbacher, 2018). This highlights the importance of examining these issues through a gendered lens and the potential utility of addressing crime and violence through community-based, and community-initiated, interventions. Research has also illustrated the potential utility of developing gender-specific models of policing in contexts where traditional policing actors do not represent a source of security or protection for women (Carrington et al., 2021). Although proposals to adopt the Brazilian model of women's only police stations for use in Australia have been met with resistance, the example illustrates the potential merits of looking to the Global South for innovative solutions to common criminological problems.

By contrast, Northern approaches to addressing the problem of crime in the developing world have historically emphasized enhancing the capabilities of formal institutions of social control. In some contexts, Northern reformers have even been unwilling to engage with informal policing and justice actors because they are not recognized by the state (Hills, 2014). The normative preoccupation with state institutions seemingly endures despite a growing body of criminological evidence suggesting that security is actually governed and delivered by a range of nodal actors and, increasingly, actants (Berg & Shearing, 2020). It is beyond the scope of this chapter to account for the problematic legacy of state-centric international criminal justice reform and police building initiatives, but it is important to acknowledge that Northern interventions, particularly those that fail to account for local circumstances and contextual differences, may prove not only ineffective but actually harmful (Ellison & Pino, 2012; Iturralde, 2020). Drawing on Ivan Illich (1974), British criminologist Stan Cohen (1998) famously associated the transposition of Western crime-control models throughout the developing world as "iatrogenic" (see also Blaustein, 2016; Bowling, 2011).

In many developing countries, this risk is particularly pronounced, as the police and other criminal justice actors were never originally established to operate within a liberal democratic framework (Ellison & Pino, 2012). Their capabilities may also be undermined by limited resources, particularly in those countries that have experienced economic crises that have impacted the public purse. At the same time, it would also be misguided to assume that Northern models or offers of technical assistance are inherently problematic or undesirable, at least from the perspective of those who face an imminent risk of urban violence and have little trust or confidence in the state and its criminal justice institutions to offer security and justice. These are all issues that need to be considered in relation to specific criminological risks and in particular contexts. Just as there can be no generalizable theory of crime and development, there should be no one-size-fits all approach to addressing the causes or consequences of criminal harms.

Finally, Moosavi (2019; 2021) has recently presented a more radical critique of the comparative project, which is grounded in postcolonial and decolonial critiques of development and the sociology of knowledge production. He argues that the intellectual contributions of influential Southern theorists, such as Syed Hussein Alatas (1974), who wrote about corruption and advocated for decolonizing the social sciences since the 1970s, have been almost entirely overlooked by Northern criminologists, including by some who today advocate for decolonizing criminology (see also Agozino, 2004). This is in our view a fair critique, and the subordination and neglect of Southern theory within the field reflects the enduring hegemonic influence of the metropole when it comes to conceptualizing, studying, and addressing the problem of crime (Bhambra, 2014; Carrington, Hogg & Sozzo, 2016; Connell, 2007). Our analysis demonstrates that, with few exceptions, Southern and subaltern perspectives have historically had a marginal impact on the international crime policy agenda and the construction of the crime-development nexus.

CONCLUSION

The conceptual ambiguity surrounding the crime-development relationship, coupled with the political nature of global crime governance, leads us to conclude that the crime-development nexus is not strictly an empirical phenomenon. Many of the Western/Northern theoretical approaches and assumptions reviewed in this chapter have certainly influenced the intellectual construction of the crime-development nexus, and there is a significant body of evidence illustrating that problems associated with criminalized harms, particularly violence, are especially pronounced in parts of the Global South. Less conventional forms of crime, including transnational organized crime and corruption, also appear to be prevalent in developing and transitional countries, where legitimate opportunities are possibly more limited and regulation perhaps less effective. Intuitively, increased access to global markets has seemingly created new opportunities, but social scientific literature on these problems, which have come to be associated with the "dark side of globalization," is comparatively thin and there is not much scope to generalize. Rather, much of the evidence base is either anecdotal or based on trends analysis (e.g., Reitano, 2018; Global Initiative, 2021), which can be useful for identifying or addressing these issues (and amplifying visibility of them) but is of limited value when it comes to theorizing their relationship with the systems of capitalist development they are said to threaten. Again, describing these problems and their uneven distribution (both globally and within societies, including those of the Global North) is important, but this is different than explaining why they exist or how they impact development.

There are certainly common historical and structural experiences that may help us to interpret some of these problems in specific contexts; however, the narrative review presented in this chapter highlights that the impacts of colonialism, modernization, or economic liberalization are mediated by a range of factors and historical experiences. For social scientists, there is nothing particularly revelatory about this claim, yet the crime-development nexus as a discursive assemblage is wedded to an ahistorical, essentialist, and reductionist characterization of the global crime problem. Framing this as a Southern problem is also problematic from a social scientific perspective, because categories like "Third World," the "Global South," or the "developing world" are only meaningful in relation to their "First World," "Northern," or "developed" counterparts who constructed to advance their own economic development through colonization, modernization, and liberalization (Escobar, 2011; Agozino, 2013; Bhambra, 2014). This is an inconvenient truth for international policy makers, because complexity, diversity, and subaltern critiques represent significant obstacles to building and maintaining the consensus that there is a *global* crime problem that must be governed collectively and addressed through cooperation, harmonization, and technical interventions.

Chapter Two

Theorizing Global Crime Governance

This chapter elaborates on our theoretical framework, which, we suggest, advances a more critical, sophisticated, and historically grounded understanding of the forms and functions of global crime governance. We begin by considering how the phenomenon of global crime governance has been theorized previously and account for the strengths and limitations of these approaches. First, we examine functionalist approaches, which conceptualize global crime governance as a natural response to the globalization of crime. The key limitation of this functionalist perspective is that it fails to consider the inherently political nature of global governance and the ways in which global policy agendas, norms, and technical capabilities are shaped by the interests of powerful international actors and negotiated through their interactions with the weak. Accordingly, we next turn to realist[1] perspectives that offer relevant, albeit superficial, insight into the politics of global governance by highlighting the influence of powerful states—most importantly the United States—in shaping elements of the international crime policy agenda to advance their foreign policy interests since the late 1940s. Realist analyses are particularly useful for historicizing the emergence of a truly *global* crime policy agenda in the post–Cold War era, one that saw the growing "securitization" of crime (Buzan et al., 1998) as states shifted their focus to less conventional transnational security threats (see chapter 6). A key limitation of realist approaches is that they offer only limited insight into how less powerful states—Italy in the 1990s, for example—shape the international policy agenda and benefit from these regimes. More significantly, realist perspectives tend to focus primarily on states, downplaying the influence of non-state actors. They also tend to categorize power in terms of military capabilities, downplaying its ideational and material dimensions.

The chapter next shifts its focus to considering the value of institutionalist and constructivist approaches to theorizing global crime governance. Institutionalist perspectives focus on the role of international institutions and regimes that are created by states to help them govern crime from a distance. These institutions and regimes play an important role in legitimizing the interests of powerful actors, including states. When international institutions are ascribed bureaucratic qualities, such as through the creation of international organizations such as the United Nations (UN) and its specialized agencies, they also exhibit a degree of autonomy that provides them with cause and scope to shape and construct policy agendas. This in turn prompts consideration of constructivist approaches that focus on the role of transnational norm entrepreneurs in constructing global crime problems in need of multilateral solutions.

Institutionalist and constructivist approaches provide relevant insight into *how* issue linkages and norms emerge as part of the international crime policy agenda. However, they offer a limited account of *why* some issues and solutions become socially constructed and embedded within international regimes but not others. Insofar as international organizations and other norm entrepreneurs are neither beholden to the interests of their sovereign architects nor wholly autonomous, we argue that it is necessary to situate institutionalist and constructivist perspectives in a political economy approach. Our integrated framework, which draws on the work of Robert Cox, is therefore the focus of the final section of this chapter.

Cox (1983, 1987, 1994) argues that global governance is shaped by the historical interplay between material, institutional, and ideological forces. Specifically, the Coxian perspective sheds light on how changes in the social relations of production give rise to new social forces, which proceed to restructure the international system to promote their interests. Cox's understanding of "production" is grounded in the Gramscian tradition of historical materialism, as opposed to orthodox Marxist interpretations that reduced material production to "economism." This distinction is important from a theoretical standpoint because a Coxian analysis treats ideas and material conditions as "bound together, mutually influencing one another, and not reducible one to the other" (see Cox, 2002, pp. 131–32). This implies that networks of global governance are structured by the interests of the dominant social forces. Since the Second World War, global governance institutions have therefore been established to facilitate and manage the expansion of global capitalism. This implies that international organizations, including the UN, exist not only to embody and promote the rules that enable this expansion but also to ideologically legitimate it, co-opt opposition, and, where necessary, neutralize potential threats. Acknowledging structural influences on the historical construction of a discursive assemblage is essential for answering the *why* question, but this is not to suggest that international organizations and other norm entrepreneurs simply act in ways that mechanically serve to reproduce hegemony. Rather, they *may* also act as sites and even sources of conflict and contestation.

FUNCTIONALISM

The first set of approaches conceptualize global crime governance as a functional response to globalization. According to this perspective, globalization— "the widening, deepening and speeding up of worldwide interconnectedness" (Held et al., 1999, p. 2)—comes with a "dark side" in the form of the emergence of transnational organized crime (Heine & Thakur, 2011). Just as legitimate business is increasingly conducted across borders, so is illicit business, especially given the revolutions in transport, technology, and communications, which have allowed previously nationally-oriented organized crime groups to go transnational (Shelley, 1995, pp. 465–66; Findlay, 2008, pp. 51–52). Thus, the global economy is underpinned by an "illicit global economy," across which illegal goods and services are traded, from drugs to humans to arms, the proceeds of which are subsequently "laundered" and enter the licit economy. The precise size and extent of this illicit economy is hard to measure, but analysts have previously cited estimates that global markets for illicit goods amount to at least $1 trillion (Jojarth, 2009, p. 7). This poses a problem not only in terms of social harms but also for the state itself, with transnational criminal networks argued to threaten the very core of sovereignty by undermining its claim to a monopoly of violence and authority within its borders (Shelley, 1995, p. 468). Indeed, the 1990s saw widespread and alarmist accounts of states overwhelmed by the "new empire of evil" of transnational organized crime, a "global Pax Mafiosa" of crime groups cooperating and dividing the world among themselves, threatening order and stability in the Global Village (Sterling, 1994; Kerry, 1997; Raine & Cilluffo, 1994).

In this context, global crime governance is simply conceptualized as a functional response to a new and emerging threat. As crime goes global, so does the response to it as societies seek to "rationalize" a chaotic and uncontrolled world by making it more transparent, understandable, and accountable (Jakobi, 2013, p. 4). This drives a plethora of actors, including states, corporations, non-governmental organizations (NGOs), international organizations, and policy networks, to pursue efforts to eliminate the illicit global economy. These efforts include enhanced cooperation between police (i.e., transnational policing; see Sheptycki, 1995; Bowling & Sheptycki,

2012), the establishment of multilateral treaties such as the United Nations Convention against Transnational Organized Crime (UNTOC) and the United Nations Convention against Corruption (UNCAC), or networked cooperation between state and non-state actors in a specific industry such as the Kimberley Process, which was developed to regulate the trade in conflict diamonds (Bieri, 2010).

Across this field of global crime governance, "best practice" policies are developed and subsequently diffused to societies facing shared global problems. For example, Simmons et al. (2018) note that policies combating human trafficking are "contagious." This suggests that once a group of countries develops successful approaches to this issue, other states will be inclined to follow suit to ensure the suppressed criminal activities are not diverted to their jurisdictions. Similarly, the anti–money laundering (AML) regime spread from a small group of states that developed recommendations on the necessary practices and institutions to combat the laundering of money to the rest of the world through the Financial Action Task Force (FATF). The FATF represents a global network of 167 states through which the recommendations are diffused and adopted as states seek to ensure that they do not become the weak link in efforts to combat money laundering (Jakobi, 2013, pp. 78–113). This highlights the growing harmonization of global crime policies as states cooperate to ensure that criminals cannot exploit differences between their legal commitments (Shelley, 1995, pp. 486–87). For functionalists, this harmonization represents the progress of a world society, with nations increasingly converging on a common culture and common definitions of crime based on universal, essentialist definitions of right and wrong (Jakobi, 2013, p. 3; Findlay, 2008, p. 52).

Functionalist approaches highlight the important role globalization has played in fostering the development of global crime governance, particularly since the 1990s. They also illuminate how these networks operate and provide insight into the dominant narratives and worldviews that provide a justification for the development of new regimes and international cooperation. This in turn influences the operations of international organizations, like the United Nations Office on Drugs and Crime (UNODC), that are responsible for facilitating functional cooperation and maintaining regimes. However, reducing global crime governance to a functionalist explanation is limiting.

As Andreas (2015) argues, the complex, dynamic, and often invisible nature of global crime makes it very difficult to accurately measure, so bold claims about its prevalence are at best guesstimates based on flawed data sets and methodologies (see also Andreas & Greenhill, 2010). As we discuss later in this book, this suggests that the work of international organizations that act as the guardians of these regimes is guided not by evidence-based policy;

rather, the evidence is driven by policy (Littoz-Monnet, 2017). Likewise, contrary to alarmist claims about a "global Pax Mafiosa," criminal networks cooperate only loosely and are more interested in avoiding or co-opting state power than challenging it (Naylor, 1995). This raises questions about whether global crime governance truly does reflect common responses to "common evils." By extension, it also prompts consideration of whether problems like transnational organized crime and corruption are really a threat to globalization or an unfortunate by-product of it rather than an integral, if undesirable, feature of our global capital order. Indeed, as this book will make clear, the architecture of global crime governance today features numerous limitations that seemingly undermine its ability to actually address these problems. Indeed, the harmonization, diffusion, and implementation of legal norms in relation to UNTOC and UNCAC is obstructed by the lack of meaningful audit or enforcement mechanisms. Another example of this is provided by Sharman (2011), who posed as a would-be money launderer to demonstrate that the AML regime actually does very little to combat money laundering. He found that AML regulations were not only ineffective but in many cases actually created perverse outcomes.

Likewise, the international crime policy agenda is riddled with omissions, which belie claims that it represents the outcome of rational and considered policy making processes. For example, one of the key instruments of fighting corruption, the 1997 OECD Anti-Bribery Convention, which criminalizes bribery of state officials by citizens or corporations, represents a very narrow conception of corruption—one that ignores the broader social practices in which bribery is embedded—thereby stifling the development of an all-encompassing approach to the problem, which may threaten the interests of Northern elites (Gutterman, 2019, pp. 210–11). The issue of measurement described by Andreas (2015) above also comes into play here, because the lack of data together with the vague and contested definitions of problems like "corruption" makes tracking progress difficult.

To address the theoretical limitations of functionalism, it is necessary to reflect on the role of power and the interests of leading actors, not least states, when it comes to influencing global crime governance and the international crime policy agenda. For example, we note that the OECD Convention was driven by the United States, where corporations were disadvantaged by the domestic criminalization of bribery through the Foreign Corrupt Practices Act (FCPA). This left them vulnerable to prosecution for accepting bribes offshore, while their European counterparts faced no such threat. Accordingly, during the negotiations that led to the Anti-Bribery Convention, US officials used their power to compel European countries to adopt a narrow focus on bribery, excluding other forms of corruption that transnational corporations relied upon (Abbott & Snidal, 2002). Likewise, the AML regime initially focused solely on money laundering associated with the drug trade, and—after 9/11—terrorist financing, both of which directly aligned with US foreign policy interests. This was at the expense of other types of illicit financial transactions, such as tax evasion or capital flight, which were understood to benefit the US economy (Helleiner, 1999). Thus, while some functionalist analyses do acknowledge the importance of states as partners or "institutional entrepreneurs" (Jacobi, 2013, pp. 230–31), their interests are typically an afterthought, because international cooperation is reduced to a rational, collective, and harmonious response to a universal threat.

REALISM

Theorizing global crime governance necessitates consideration of power. Realist approaches provide a useful starting point because they highlight the role that powerful states play in defining international policy agendas to suit their interests.[2] For our purposes, this implies that global crime governance and the international crime policy agenda have been disproportionately influenced by the United States via a combination of international political advocacy and the export of criminal justice norms, law enforcement priorities, and policing practices (Andreas & Nadelmann, 2006, p. 10). This influence is probably most frequently discussed in relation to America's role in shaping the global efforts to combat drugs and drug trafficking. Consequently, the international drug policy agenda has historically emphasized policies associated with prohibition rather than regulation or legalization (Woodiwiss, 2003a, pp. 19–20).

For powerful countries, influencing the international crime policy agenda may also offer a strategy for advancing other policy priorities. As noted above, the United States uses the OECD Anti-Bribery Convention to promote its strategic trade interests rather than as a vehicle for actually addressing corruption (Joutsen, 2018, pp. 321–22). Similarly, the US certification system for monitoring compliance with international obligations relating to human trafficking and drug trafficking advances national security interests, and states considered threats are sanctioned while allies are typically given a free pass (Friman, 2010). From a realist perspective, this suggests that global crime governance is not a universal project to promote collective security interests or advance the common good. Rather, it allows powerful states to selectively police those problems (issues and actors) that conflict with their interests. The expansion of global crime governance networks and the creation of new regimes are thus explained by their power and influence rather than a consensus that a problem exists.

Realist analyses are also useful in historicizing global crime governance. Contrary to ahistorical functionalist accounts, realists point to the significance of the post–Cold War context. Specifically, they illustrate how alarmist accounts of a "global Pax Mafiosa" served the interests of the security agencies of Western countries whose mandates and budgets were threatened by the demise of the Soviet Union. These agencies shifted their focus from war to crime, thereby redefining their missions and blurring the boundaries between international and domestic security (Andreas & Price, 2001; Naylor, 1995), with policy discourses associated with the latter becoming increasingly "securitized" (Buzan et al., 1998). For example, the United States framed the issue of money laundering as a national security threat by linking it to the war on drugs and later terrorism, thereby elevating it to a global governance problem (Hameiri & Jones, 2015, pp. 169–73). This occurred despite limited evidence of links between Islamic terrorist groups and organized crime, so the issue linkage makes little sense from a functional standpoint (de Goede, 2009). Nevertheless, once framed as a national security threat, it became a priority for the United States, which used institutions such as FATF to coerce other states into adopting its recommendations (Drezner, 2007, pp. 133–36). The role of bodies such as FATF therefore illustrates the value of supplementing the realist perspective with an institutionalist lens in order to analyze the role of international regimes and organizations.

INSTITUTIONALISM

Institutionalists argue that states create international institutions because these reduce the transaction costs of cooperation by acting as impartial brokers in negotiations, sharing information, promoting norms and standards, and monitoring compliance (Keohane, 1984; Krasner, 1983). For example, the various UN organs tasked with dealing with crime, including UNODC, serve states' interests by articulating common standards and norms relating to criminal justice and providing technical assistance to implement them (Redo & Platzer, 2013). A good example is UNTOC, negotiated at the UN during the 1990s to combat transnational organized crime. The negotiations were initially driven by several European states and saw the establishment of the UN Office for Drug Control and Crime Prevention (UN-ODCCP)—the forerunner to UNODC—in 1997 to facilitate the drafting of the convention and its protocols (Vlassis, 2002, pp. 85–87). UNTOC was embraced by the United States because, according to a senior State Department official, it "promoted practices already adopted in the United States to commit other signatories to do the same on a global basis" (cited in Andreas & Nadelmann, 2006,

p. 173). Thus, from a US perspective, an international institution such as UNTOC is more efficient because it legitimizes the imposition of the country's policy agenda on other states, thus negating the need to negotiate individual bilateral agreements with them (Andreas & Nadelmann, 2006, p. 9). Moreover, the value of UNTOC and UNCAC is that they subsequently promoted and monitored the implementation of the necessary legal instruments to fight transnational crime, to ensure there were no "safe havens" where it could flourish (Williams & Baudin-O'Hayon, 2002, pp. 135–37). This established a mandate for UNODC to provide technical assistance to developing countries that lacked the expertise to implement them, and for UNCAC (and much later UNTOC) a peer review mechanism for monitoring progress and compliance (Vlassis, 2002, pp. 91–93). Thus, from an institutionalist perspective, global crime governance remains a state-driven project, albeit one that involves multilateral efforts to facilitate international cooperation.

Institutionalist accounts share some ground with functionalist analyses and stress that international institutions have, at best, limited autonomy from states. That is, they are said to exist to serve states, especially the most powerful among them. Accordingly, the shortcomings and failures of global crime governance are typically attributed to the interference or indifference of powerful actors. For example, the main international institution for combating the illicit trade in small arms, the UN Program of Action on Small Arms and Light Weapons, is a soft-law, non–legally binding agreement that has failed to stem the proliferation of small arms to conflict zones. This, according to Jojarth (2009, pp. 281–84), is because the United States (and its domestic gun lobby) opposed creation of a stronger agreement, preferring instead to create a "shallow and weak" institution (also Efrat, 2012).

While realist and institutionalist perspectives helpfully draw attention to the role of state power, they are limited when it comes to making sense of policy developments in cases where sovereign interests are less apparent. As discussed in chapters 7 and 8, the inclusion of crime as an element of the SDGs was therefore most directly attributable to the advocacy of UNODC, albeit within a broader rule-of-law framework. Likewise, as illustrated in chapter 5, prior to the 1990s, UNODC's predecessors have often framed the problem of crime in ways that did not directly reflect the interests of the United States, which, for most of the Cold War, was indifferent to or dismissive of the UN as a vehicle for advancing its foreign policy objectives. Accordingly, understanding the crime-development nexus—and global crime governance more broadly—requires consideration of international institutions as semiautonomous actors.

CONSTRUCTIVISM

Constructivist approaches illustrate how problems are framed, emphasized, or de-emphasized. Constructivism therefore treats problems as the outcome of a political process rather than simply accepting that they exist, or that their reality is consistent with their representation. Accordingly, those issues that are considered crimes, in this case crimes worthy of global attention, reflect the wider political context (Hülsse, 2007, p. 156). The perspective is particularly influential among critical criminologists, who are interested in the politics of criminalization and its impact on marginalized communities, which are typically over-policed and under-protected (e.g., Weber et al., 2021). In International Relations, constructivists typically focus on the role of transnational norm entrepreneurs—individuals, NGOs, and advocacy networks—who convince states and other powerful actors that certain issues are problems that necessitate global responses (Finnemore & Sikkink, 1998; Wendt, 1995). They do so by mobilizing public opinion, framing issues as common problems, and presenting responses as reflecting universally shared moral imperatives. With regard to the international crime policy agenda, state and non-actors have attempted to construct international prohibition regimes to criminalize and suppress "global crimes" (Nadelmann, 1990). To the extent that they succeed, these regimes are spread and implemented through socialization and processes of social pressure, such as naming and shaming (Sharman, 2011). Thus, for constructivists global crime governance is driven not only by the economic and political interests of states but also by norms and moral arguments, which are utilized by non-state actors to champion issues or positions they care about.

This is evident from global efforts to combat bribery and corruption. Until the 1980s, these were not widely perceived as global problems. Indeed, states and international organizations considered them unavoidable and perhaps even necessary for cutting through bureaucratic red tape to implement development projects. However, this began to change in the 1980s and 1990s due to the advocacy of several norm entrepreneurs, including the World Bank, multinational corporations, practitioners, and civil society organizations (Abbott & Snidal, 2002, pp. 158–60). Notably, the aforementioned FCPA (1977) prompted American corporations to assume the role of "moral entrepreneurs" (Nadelmann, 1990) and actively lobby for the creation of a global anti-bribery regime (Wrage & Wrage, 2005). NGOs and advocacy networks, most notably Transparency International (TI), were later created to champion this agenda and establish a global prohibition regime designed to "civilize" global markets (Larmour, 2005). Since 1993, TI has played a leading role in framing anti-corruption not only as a moral imperative but also as integral to other issues already on the global agenda, namely the promotion of development and good governance (Wang & Rosenau, 2001). This messaging was backed by a wave of economic research that highlighted how corruption was a threat to economic development as countries with high levels of corruption saw lower levels of foreign investment in a globalized economy (see Wang & Rosenau, 2001, endnote 52). As discussed in chapter 6, advocacy from actors such as TI established a normative consensus among states that corruption was both a moral scourge and, more importantly, an obstacle to economic liberalization and development.

Once the global anti-corruption regime was established, TI, the UNCAC Civil Society Coalition, and the International Anti-Corruption Conference Council campaigned for the implementation of the norm by working with governments to develop the necessary policies to do so, while resorting to social pressure to name and shame those who fail to do so (Gutterman & Lohaus, 2018). Thus constructivist approaches to global crime governance highlight not only the *processes* through which global crime problems are socially constructed but also the crucial role of *non-state actors* in this process. The social construction of the crime-development nexus in the lead-up to the SDGs similarly involved networks of non-state actors, including civil society organizations, academic experts, and international institutions.

These networks have been described as a "transnational legal order" by some constructivist scholars, who argue that domestic legal systems are increasingly enmeshed within formal and informal institutions that span the international, national, and local levels (see Halliday & Shaffer, 2015; Shaffer & Aaronson, 2020; Aaronson & Shaffer, 2021). Across these orders, criminal justice norms are constructed, contested, and implemented as actors seek to align domestic legal systems with international standards. These harmonization efforts are supported by international organizations, which not only define these norms through international agreements but also provide symbolic and technical assistance through summits, working groups, training workshops, and other practices aimed at promoting the implementation of global norms locally. This points to another theoretical dimension of the construction of the crime-development nexus, namely the agentive qualities of the international organizations created to uphold the transnational legal order.

The idea that international organizations do not simply reproduce the interests of states is located in the influential work of Barnett and Finnemore (1999, 2004). Their autonomy is said to stem from their rational legal authority as bureaucracies. This enables them to present themselves as impartial servants of the common good, deriving legitimacy from their expertise and political neutrality. With this autonomy, international organizations can draw attention to global problems they believe are in need of attention. They do this through a combination of research, diplomacy, and advocacy, which they use to highlight issues that fall within their portfolios, and prompt action. The ability of international organizations to produce and disseminate evidence is particularly important because it enables them to shape policy, legitimize, or de-politicize issues or initiatives by presenting them as "technical matters" or by invoking their "epistemic authority" (Littoz-Monnet, 2017, pp. 7–8).

International organizations do this for material reasons. For example, they typically have a bureaucratic disposition toward expansion and self-preservation (Barnett & Finnemore, 1999). "Minimizing institutional insecurity" is therefore essential for maintaining their relevance and ensuring they have "sufficient resources to carry out their goals" (Littoz-Monnet, 2017, p. 8). During periods of change or uncertainty, survival may entail creating new roles or mandates by constructing problems or issue linkages (Betts & Pilath, 2017) that require their intervention, funding, and more responsibility. Ironically, in the context of the UN system, self-preservation may actually undermine the autonomy of international organizations by increasing material dependency on voluntary contributions from powerful countries (Browne, 2006).

How organizations interpret and respond to material pressures is ultimately mitigated by their institutional cultures, with their values, ideals, and missions shaping their responses. Again, this speaks to their (semi-)autonomous status. Since the Second World War, the work of international organizations has been overwhelmingly shaped by a combination of liberal and cosmopolitan values, and their expansionist tendencies reflect their desire to promote their interpretation of a particular ideological agenda to all corners of the globe. The ideational motives are alternatively linked with the fact that members of international organizations typically believe their work is important and beneficial (Barnett & Finnemore, 1999). The cultures of international organizations are therefore shaped by narratives linked with the functionalist assumptions described above. This is often conducive to a universalist outlook as liberal internationalism provides a cultural lens through which bureaucrats identify, analyze, and address problems. These values do not always align with the strategic interests of powerful states, but the work of international organizations may nevertheless serve their interests by constructing and maintaining a transnational legal order that serves to reproduce and universalize Anglo-European norms and institutions that were themselves designed to support a particular model of capitalist development. This perspective is certainly relevant insofar as the crime-development nexus is ultimately a discursive assemblage that cannot be analyzed using traditional social-scientific methods. At the same time, the construction of a problem or an issue linkage is shaped by the interactions between the norm entrepreneur and the ideological, institutional, and structural forces they encounter. It is through these interactions that problems are negotiated, assembled, and translated into action.

POLITICAL ECONOMY

Constructivist readings of global crime governance provide valuable insight into *how* global prohibition norms and issue linkages are socially constructed and institutionalized, but are less convincing when it comes to explaining *why* this occurs. In short, constructivists struggle to explain why certain issues and norms attract attention or gain purchase among entrepreneurial actors and the wider international community while others do not. Constructivist scholars including Barnett and Finnemore (2018, p. 70) acknowledge this shortcoming and concede that in the end, it is power that determines which social constructions succeed and fail (also Sharman, 2011; Barnett & Finnemore, 2004; Nadelmann, 1990; Abbott & Snidal, 2002). The problem is that constructivists tend to conceptualize power as being overwhelmingly political in nature. Consequently, they tend to associate power with the interests of influential actors, state or non-state, but ignore its material basis. This, in our view, is a significant limitation of the constructivist approach, particularly when applied to the study of global crime governance.

The importance of material forces in shaping the global crime policy agenda is evident from TI's construction of the anti-corruption norm and the backing it received from TNCs based in the United States, which feared losing their competitive edge against their European-based counterparts due to the FCPA (Wang & Rosenau, 2001, p. 41). Over time, this support wasn't confined to just American corporations, and the International Chamber of Commerce would later play a significant role in supporting the negotiation of the OECD Convention because corruption came to be recognized by transnational capital interests as an unacceptable cost of doing business (Abbott & Snidal, 2002, p. 167). To this day, the work of TI is funded by government agencies, multilateral institutions, and corporate and individual donors. What unites this diverse group of benefactors is a collective material interest in creating open and transparent markets so that economic liberalization can flourish. Likewise, the construction of the crime-development nexus is invariably linked with material interests, and not just those of states. Accounting for how these material interests influenced the construction of the crime-development nexus requires examining the role of changing social relations of production (specifically the onset of neoliberal globalization) and how these changes produced, and were produced, by different types of non-state actors and governance models. In short, unraveling the crime-development nexus—and global crime governance, more broadly—requires a political economy focus.

The analytical framework utilized in this book builds on these existing analyses by adopting a Coxian approach to global governance. The work of Robert Cox, based on the writings of Antonio Gramsci (1971), perceives the international system—or what Cox refers to as a "world order"—as grounded in the social relations of production of capitalism (Cox, 1983, p. 173). Capitalism is understood as more than a system of organizing the economy; it is an associated system of values, its social structures, and forms of state. These are not fixed but constantly evolving and changing due to struggles over the social relations of production (Cox, 1994, 103). The changes in the social relations of production give rise to new social forces—not only classes but also class factions, distributional coalitions, and any other societal groups whose emergence and relative power are rooted in political economy. These forces seek to restructure domestic societies and transform the state to sustain and facilitate their dominance. This is not simply achieved through coercive means but rather by promoting norms and values that legitimize domination. For dominant groups, the legitimation of power necessitates making concessions to subordinated groups to secure their consent. To the extent they succeed, dominant social forces secure "hegemony," which refers to a form of class rule that relies predominantly on governance by consent, with coercion remaining in the background (Gramsci, 1971, p. 55–60; Cox, 1983, p. 163).

Since the 19th century, hegemonic rule has originated in powerful states and subsequently spread across borders as dominant social forces seek to restructure the global economy and world order to advance their material interests and sustain their dominance. This necessitates the development of international (and ideally global) institutions to establish a general set of rules or norms that support the international diffusion of the dominant mode of production (Cox, 1983, p. 171–72). Cox refers to these institutions as *nébuleuse*: the "unofficial and official transnational and international networks of state and corporate representatives and intellectuals who work towards the formulation of a policy consensus for global capitalism" (Cox, 2002, p. 33). Once established, they work to construct and secure a global policy consensus, which is then, *in theory*, implemented by social forces seeking to bring their states in line with the dominant mode of production (Cox, 1987, p. 254). *In practice*, harmonization or the diffusion of global policy agendas occurs unevenly and often encounters resistance from competing social forces. Resistance, domestic or international, can thus be studied as a form of counter-hegemony that must be managed by dominant forces.

For power to be characterized as hegemonic, resistance must be managed primarily via concessions rather than coercion. From a global governance standpoint, formal international organizations play a crucial role in orchestrating this process. According to Cox, they fulfill three functions: embodying and promoting the rules that facilitate the expansion of global capitalism; ideologically legitimating the norms of the world order; and co-opting and marginalizing opposition (Cox, 1983, pp. 172–73). Accordingly, staff within them seek to facilitate the spread of global capitalism that underpins and legitimizes the transnational legal order. This entails the universalization of the norms and presenting them as serving the common global good, as opposed to specific material interests (Cox, 1980, p. 377).

For example, the unifying logic of the international crime policy agenda since 1948 has been to promote liberal order by establishing or strengthening the capacities of various institutions to prevent or mitigate the impacts of crime. For much of the Cold War, this agenda was overwhelmingly guided by liberal paradigms of Modernization Theory and "Keynesian" economics, which envisaged a prominent role for the state in restructuring societies to facilitate capitalist development. However, the ideological fault lines of the bipolar international system and resistance from the "Third World" meant that the embedded liberal model was not universally accepted or supported. Maintaining an institutional space for international crime prevention within the UN system thus necessitated concessions, namely opportunities for states to air dissenting views. These geopolitical and ideological conditions negated the possibility of establishing a consensus understanding of the global crime problem. By extension, meaningful institutions and regimes for advancing this agenda could not be established until after the collapse of the Soviet Union.

Legitimation also entails diffusing the backlash against the hegemonic agenda. International organizations achieve this by devising policies or initiatives to attenuate its negative consequences. This requires a long-term vision that foresees the conditions leading to the backlash and develops the necessary policy responses (Cox, 1994, pp. 101–2). In the crime space, this role is evident from the UN's push to address the consequences of rapid urbanization and development in the 1950s and 1960s via its "social defense" program, discussed in chapter 4. This initiative was prompted by genuine concerns that the social instability and anomie generated by capitalist development would lead to rising levels or urban criminality. Similarly, the subsequent framing of crime as an obstacle to development during the 2000s was prompted by concerns about the social consequences of structural adjustment policies and acknowledgment that economic liberalization was failing to deliver positive human development outcomes in the Global South. Thus, from a Coxian perspective, even progressive institutions like the UN serve the interests of dominant social forces in the world order.

At the same time, international organizations have also been theorized as potential sites for counter-hegemony. As Murphy points out, international organizations need to make material and ideological concessions to less powerful actors—both state and non-state—creating opportunities for them to pursue their interests (Murphy, 1994, p. 32; Cox, 1980, p. 377). For example, during the 1970s the crime policy agenda was influenced by demands of the Third World as articulated through the NIEO (see chapter 5). Subsequently, the establishment of international regimes in the early 2000s (e.g., UNTOC and UNCAC) has created greater opportunities for civil society organizations to participate in global crime governance and influence the policy agenda. This has occurred both within and beyond the UN system. It is important to acknowledge these opportunities for contestation, but it is questionable whether they are actually consequential, as international organizations like the UN have been designed to co-opt the leadership of counter-hegemonic forces and neutralize more radical agendas. In this regard, they might be said to embody the idea of hegemony, which Cox (1983, p. 173) famously equated with "a pillow: it absorbs blows and sooner or later the would-be assailant will find it comfortable to rest upon."

Chapter Three

Historicizing the Crime-Development Nexus

The link between crime and development only emerged as an international policy concern following the establishment of the United Nations (UN). Prior to this, both crime and development had represented distinct areas of concern for the international community, or, perhaps more accurately, the European imperial powers who, together with the United States, established the institutional and ideological foundations of the transnational legal order that exists today. Historicizing the crime-development nexus as an element of the UN crime policy agenda therefore necessitates consideration of its antecedents and their relation to the history of capitalist development in both the metropole and its dependencies.

Contextualizing these expansive and complex historical developments is no simple feat, and we do not present this chapter as a comprehensive or definitive history. Rather, it should be read as a broad-strokes, historical primer for criminologists and International Relations scholars who are unfamiliar with the history of early European attempts to govern international crime, colonialism, and the legacy of the League of Nations. In presenting this narrative, we attempt to illuminate key historical continuities and shifts and to consider how these were shaped and connected by an interplay between ideological, institutional, and material forces (Cox, 1987). In this regard, the chapter presents a Gramscian history of the modern origins of global crime governance today, one that challenges the idea that the problems that emerged in the 1990s were particularly novel. It further illuminates why global crime governance today is overwhelmingly shaped by Northern states for the purpose of advancing and securing an economic order that aligns with their interests.

CAPITALIST DEVELOPMENT AND INTERNATIONAL CRIME

Historical criminologists and socio-legal scholars have traced the emergence of crime as an object of international concern to the latter decades of the 19th century. For example, Knepper (2009, p. 5) attributes the invention of the international crime problem between 1881 and 1914 to concerns "about the social effects of 'world shrinking' technologies and associated cultural, economic and social changes on criminal behavior." These changes were largely a product of, and contributing factor to, the Second Industrial Revolution, which emerged in Europe and North America during this period. They included innovations in transport (e.g., railroads and steamships), manufacturing, and communication (e.g., undersea cables and telegraphs) that had a significant impact on the mobility of people and commerce (Hobsbawm, 1989). From a criminological standpoint, Knepper (2009) argues that heightened awareness of these changes prompted concerns among journalists, social commentators, police, and government officials about criminal and political threats to the emergent capitalist order. This section considers how Western elites worked to address these issues through multilateralism while transposing Anglo-European criminal justice institutions and legal norms upon the colonized peoples of the dependencies, the descendants of whom today are the intended "beneficiaries" of the SDGs.

THE "ANARCHIST WAVE"

The most significant threats to the emerging capitalist order of the Gilded Age were ideological rather than criminal. Notably, anarchism emerged as an international concern in the second half of the 19th century following a wave of assassinations and bombings across Europe and, later, the United States (Levy, 2004). Classical anarchism, like Marxism,[1] evolved in response to the perceived deficiencies of capitalist development. The violence that came to be associated with anarchism has since been characterized as early modern acts of terrorism (Rapoport, 2004; cited by Jensen, 2009, p. 89). High-profile bombings and assassinations attracted significant attention from governments, police, and newspapers, which in turn contributed to amplification of concerns about the problem (Hobsbawm, 1989). The concern among ruling European elites was that anarchism would gain purchase among the growing proletariats of rapidly industrializing countries due to growing disillusionment about working conditions and inadequate wages (Jensen, 2014).

Due to the aforementioned innovations in transportation that enabled mass and, for the most part, unrestricted migration, there was also growing awareness that the anarchist movement had spread globally to the United States, Latin America, Japan, and colonies administered by the European imperial powers (Knepper, 2009). The spread and appeal of anarchism was uneven, and Jensen (2014) stresses that contrary to newspaper reports of the era, there was limited evidence of a coordinated, global anarchist conspiracy to overthrow the imperial powers of the era. Nevertheless, concerns about this transnational movement prompted ruling elites and police from rival empires to develop new modes of cooperation to collectively address a common threat. This was part of a larger process of the emergence of a liberal internationalist elite committed to constructing a global governance system that would facilitate the emergence of a truly global economy by removing political and technical obstacles (Murphy, 1994).

International cooperation was pursued through various initiatives, including the 1898 International Anti-Anarchist Conference of Rome and later the St. Petersburg Anti-Anarchist Protocol, where Germany and Austria pushed for the creation of an international anti-anarchist league (Jensen, 2014; Knepper, 2009). This was aided by the emergence of a relatively new "scientific" body of knowledge, criminal anthropology, that located the pathology of offending with the physical and moral defects of individuals (rather than social or economic conditions). Essentially, this knowledge supported the depoliticization of the issue, which in turn created scope for it to be framed and addressed as a technical matter. This prompted greater cooperation between bureaucratic police organizations, which in turn helped to establish the foundations for international police cooperation (Deflem, 2009). Political cooperation remained limited, however, and different countries adopted their own strategies for addressing the anarchist threat (Jensen, 2009).

In Italy, criminal anthropology provided the government with a means of "refram[ing] the whole question of anarchist assassination attempts, defusing and diminishing their impact by looking at them as the deeds of the mentally unbalanced, juvenile delinquents, and common criminals rather than of social reformers or political activists" (Jensen, 2001, pp. 31–32). This helped to delegitimize the economic, social, and political grievances of anarchists and, by extension, reduce the appeal of this radical ideology. As argued later in this book, similar strategies are utilized today by international actors as a means of deflecting attention away from the structural causes of global crime problems, namely inequality. By contrast, the ruling elites in Britain readily acknowledged the structural and political instabilities of capitalism and managed to avoid an "anarchist wave" by making concessions to trade unionists, thereby affording socialists (as potential Marxists and anarchists) with meaningful opportunities to participate in the political sphere.[2] From a Gramscian perspective, these concessions functioned as a "safety valve for proletarian energies" (Jensen, 2009, p. 99), thereby reducing the domestic appeal of anarchism, delegitimizing its radical prescriptions, and reinforcing the hegemonic position of the ruling class and its imperialist aspirations amid growing resistance from liberal progressives. Policing and surveillance tactics also played a role in preventing acts of anarchist violence, but Britain ultimately managed the anarchist threat domestically through interventions that alleviated (or at least deflected attention from) the economic, political, and social conditions that potentially made it appealing.

There are parallels between Britain's strategy and the West's embrace of "embedded liberalism" as a model for capitalist development following the Great Depression, and this is not coincidental (see Ruggie, 1982). This model served as the dominant framework for economic policy between the 1940s and 1970s, when the United States and its allies feared that the instabilities caused by free market liberalism might increase the appeal of communism. Thus, the example illustrates that embedded liberalism involves making concessions, and that this offers those in power a way to co-opt and pacify political and ideological threats. This strategy is particularly appealing when the disenfranchised openly question the legitimacy of the order and become aware of radical alternatives. Opening up or creating institutions as political spaces for managing these conflicts allows political and economic elites to maintain hegemony.

Spain's approach to dealing with anarchism was less successful. It relied on aggressive policing and targeted legislation to crack down on this political threat. This heavy-handed approach, together with the absence of a well-organized labor movement, exacerbated the problem and enhanced the domestic appeal of this radical ideology (Jensen, 2009). Consequently, the anarchist movement persisted in Spain long after it had been suppressed in other European countries. From a theoretical standpoint, Spain's approach illustrates why managing a political threat through coercion and state violence is unlikely to succeed, and may actually exacerbate the problem. This is widely acknowledged by criminologists and counterinsurgency experts, yet even today, many governments continue to adopt a punitive and repressive approach to dealing with political dissidents. As noted above, governments often legitimize state violence and repression by labeling the targets criminal or terrorist threats. State violence is naturally frowned upon by the sovereign and institutional custodians of transnational legal order, but it's also tolerated, ignored, and in some cases accommodated because this is necessary for preserving functional cooperation and the illusion of political consensus (for example, in relation to global drug policy, see Bewley-Taylor, 2006).

Acknowledging these different approaches prompts a number of considerations. First, issues that come to be collectively defined as transnational criminal threats manifest distinctly in different contexts, meaning their domestic causes and impacts are typically complex and varied. Second, technical cooperation can occur in the absence of political cooperation (see also Bowling & Sheptycki, 2012). Indeed, such cooperation is often the foundation on which more explicitly "political" institutions are constructed down the line, something that is certainly true of global crime governance, as we will show in subsequent chapters (see also Murphy, 1994). Third, even where transnational legal order and functional cooperation exist, domestic government policies ultimately play an instrumental role in determining how problems of this nature are framed and addressed (Aaronson & Shaffer, 2021). Finally, both the viability and desirability of developing "functional" multilateral frameworks to address complex problems through a criminal lens are questionable, particularly in cases where this may serve to legitimize repressive state policies that conflict with liberal internationalist values. We revisit these themes in the following chapters, but raising them here is useful for signposting continuities between these early attempts to secure the conditions of capitalist development and our current system of global crime governance.

TOWARD THE GLOBAL PROHIBITION OF ILLICIT ENTERPRISES, REAL OR IMAGINED

International cooperation during the 19th century was also evident from attempts to prohibit or regulate certain commercial activities. Arguably the most successful prohibition regime of the 19th century was the international ban on the traffic in African slaves (Andreas & Nadelmann, 2006). The leading sovereign proponent of abolitionism throughout the 19th century was Britain, a country that derived its hegemonic influence from its accelerated economic development, extensive colonial holdings, and unrivaled naval power. Ironically, Britain's global empire and domestic economic development, which enabled it to act as a global norm entrepreneur and enforcer, were in no small part attributable to its active involvement in, and support for, the international slave trade during the 17th and 18th centuries (Morgan, 2000). What was once considered a legitimate economic activity, and one that had been integral to early modern development of Britain and other European nations, was deemed illegitimate once it was no longer considered a desirable model for capitalist growth and imperial expansion.

The abolition of the African slave trade was undeniably a positive development from a moral standpoint, but at the time it went against the interests of some economic and political elites in the Americas who derived their material wealth from an agrarian economy and required a cheap source of labor. This early example therefore illustrates that global prohibition regimes, like the systems of capitalist development to which they are bound, produce winners and losers. More developed countries (or perhaps, more accurately, their elites) are in a position to shape the international normative agenda and establish and enforce institutions that advance their interests (Andreas & Nadelmann, 2006). We see similar dynamics today in relation to a wide range of regimes that involve the criminalization or regulation of morally questionable, albeit economically lucrative, activities that are perceived as a threat to Western capitalism (or liberal sensibilities) in the Global South. For example, there are few today who would openly question the need for an international norm against human slavery (which persists in various forms), yet other prohibition regimes, including those that relate to the cultivation of illicit crops, wildlife trafficking, and poaching, are more contentious because they provide income for people in economically disadvantaged regions with limited opportunities. As Hübschle (2018) argues, security-driven responses thus typically fail to address their material needs, and prohibition may actually generate new sources of risk and insecurity while rendering these populations dependent on illicit economies.

The abolition of the African slave trade also speaks to the important role that non-state actors and transnational advocacy networks play in generating public and political support for the criminalization of commercial practices that are labeled immoral (Andreas & Nadelmann, 2006). In this case, the Christian abolitionist movement in Britain gained steam domestically in the late 18th century due primarily to the progressive forces of evangelicalism and Enlightenment-era thinking. This moral entrepreneurship created pressure for politicians to "[turn] against a system which could not be defeated in 1800 by the unaided operation of the invisible hand" (Drescher, 2010, p. 199). The movement then took on a transnational dimension and spread to other European countries through the work of the Anti-Slavery Society and later the British and Foreign Anti-Slavery Society, and this contributed to the "powerful diffusion of religious and liberal abolitionist sentiments throughout much of the world" (Andreas & Nadelman, 2006, p. 30). For reasons described above, the antislavery norm was not universally accepted or celebrated by governments in the 19th century, but it did attract support from other industrializing nations, which recognized that slavery was becoming obsolete and probably counterproductive from a development standpoint. The norm was therefore institutionalized via multilateral agreement with the General Act of the Brussels Conference of 1889–1890, which proceeded the 1926 Slavery Convention.

During the 19th century, religious and progressive moral entrepreneurship in Europe and the United States also gave rise to an international campaign to combat "white slavery," or the trafficking of women and girls for commercialized sexual purposes (Knepper, 2009). Much like the anarchist threat, hysteria about white slavery from the 1880s onward was largely fueled by sensationalist media coverage that centered on vivid accounts of vulnerable young women and girls, typically white and Christian, reportedly abducted or deceived into prostitution or other sexually exploitative practices by international crime syndicates. Much has been written about the factually dubious accounts that contributed to the emergence of a diverse coalition of philanthropic organizations and religious movements, which used their international connections and material resources to amplify the visibility of the issue. These advocacy groups thus successfully lobbied Western governments to take cooperative action, and this led to the widespread adoption of the 1904 International Agreement for the Suppression of the White Slave Traffic and later, in 1910, the International Convention for the Suppression of White Slavery (Andreas & Nadelmann, 2006).

Abolitionists and reformers derived much of their support from the growing middle classes of Western industrializing countries during this period. In this regard, Jäger (2002, p. 569) argues that the problem of "white slavery" instantly resonated with the "moral climate" of the middle class, specifically concerns about respectability and the forces of modernization as a threat to the traditional family, which was seen as the moral building block of a liberal, orderly society. These sentiments were particularly strong among members of the socially conservative middle classes, who opposed legalized prostitution and thus embraced the anti–white slavery movement as a platform for advancing their social reforms. The political influence of a growing middle class was itself a product of economic and social development, and their conservative, xenophobic, and protectionist views reflected contemporary anxieties about free trade, cosmopolitanism, and free migration (Hobsbawm, 1989). These anxieties fueled "the idea that international crime was on the rise as a consequence of a general modernization of social life" (Deflem 2004, p. 96). We note there are important parallels between the cultural effects of capitalist development at this time and today, particularly following the decline of embedded liberalism and the rise of neoliberal globalization, which is widely associated with the condition of "late modernity" (Bauman, 2000; Garland, 2001). It is not our contention that these ontological anxieties are entirely unfounded, but rather that they are often disproportionate to the actual severity of the problem and misdirected (Holloway & Jefferson, 1997). From a Gramscian perspective, misdirection is not simply a natural response to structural crises, but rather an attempt by elites to frame structural crises as cultural, moral, and, increasingly, security threats as a strategy for shoring up their hegemony (Hall et al., 1978; Buzan et al., 1998).

Finally, it is worth very briefly reflecting on the foundations of the global drug prohibition regime established in the decades preceding the First World War. Like regimes created to prohibit the trade in African slaves and later white slavery, drug prohibition was a product of moral entrepreneurship from religious groups and social reformers. In this case, however, the leading sovereign proponent of international drug control was not a hegemonic, industrialized global power, but rather a rising industrial power, the United States, which had historically adhered to an isolationist and protectionist foreign policy platform. As Andreas and Nadelmann (2006, p. 40) write, America's advocacy of global prohibition reflected contemporary domestic concerns about the impact of "unregulated drug sales" and highly addictive and potentially dangerous products on the economic productivity of the lower classes during the Second Industrial Revolution. In other words, these substances were seen as a potential barrier to capitalist development, and this created an incentive for the United States to propose an international regime to address this problem.

America's most pressing concern was the international opium trade, and in 1909 the country convened the Shanghai Opium Commission, which was attended by representatives of thirteen governments that overwhelmingly favored a softer approach, "urging gradual suppression of opium smoking and measures intended to stop the smuggling of narcotics" (UN, 1959). This led to adoption of the International Opium Convention in 1912, which introduced restrictions on the export of this substance but stopped short of introducing global prohibitions or obligating signatories to criminalize its importation or consumption (Wright, 1924). These initiatives are noteworthy because they established the institutional foundations for the global drug prohibition regime that survives today.[3] They also foreshadowed America's future role as a hegemon that would shape the contours of global governance in a manner that reflected its economic and geopolitical interests in the decades to come (Andreas & Nadelmann, 2006).

All of these examples are illustrative of a wider attempt by the European imperial powers and later the United States to establish a transnational legal order based predominantly, if not exclusively, on Western cultural norms and interests. As with the previous examples of African slavery and white slavery, international cooperation was cautiously embraced as a vehicle for establishing and safeguarding norms and frameworks for cooperation that advanced collective imperial interests. Cooperation of this nature was oriented toward managing or pacifying any potential threats to capitalist development, real or imagined. It also represented a collective political strategy for managing the aforementioned anxieties of an increasingly influential middle class during a period of rapid structural change.

Domestically, the perceived need to manage these instabilities in the West also contributed to the development of modern criminal justice systems, including police, together with legal systems that were developed (at least in part) to safeguard a liberal economy, control the working classes, and uphold the status quo (Robinson & Scaglion, 1987). Internationally, as detailed in the following section, systems of social control were simultaneously transposed upon colonized peoples, whose resources and markets were seen as essential for driving economic and social progress in the West. Consequently, the institutions, ideologies, and technologies used to manage crime throughout what is today known as the Global South are overwhelmingly rooted in systems of colonial administration established to facilitate economic imperialism (Agozino, 2003).

IMPERIALISM, COLONIAL ADMINISTRATION, AND POLICING

The economic and social development of the European metropole was fueled by its exploitative material relationship with the rest of the world (Rodney, 1972; Prashad, 2007, 2014). Put simply, Western European nations were the first to progress from feudalism to capitalism, and this gave them a significant material and technological advantage over other parts of the world. The pursuit of profit and material resources abroad thus contributed to the global spread of capitalism and its accompanying ideologies, and this also stimulated industrialization at home, initially in Britain and later throughout Europe, North America, and Japan. It is therefore important to stress that the foundations of modern capitalism spread unevenly beyond Europe over a number of centuries via a combination of international trade, colonialism, and other mechanisms of economic and cultural imperialism. Consequently, by the late 19th century, European nations had solidified their status as imperial powers, and their material prosperity enabled them to construct an international legal order that would support international commerce (Murphy, 1994).

The economic and social development of the imperial powers from the 15th century onward directly contributed to the "underdevelopment" of their "dependencies" (Frank, 1966; Rodney, 1972). Although the nature of the metropole-dependency relationships varied, the basic dynamic was broadly consistent. European nations used their superior military and economic power to extract raw materials through international trade and colonization. In some colonies, resources were also initially extracted or cultivated using African slave labor until this was eventually deemed immoral by the metropole and incompatible with its development. Raw materials were shipped back to

Europe, where they were sold at market for profit or manufactured into consumer products that were sold domestically or exported. Naturally, the metropole accumulated the vast majority of these profits, which it reinvested in its own economic, social, and technological development. This increased the gap between the metropoles and their dependencies and undermined the latter's economic, political, and cultural autonomy (Prashad, 2013; Rodney, 1974).

The "underdeveloped" characterization of "Third World" countries and the perceived need for the international community to promote economic and social development are directly rooted in this colonial legacy. Consequently, international institutions established to govern crime globally remain overwhelmingly oriented toward addressing "Southern" problems or enhancing "Southern" capabilities, typically through legal or technical interventions that are informed and inspired by the knowledge of their former colonizers in the Global North. This illustrates that systems of colonial administration supplied the foundations for modern criminal justice systems throughout the Global South today. They also represent an important building block of the transnational legal order described by Halliday and Shaffer (2015).

As noted above, colonial police and criminal justice systems were never intended to be democratic or liberal institutions, and nor were they developed with the aspiration of cultivating legitimacy (Brogden, 1987; Brown, 2014). Perhaps the key distinction between social control in the metropole and their dependencies was simply that the consent of colonized peoples was seen as less consequential by ruling elites in the metropole, both strategically[4] and morally (due in no small part to the influence of racial ideologies at the time; see Jenkins & Leroy, 2021).

This is not to suggest that colonial administration relied exclusively on coercion, although this was certainly evident from policing practices, draconian punishments, and the colonizers' indifference to the rights and freedoms of colonized peoples. Rather, colonization was a political project oriented toward producing obedient subjects who would consent to these systems of exploitative rule and the racial ideologies used to justify them (Brown, 2006). Throughout the dependencies, this was primarily achieved not through policing or coercion but rather through education and the transposition of Western cultural values and economic, political, and religious institutions. Manufacturing consent for imperialism was therefore the long-term strategic aim of metropole elites, whereas the police, the military, and colonial justice systems provided a more immediate means of ensuring compliance, managing conflict, and suppressing resistance.

Consequently, one of the challenges that emerged during decolonization (and persists today) is that of "modernizing" and "democratizing" institutions, which were never established to serve the interests of the subaltern subjects. Decolonization also brought other challenges, as many newly independent nation-states featured significant divisions, which European imperial powers had used to their advantage as part of a "divide and rule" strategy. Consequently, police and criminal justice institutions throughout the Global South have developed in such a way that they serve to reproduce and entrench social, cultural, political, and economic fault lines (Brown, 2006).[5]

Finally, the development of criminology also directly contributed to the imperialist project by functioning "as a tool to aid the control of the other" (Agozino 2004, p. 348), both foreign and domestic. It did this by scientifically constructing these "others" as inferior, deficient, or incapable of acting as rational, liberal subjects. The colonial project therefore contributed to the universalization of dominant criminological and Western legal traditions and, by extension, the displacement and marginalization of traditional systems and methods for dealing with conflict and delivering justice (Carrington et al., 2016).

Admittedly, this is a broad-strokes account of imperialism and colonialism with notable limitations that must be acknowledged. Notably, colonialism was not a homogeneous project, nor was it simply imposed upon colonized people by colonizers. Rather, as Sen (2004) observes, colonization was negotiated by colonized people who were in some cases participants in the imperialist project. This is undoubtedly at least in part a reflection of colonial attempts to cultivate local elites and capitalize on preexisting conflicts and divisions to form alliances with colonized subjects who would serve as important allies and proponents of the imperialist project (Brown, 2006; Rodney, 1972). In many cases, colonized peoples assumed the role of agents of colonization as low-level administrators in other parts of the world, where their experience, skills, and cultural knowledge were considered assets. Local elites who were complicit in and benefited from colonization would then later inherit and lead their nations following decolonization. Indeed, Hobsbawm (1994) observes that the spread of liberalism fueled the decolonization movement during the interwar period and that calls for autonomy and anti-colonialism were in many cases guided by the aspiration of these subaltern elites to participate in the global capitalist economy, not abolish it.

INTERNATIONAL CRIME AND "BENEVOLENT IMPERIALISM"

The League of Nations is typically remembered as a failed experiment in global governance, but as the direct predecessor to the UN, it is worth reflecting on two key elements of its work during the interwar period. The first relates to the work of "several technical organizations which had to do with aspects of crime" (Knepper, 2011, p. 2). The second relates to the League's Mandate System that preceded the demise of European imperialism and the decolonization movement (Pedersen, 2015). Both elements of the League's work program shaped the form and functions of the UN so reviewing its legacy highlights an important institutional link between the "Age of Imperialism" (Hobsbawm, 1989) and the rise of liberal internationalism (Cottrell, 2017). As Susan Pedersen (2007, p. 1092) writes:

> The League appears as a key agent in the transition from a world of formal empires to a world of formally sovereign states. By contrast, if one notes its efforts to regulate cross-border traffics or problems of all kinds, it emerges rather as a harbinger of global governance.

FROM ANTI-TRAFFICKING TO "SOCIAL QUESTIONS"

Knepper (2011) argues that the work of the League of Nations contributed to the construction of a global imaginary about the problem of "international crime." This was fueled by wider postwar anxieties about rising crime rates, the internationalization of organized crime, and xenophobic and anti-Semitic narratives about international criminals. Underpinning these anxieties was a growing sense that there was something novel about crime that could only be understood and addressed via an internationalist outlook. Beyond this, Knepper argues that contemporary narratives about the international crime problem recognized its complexity and the intersections between different forms of illicit activity. Finally, he notes there was a sense that successfully managing these issues required the involvement of all sovereign countries, even if their interests were not naturally aligned. An institutional forum was therefore required to facilitate and support international governance in this area, and the League of Nations provided this.

The League's contribution to what we today describe as global crime governance is particularly evident in relation to two problems that had previously generated limited forms of international cooperation: white slavery and the international opium trade. Specifically, Article 23a of the League's Covenant "entrust[ed] the League with the general supervision over the execution of agreements with regard to the traffic in women and children, and the traffic in opium and other dangerous drugs" (The Covenant of the League of Nations, 1920). The continuities between the work of the League of Nations on these issues and previous attempts to regulate them through treaties and international agreements is noteworthy, but the League (which reached a membership of 58 countries in 1934–1935) represented an important departure from these previous, ad hoc efforts to regulate illicit activities. It afforded them (near) universal recognition and an institutional architecture for cooperation and coordination on an ongoing basis.

The League consisted of three main organs. The League Assembly was essentially the predecessor to the United Nations General Assembly (UNGA) and consisted of delegates from all Member States, who met annually in Geneva. It's significance was largely symbolic, argues Pedersen (2015, p. 7), who describes the Assembly as "a public arena where [representatives] had to perform civility and espouse internationalism, whatever their private or even political inclinations." The second organ was the League Council, a predecessor of sorts to the United Nations Security Council (UNSC). The Council met four times annually to settle disputes between League members, and, much like the UNSC today, it was dominated by powerful countries. Although it is credited with some political successes in the 1920s, the Council's expanded membership in the 1930s contributed to its diminishing power and influence (Pedersen, 2007, p. 1099). The final organ was the League Secretariat, which supplied a bureaucratic apparatus for the organization, much like the UN Secretariat. This functioned as an international civil service and was responsible for overseeing the implementation of policies that were adopted by the Assembly, typically on the advice of the Council.

The Secretariat included a Social Section staffed by a small team of international bureaucrats who supported the work of expert committees, which provided the Council with recommendations relating to Article 23a. These included a Committee on the Traffic in Women and Children, a Child Welfare Committee, and, until 1930, an Advisory Committee on the Traffic in Opium and Other Dangerous Drugs. The committees were unique in their composition (which changed over time) but typically included diplomatic delegates (mostly men) and "experts" representing transnational voluntary organizations (often women; Miller, 2009). For the Committee on the Traffic in Women and Children, these experts included members of activist networks and organizations who previously played a role in raising the profile of "white slavery" both domestically and internationally. Their involvement evidences the aforementioned continuity between the prewar anti-trafficking agenda and the work of the Committee and Social Section. It further illustrates how civil society actors shape the international crime policy agenda, and not always for the better. Their involvement was not coincidental, because the 1904 and 1910 treaties supplied the League with a normative mandate to undertake work in this space.[6] These treaties and domestic political support for their implementation established transnational infrastructures (both legal and bureaucratic) that were necessary for promoting technical cooperation (Miller, 2009).

It is difficult to assess the impact of the League's work on international crime, but by the 1930s it seemingly emerged as "a primary justification for its relevance to world affairs" (Knepper, 2011, p. 69). In other words, despite the League's failure as a political project, proponents of liberal internationalism pointed to its technical successes to defend the institution. The centrality of the League's anti-crime work to these legitimizing, functionalist narratives is perhaps overstated by Knepper,[7] but its purported successes were said to include creating and sustaining networks that actually contributed to the eradication of the white slave trade and the establishment of an international system for regulating the opium trade. Knepper (2011, p. 70) argues that by the 1930s, Article 23, originally of marginal importance, became a key justification for the League's continued existence. It was, as argued by Pedersen (2007, p. 1092) above, a key element of the League's legacy as a "a harbinger of global governance."

In the 1930s, the economic and social impacts of the Great Depression created international demand for expertise that could help to address social welfare issues. Accordingly, these material conditions and their social consequences contributed to the redefinition of the League's work on social problems, with less emphasis thereafter being placed on the vulnerability of women (Miller, 2005, p. 166). Henceforth, there was a heightened emphasis on reducing the vulnerability of children to delinquency, an issue that had been neglected up to this point. In response to international concerns about the social instabilities caused by the Great Depression, the League of Nations published a comparative study on juvenile delinquency in 1934 that concluded: "the causes of . . . this waste of young human lives, are familiar, and are invariably the same" (League of Nations, 1934, p. 7). These included "disintegration of the family," "the absence of the mother . . . as frequently happens for economic reasons," and "the present world economic depression" (pp. 7–9), which deprived children of "the necessities of life" (p. 84), a limited scope for government interventions and social reforms due to budgetary constraints (p. 9).

The League's recommendations for "safeguarding children from moral danger" appear to be consistent with the UN's early work on juvenile delinquency as part of the "social defense" movement (see chapter 4). Specifically, its 1934 report outlined a program of Keynesian reforms to mitigate the economic impacts on the working class along with public investment in social services to strengthen what criminologists would later describe as social bonds (see League of Nations, 1934, p. 175). The continuity between these prescriptions and the social defense movement is perhaps unsurprising, as both advocated a model of embedded liberalism. In the former case, the emphasis was on promoting social development in the industrialized world, whereas the UN's focus was the developing world. The League's work on "Social Questions" indicated growing recognition of the link between economic and social development, but in the 1930s this remained poorly understood. From a criminological perspective, research on social disorganization and strain was still relatively new, albeit increasingly popular due to the aforementioned consequences of the Great Depression. However, their international influence was seemingly limited at the time because of America's isolationist and protectionist policies. In any event, Miller (2005) argues that reports such as this one prompted greater recognition that economic and social issues were connected and should therefore be studied and addressed in a manner that acknowledged the economic roots of social problems.

In 1936 the League replaced the Committee on the Traffic in Women and Children and the Child Welfare Committee with a single Committee on Social Questions. With social welfare now the dominant concern (and approach), the League's interest in international crime seemingly declined. There appear to be two possible explanations for the decline of international crime as a central element of the League's social agenda. First, Miller (2005) notes that the composition of the Committee on Social Questions differed from that of its predecessors, because it no longer included activists representing transnational voluntary organizations. They were instead replaced by experts who were nominated by delegates from the Council to undertake research or provide advice on welfare issues. As discussed in the following chapter, similar expert committees would play a role in shaping the international crime policy agenda of the UN during the Cold War. Second, compared to the anti-trafficking agenda, the welfare agenda provided relatively limited scope for members of the Social Section to collaborate with other organizations, including the International Criminal Police Commission, which was more concerned with international police cooperation than social policy (Knepper, 2011). Essentially, there was less scope for technical cooperation to occur.

A final point to stress is that the League's welfare-based approach to addressing "Social Questions" was anchored in universalizing Anglo-European assumptions about the nature of crime and its structural causes. This is hardly surprising insofar as the League of Nations was never developed to function as a truly global organization, but rather as "a modified Concert of Europe" (Pedersen, 2007, p. 1195) that would ensure peace between the great powers and establish an order that would allow them to pursue their material interests. It was increasingly recognized by the European powers that in the long run, colonialism was not a sustainable model for economic growth, and thus an alternative was needed. The United States, which created the League but never joined, was naturally more enthusiastic about decolonization than its European imperial counterparts. Nevertheless, they all agreed that the new system should preserve imperialist, economic relations and the cultural and political dominance of Anglo-European institutions (Anghie, 2005).

THE MANDATE SYSTEM AND "BENEVOLENT IMPERIALISM"

The League of Nations' Mandate System was established by Article 22 of the Covenant to oversee the administration of former colonies of Germany and the Ottoman Empire (Pedersen, 2015). The system, which permitted occupying imperial victors to administer these colonies, represented a compromise between proponents of annexation (as had previously been the norm) and those who called for these territories to be administered by the League of Nations. A Mandate Commission, consisting of nine "former diplomats and colonial officials" who were based in Geneva, was therefore established to manage this system and provide oversight and report to the Council (p. 3).

The Mandate System was never actually designed to advance self-determination or to facilitate the shift toward decolonization, which was debatably inevitable by this point. In other words, it was never intended to be a radical project, but rather a "progressive" experiment with aspirations akin to a form of "benevolent imperialism" (Pedersen, 2015, p. 403) that reflected the dominant, liberal internationalist ideals of the 1920s.[8] For example, Pedersen explains that William Rappard, who was appointed director of the Mandates Section and worked closely with the Commission, "did not think the occupied areas ready for self-government; [and] the language of civilizational stages, of 'backward' peoples, and Western guidance, fell easily from his lips" (p. 4). At the same time, he believed that colonies should be administered to advance their own interests—as defined by Anglo-European experts, of course. From this "benevolent" perspective, the Mandate System was envisioned as a model for advancing the social and economic development of "backward" peoples. This was understood to represent a long-term project that required expert knowledge from the metropole, and the League of Nations as an international organization was embraced as the ideal platform for providing this.

By extension, "civilizing" colonized peoples of the dependencies was understood to represent a necessary prerequisite for self-determination among progressive liberal internationalists. These ideas are readily apparent from Article 22 of the League Covenant, which established that "the tutelage of such peoples [not yet able to stand by themselves under the strenuous conditions of the modern world] should be entrusted to advanced nations who, by reason of their resources, their experience or their geographical position, can best undertake this responsibility and who are willing to accept it" (League of Nations Covenant, 1920, Article 22, par. 1–2). This notion reasserted the superiority of European nations together with their legal and political institutions and would later influence the development of an efficiency model, described by Murphy (2006), which was instrumental to the UN's efforts to promote economic and social development in the context of decolonization from the 1950s onward.

Pedersen's (2015) analysis of the Mandate System further evidences that the League as an international organization served as both a site and a platform of counter-hegemony (Murphy 1994) because it inadvertently facilitated the spread and growth of the international decolonization movement. It did this by providing prominent critics of colonization and advocates of self-determination a public platform to voice their concerns in Geneva, where there was an international media presence. Pedersen (2015, p. 407) argues that this "opened up imperial rule to an uncontainable wave of scrutiny," because "[t]heir words were out in the world, a world now remade by literacy, print, air travel, and radio waves, and could not be recalled." These calls for self-determination found an audience with the aforementioned population of "civilized" and educated liberal elites who formed part of a growing middle class. They had come to embrace Western values and capitalism, yet rejected "white (i.e., North Atlantic) racism" (Hobsbawm, 1994, p. 203).

The Mandate System contributed to the decolonization movement, but this would not have occurred without the support of the Western powers. For example, President Woodrow Wilson of the United States, a key political proponent of the Mandate System, opposed annexation. From his perspective, writes Anghie (2005, p. 119), "the essential purpose of the system was to protect the interests of backward people, to promote their welfare and development and to guide them toward self-government and, in certain cases, independence." As noted above, the European imperial victors of the First World War were initially reluctant to embrace this approach but did so in the interest of compromise. The subsequent willingness of the European imperial powers to accept that decolonization was inevitable was therefore shaped by changing material conditions during the 1930s, which rendered their empires unsustainable.

To this effect, Hobsbawm (1994) masterfully explains how the global impacts of the Great Depression (1929–1933), specifically the collapse in demand for primary products, disrupted economic relations between the metropole and its dependencies. Support for colonialism among "native" elites who had previously benefited from their participation in this exploitative system quickly disappeared, while the generalized effects of this economic shift on "peasants" rendered them a potential ally. Despite ideological differences between these local elites and those who had not historically benefited from colonialism, cooperation and mass mobilization was often achieved through appeals to nationalism. Many decolonization movements then gained further steam in the 1940s as news of successful independence movements traveled around the world and former imperial powers were defeated in the Second World War. The UN system was therefore designed in part to function as the next stage of this "civilizing" project, one that would provide newly independent nation-states with access to Western expertise to support their integration into a global capitalist economy (Jolly, Emmerij, & Weiss, 2009).

In this regard, Anghie (2005) argues that the creation of the Mandate System signified the start of a gradual shift toward an international liberal order grounded in legal universalism and paternalism. The new system could accommodate political freedom (i.e., self-determination) so long as states developed and governed in ways that aligned with the ideological and material interests of the West. The creation of the Mandate System thus institutionalized a liberal humanist construction of non-European sovereignty that "reinforced the idea that a single process of development—that which was followed by the European states—was to be imitated and reproduced in non-European societies, which had to strive to conform to this model" (p. 145). Thus, as the prototype for a neocolonial order, the Mandate System established the institutional foundations of "the contemporary discipline of development" (Anghie, 2005, p. 119).

An ideological justification for this liberal humanist shift was found in the work of 16th-century Spanish theologian Francisco de Vitoria, who "had been concerned with protecting the welfare of dependent peoples" (quoting Anghie, 2005, p. 45). This was seemingly exemplified by Wilson's support and advocacy of self-determination and decolonization, but it would be misleading to suggest that his motives were purely ideological. Rather, his support was driven primarily by the material interests of the United States. Specifically, Wilson viewed self-determination and decolonization as preferable to the protectionist policies of European imperial powers, which limited American access to both primary commodities and export markets (Hobsbawm, 1994). Opening these markets for free trade was therefore seen as essential for America's economic growth and rise as a great power. The Mandate System represented an important first step toward constructing a new capitalist order, which persists to this day.

Chapter Four

Development and Social Defense

This chapter accounts for how crime was governed as an international development issue through the United Nations (UN) system during the first two decades of the Cold War. We begin by reflecting on the creation of the UN and describe some important ideological and institutional continuities with the League of Nations. These are particularly evident in relation to the role that was envisioned for the UN when it came to supporting newly or soon-to-be independent states with their economic, social, and political development. This highlights the UN's significance as an institutional locus for advancing the liberal project at a time when the capitalist development model faced a challenge from the Soviet Union. In this regard, the UN was envisioned as a vehicle for legitimizing and advancing a liberal internationalist project.

The UN's approach to development also represented an extension of the liberal humanist ideals embedded within the League's Mandate System. This was particularly evident in relation to the presumed superiority of Western institutions and knowledge systems. Our analysis stresses, however, that the geopolitical conditions of the Cold War era represented an important barrier to the realization of a universal liberal order, and this was acknowledged by the architects of the UN development system. Nevertheless, the system was initially anchored in what Murphy (2006) describes as the "development as efficiency" model, and it was only in the late 1960s that sections of it, notably the United Nations Development Programme (UNDP), embraced the "development as freedom" model.

Against this institutional backdrop, we account for the establishment of the UN's Social Defense program and its efforts to support "underdeveloped" countries with managing the criminological consequences of modernization. The social defense movement was primarily anchored in the "development as efficiency" model and emphasized the transfer of Western expertise and assistance to the developing world to facilitate economic and social development. Unsurprisingly then, the work of the Social Defence Section on crime prevention was heavily influenced by the American criminological tradition of sociological positivism, which was in turn influenced by Durkheim's ideas about anomie and modernization. This represented a significant departure from previous attempts to address crime as an international issue that did not account for social development, or focused exclusively on transnational issues such as "white slavery" or narcotics trafficking. The fundamental assumption of the new social defense paradigm was that newly independent states would follow a similar trajectory as their industrialized counterparts and face similar problems, which could be anticipated and managed through policy interventions.

The early work of the Social Defence Section served to reproduce and validate a universal assumption: that crime is a consequence of modernization. The social defense paradigm was therefore designed to assist governments of "Third World" nations with managing the criminogenic consequences of modernization through state planning and criminal justice policies. Social defense was essentially an attempt to develop an embedded liberal playbook for addressing these issues. Consequently, while alternative perspectives on the nature and causes of criminality were afforded representation in this institutional sphere, their influence on the work of the Secretariat in relation to crime prevention was limited until the 1970s.

THE UN DEVELOPMENT SYSTEM

Development is one of the three foundational pillars of the UN, which was formally established in 1945.[1] Specifically, Article 1(3) of the UN Charter establishes that one purpose of the UN is "To achieve international cooperation in solving international problems of an economic, social, cultural, or humanitarian character." The need for international cooperation to address matters previously treated as either domestic concerns for sovereign nations or issues of colonial administration was linked with a number of important assumptions that underpinned the Western vision for a postwar liberal order at the time.

First, the United States' role as the primary architect of the postwar liberal order all but guaranteed widespread decolonization, which it had long advocated. Self-determination was therefore formally acknowledged in the UN Charter, and the UN was formally charged with promoting "higher standards of living, full employment, and conditions of economic and social progress and development" (Article 55a). Second, both the American and European architects of the UN believed that establishing a stable, integrated international economy represented the cornerstone for peace and stability, and was necessary to avoid another Great Depression. Third, and relatedly, the same American and European architects wanted to ensure that the economic, social, and political development models adopted by newly independent states would ensure their participation in this international capitalist economy rather than the Soviet Bloc. As Murphy (2006, p. 36) argues, the use of development to shore up hegemony was not a new idea but rather a direct extension of Roosevelt's policies toward Latin America during the Second World War, when "US officials feared growing Nazi influence in the hemisphere where leading US companies had, for decades, relied on strategic raw materials, profitable investments, and key export markets."

The West's concerns were amplified by the success of the Soviet five-year plans during the interwar period, which transformed the country into a modern, industrial power within a relatively short period (Hobsbawm, 1994). Furthermore, international socialism potentially offered newly decolonized countries an appealing political ideology because it embodied a critique of European imperialism. Fortunately for the West, most ruling elites who came to power throughout the Third World were interested in joining rather than overthrowing the global capitalist economy. As noted in chapter 3, this was a legacy of colonialism and its cultivation of local elites, which reproduced a commitment to political and economic modernization along Western lines. The inclusion of "development" as a pillar of the UN agenda can therefore be interpreted as a necessary concession by the UN's Western architects, who were ultimately concerned with maintaining their influence. The sovereignty of newly independent countries was tolerated so long as they governed themselves in a manner that was compatible with, or at least did not conflict with, Western interests. This was important not just for ideological or political reasons but also, as was the case with Roosevelt's Latin American policies, for preserving continued access to the markets and natural resources of the developing world (Anghie, 2006).

Within the UN system, political responsibility for setting the international development agenda is formally vested in the Economic and Social Council (ECOSOC; see Article 62). ECOSOC, composed of elected representatives of UN member states, is responsible for negotiating and adopting resolutions, drafting conventions, and monitoring development outcomes (Rosenthal, 2018). ECOSOC was designed to function as a deliberative forum, but not as an efficient or effective site of policy making. This is evident from the fact that ECOSOC resolutions, unlike those of the UN Security Council (UNSC), are not legally binding.[2] This is important for two reasons.

First, it suggests that development was never intended to serve as the primary function or purpose of the UN. This is evident from the fact that the UN's technical assistance program, the Extended Program for Technical Assistance (EPTA), was only established in 1950. This was prompted by President Truman's inaugural address of January 1949, in which he stated, "we [the developed West] must embark on a bold new program for making the benefits of our scientific advances and industrial progress available for the improvement and growth of underdeveloped areas" (Truman, 1949). This portion of the statement, reportedly "a rhetorical afterthought," evidences America's early preference for a model of development that linked efficiency with growth. In other words, it assumed that development could best be achieved if newly independent countries "adopt procedures and skills that originate [in the West]" and that integrating these countries into the global economy would produce an "abundance of goods that promise[d] to eliminate destitution, and with it, the deepest of human inequalities" (quoting Murphy, 2006, p. 44; see also Hickel, 2017, pp. 1–3). It is unclear what plans Truman had for the UN as a development actor, but his statement afforded proponents of a multilateral development system a chance to establish the EPTA.

Second and relatedly, the subordination of development to security by the Western architects of the UN and the neocolonial overtones of Truman's speech suggest that this multilateral institution was never intended to function as the primary channel through which the West would promote its international economic and political interests. Rather, as noted below, this was to occur through bilateral aid and the Bretton Woods institutions. Thus, the expansion of the UN development system and the creation of its technical assistance program was an inadvertent consequence of US attempts to consolidate its hegemony in the aftermath of the Second World War. It was also an institutional extension of the enduring, liberal humanist belief in the West's responsibility to "civilize" the "backward" people of the dependencies. In this context, Anghie (2005) argues that "backwardness" came to be associated with the economic and social "underdevelopment" of the same subaltern populations that were previously treated as inferior based on their ascribed cultural and racial characteristics.

The inclusion of development as a pillar of the UN mandate was nevertheless widely supported by independent, non-European countries in the late 1940s (particularly those in Latin America and Asia, including China, that benefited from technical assistance from the League of Nations). It was not, however, supported by the Soviets, who viewed the UN's economic and social development mandate together with the semiautonomous Bretton Woods institutions as vehicles for advancing an ideological and economic agenda that was antithetical to their own. This resistance, together with the ability of Western powers to promote their economic interests through bilateral aid and later the Bretton Woods institutions, meant that the actual impact of the UN's contributions to economic and social development were somewhat limited until the 1960s. One key explanation for this delay is that political support for development increased following the proliferation of newly independent, developing countries in the 1950s and 1960s. This enabled decolonized countries to shape the UN policy agenda through the United Nations General Assembly (UNGA) and ECOSOC, and these in turn provided valuable forums for advancing their collective interests and contesting neocolonial agendas (Hettne, 1995; Murphy, 1994). It is no coincidence then that the growth of the UN development system coincided with the rise of Third-Worldism (Berger, 2008) and the establishment of the Non-Aligned Movement in 1961, which attempted to shift the focus from East-West to North-South relations (Dinkel, 2018). This suggests that even though the UN development system was originally structured by the ideological and material interests of the West, it became an important sphere where the idea of development was negotiated and concessions were made.

Even the West's relationship with the UN development system changed during this time. Notably, US enthusiasm for establishing a multilateral UN aid budget gained limited support from President John F. Kennedy, who declared the 1960s to be the [first] "United Nations Decade of Development" (Kennedy, 1963). More significantly, however, the Kennedy administration also established its own bilateral assistance program at this time, which included the Alliance for Progress, designed to strengthen economic links with Latin America, and the US Agency for International Development (USAID). What became known as the "law and development movement" also emerged during this time, driven by Ivy League American legal scholars with the financial backing of USAID (Salas, 2001). The aim of the movement was to promote legislative reforms, legal norms, and education to support democratization efforts in the Third World and ultimately establish stable, capitalist economies, often in the form of US-friendly client states. A range of projects were funded by USAID, which even established a Division of Public Safety in 1962 to promote technical assistance to police as part of a wider counterinsurgency strategy (McClintock, 1986).

There is little evidence of direct cooperation between the UN and the United States when it came to development work, and the UN development system was not simply a vehicle for promoting American foreign policy interests. Nevertheless, in the 1960s both development actors shared an overarching belief in the modernization theory, with one of its chief proponents, Walt Rostow, serving as a key member of the Kennedy and Johnson administrations. Prior to the publication of Rostow's seminal book in 1960, Murphy (2006) notes that his ideas had already been in circulation during the 1950s and therefore directly shaped the UN's approach to development.

This ideational link was significant because it ensured that the work of the UN development system would remain fundamentally compatible with the ideological and materialist aspirations of the United States. Institutionalizing this approach within the UN development system also limited scope for the Soviets to use political forums like the UNGA or ECOSOC to promote or legitimize their own prescriptions for economic and social development, which threatened the interests of Western capital.

It is also interesting to note that the dominant UN model for economic and social development at this time emphasized the importance of state planning and embedded liberalism (Murphy, 2006). This was in large part a continuation of the Keynesian prescriptions for economic development that became dominant throughout the West following the Great Depression. For newly independent countries, a model that emphasized the importance of state planning was appealing, for both symbolic[3] and economic reasons. It was not, however, the West's experience that signaled the potential benefits of state-planning but rather the Soviet Union's rapid industrialization during the interwar period (Hobsbawm, 1994). State planning was seen by developing countries as a means of accelerating their modernization, thereby allowing them to compete with their developed counterparts. The West recognized this, and Rostow's (1960) aptly titled "Non-Communist Manifesto" was presented as an alternative recipe for accelerated economic growth that promised to keep newly independent countries within the capitalist sphere.

Western countries were tolerant of the UN's technical assistance capabilities, which aligned with and advanced the modernization project, but less enthusiastic about the prospect of entrusting the UN with financial resources. A UN "Special Fund" was eventually established in 1959. However, its role as the preeminent development investment fund was immediately challenged by the establishment of the International Development Authority as part of the World Bank the following year (Murphy, 2006). This is important, because lending and investment decisions at the World Bank are more directly responsive to the interests of the sovereign donors, whose influence is proportional to their investment. By comparison, donors and borrowers have equal representation in the UNGA, which controls the UN development budget. Accordingly, the World Bank, which later became a key proponent of structural adjustment policies and the "rule of law" revival in the 1990s (discussed in the following chapters), was the preferred multilateral institution for soft lending by the United States. The World Bank was therefore both a partner and competitor of UN development agencies (Browne, 2011). It had greater access to Western capital but limited autonomy, weak legitimacy in the Third World, and few capabilities when it came to implementation (Payer, 1982).

Finally, at an institutional level, it is important to note that the UN development system is, and has always been, highly decentralized. This means that technical assistance work is performed by specialized agencies with their own bureaucratic cultures and objectives, which originally focused on *either* economic or social development issues. Coordination has long been a challenge, as has interagency competition (Browne, 2011). What did connect these various agencies during the 1950s and 1960s was an overarching belief in liberal internationalism and the modernization project. Together, these provided international civil servants with a universal philosophy of development that legitimized their mission as providers of technical expertise and assistance. There were of course disagreements and debates among the key bureaucratic entities within the system, and these helped to shape its values and culture. For example, Argentinian economist Raúl Prebisch, whose ideas would later influence the development of dependency theory, was actively involved with the program, as was Paul Hoffman, who was involved with the Marshall Plan and later became the first administrator of UNDP (Murphy, 2006; Browne, 2011). These diverse individuals shared a belief that as a multilateral entity, the UN was better positioned to support modernization projects and advance the interests of the developing world than bilateral aid.

In practice, the technical assistance work of the UN in the 1950s and 1960s often diverged from this ideal. It has since been characterized as having privileged donor interests over local needs, diverting local resources to projects that are aligned with donor or organizational interests, creating material and behavioral dependency (Browne, 2011). Although there have been important shifts in the international development agenda since the 1960s, most notably in relation to the heightened influence of the development as freedom paradigm, particularly following the creation of UNDP in 1965, many of these problems endure. The reasons for this are discussed in the following chapters, but for now it is important to signpost them, because they were also evident in relation to the early work of the UN crime program, which was created as a component of the UN development system yet operated at its fringes.

SOCIAL DEFENSE

The UN crime program was established in 1947 as the Social Defence Section of the Secretariat's Bureau for Social Affairs, which reported to the Social Commission of ECOSOC. The original purpose of the Social Defence Section, as defined by ECOSOC (Resolution 155 VIIc), was to function as a continuation of the work that had been previously undertaken by the League of Nations on "Social Questions" following the Great Depression (Walters, 2001). The formal mandate centered on "crime prevention" and the "treatment of offenders," and this was anchored in the development pillar of the UN Charter.[4] The key point here is that the Social Defence Section was established as part of a wider development system that aspired to promote economic and social development as the foundation for peace and order. At the same time, the UN's work on economic and social development remained institutionally siloed, and the Social Defence Section was distinct from other social development entities due to its niche portfolio. It was also distinct from its predecessor in the League's Secretariat, which had been primarily concerned with international crime problems in the 1920s. The first two decades of the UN crime program were therefore shaped by what became known as the social defense movement (Ancel, 1965; Redo, 2012).

It is worth reflecting on the genealogy of "social defense" because prior to its adoption by the UN, it had previously been associated with a variety of modern criminological and legal traditions. Marc Ancel, one of the chief architects and proponents of the social defense movement in the 1950s and 1960s, noted for example that early classicists associated the concept with the development of a modern system of criminal law and punishments, which they argued would contribute to the protection and preservation of society (Ancel, 1965). Italian positivists, on the other hand, later associated it with their revised theory of punishment, which advocated preventative measures to protect society from dangerous individuals (Canals, 1960). Variations of the concept had also been associated with modern, authoritarian regimes. For example, the Nazis appealed to the social defense of the community at the expense of individual rights, and prior to this the Soviets invoked it to justify measures to preserve "the order created by the power of the workers and peasants" (Ancel, 1965, p. 12).

What Ancel (1965) described as the "modern" idea of social defense thus occupied a middle ground between classical traditions, which centered on the criminal law and the issue of moral culpability, and early positivist traditions, which were focused on the causes of criminality, albeit in relation to individual-level explanations. The progressive, internationalist orientation of the modern social defense movement, which aspired "to promote the international interchange of ideas and to foster scientific studies and advanced human views in the field of criminal law," was also shaped by its proponents' awareness of its past authoritarian connotations, and this imbued it with a further emphasis on the importance of promoting humane policies and the protection of individual rights (Ancel, 1965, p. 4). What the modern social defense paradigm prescribed then was "organizing and directing the social reaction against crime, as effectively as possible and after a rigorous study of the question" (Ancel, 1965, p. 4).

The emphasis on "rigorous study of the question" suggests a further influence on the social defense movement, which is directly relevant to our discussion, and the work of the UN crime program: Durkheimian functionalism, which theorized crime as a *social* fact (see chapter 1). Accordingly, there was a strong degree of resonance between social defense and the work of "Anglo-American criminologists . . . in particular to sociologists from the United States" (Ancel, 1965, p. 6). Consequently, the social defense movement developed an interest in the structural causes of crime, both economic and social, and it aspired to help developing governments establish conditions and develop policies that would allow them to manage the anticipated criminological consequences of rapid modernization under their five-year plans. The assumption that these consequences were inevitable was shaped by Rostow's Anglo-centric view of modernization and a growing body of criminological literature that offered theoretical insight into the relationship between industrialization, urbanization, and crime in the United States. Put simply, social defense was established as a Western program for effectively managing what might be described as the dark side of modernization. As noted in chapter 6, important parallels exist between the functionalist assumptions underpinning this paradigm and those that would later shape international attempts to address the "dark side of globalization" in the 1990s.

For liberal internationalists, social defense provided an attractive vehicle for addressing the criminological consequences of modernization through research and cooperation. Ironically, the ambiguity of the concept and the fact that "it [did] not aim at imposing a new dogma or establishing a single doctrine in place of all other theories of criminal law and criminology" also rendered it relatively palatable to the Soviets following Stalin's death in 1953 (Ancel, 1965, p. 7). Indeed, expert committees and the UN crime congresses even offered the Soviets institutional forums for contesting Western theories of crime and proposing alternative prescriptions for the prevention and treatment of offenders that highlighted the inherent superiority of the Soviet system (discussed below).

Furthermore, the fact that any UN resolutions or recommendations relating to social defense were ultimately nonbinding also ensured that any country could simply ignore or selectively adhere to those norms they perceived to be unpalatable or incompatible with its own model of social development. The viability of this transnational legal order was therefore linked with its flexibility and the lack of an effective regulatory mechanism. Once again we argue that these are enduring issues that undermine the efficacy of global crime governance today.

The establishment of the Social Defence Section signified institutional recognition that crime was a social development issue. At the same time, it is important not to overstate the importance of social defense during the early decades of the Cold War. Even in its heyday of the 1960s, social defense was a niche issue within the UN system, and the Social Defence Section failed to attract funding from donors (Clifford, 1979, p. 1). The significance of the Social Defence Section is thus twofold. First, as a bureaucratic node it contributed to the consolidation, institutionalization, and expansion of international networks of experts with a shared interest in matters relating to criminal policy. Second, it worked to generate and disseminate scientific knowledge that shaped the international crime policy agenda. This knowledge directly contributed to the universalization of the idea that Western, social scientific approaches to theorizing crime were essential for understanding and addressing the criminological effects of economic development.

THE INSTITUTIONAL ARCHITECTURE OF GLOBAL CRIME GOVERNANCE

The UN crime program was not the first institution established to promote intergovernmental cooperation in matters relating to crime and penal policy. It was, however, unique from its predecessors for five reasons, which were outlined by Manuel López-Rey, chief of the Social Defence Section from 1952 until 1960. First, López-Rey (1954) emphasized that the UN crime program created a space for international criminal policy development that emphasized social problems and policies. By contrast, the previous intergovernmental organizations had approached crime as either a legal problem or through the lens of biological positivism.

Second, López -Rey described the UN's capacity for leadership in promoting universal recognition of the need for an international criminal policy. At the same time, the Social Defence Section accepted that "standardization is not possible" on account of the unique "cultural, social and economic conditions" of every country (p. 128). Its focus was therefore on promoting coordination and establishing international and regional frameworks for cooperation, knowledge sharing, and norm development under the aegis of social defense.

Third, as an element of the UN's wider social development program, López-Rey (1954) suggested that the crime program had the capacity to provide technical assistance to governments. As noted above, the UN's approach to technical assistance was directly informed by the legacy of the Mandate System, but the League's work on juvenile delinquency through the Commission on Social Questions in the 1930s did not include provision for technical assistance. The technical assistance capability of the UN crime program was therefore unique, and throughout the 1950s and 1960s the Social Defence Section provided training for governments of developing countries via workshops, expert missions, and funded fellowships.

Fourth, the research capabilities of the UN crime program enabled it to function as an international source of information about criminal trends and best practices for developed and developing countries alike (López-Rey, 1954). However, the program was more than a repository or distributor of existing knowledge. Rather, it produced knowledge that came to shape the international crime policy agenda and reaffirmed the validity and universality of the social defense paradigm and American criminological theories (Walters, 2001).

Finally, López-Rey (1954) notes that the UN crime program was distinct because it featured a permanent administrative body via the Social Defence Section, which allowed it to fulfill the roles and functions outlined above. The Section itself was composed of a small team of individuals selected for their expertise on a range of issues that fell within the broad scope of the paradigm. The Section, in its various subsequent iterations, would have a significant impact on the work of the UN crime program during the Cold War era and thus represents an important site of institutional continuity and memory within a UN system that has undergone several restructures and transformations since the 1950s.

During the Cold War, the UN crime program also featured an expert advisory committee established in 1949 to assist the Secretariat and Social Commission with developing "policies and programs appropriate to: (a) The study on an international basis of the problem of prevention of crime and the treatment of offenders; and (b) International action in this field" (ECOSOC Res. 155(VII) c). The committee, which originally included seven members representing different countries who were appointed by the secretary general, was established as the "International Group of Experts on the Prevention of Crime and the Treatment of Offenders" but later rebranded as the "Ad Hoc Advisory Committee of Experts" by UNGA 415(V) in 1950. This rebranding coincided with the UN's decision to absorb the functions of the International Penal and Penitentiary Commission (IPCC), which had previously been affiliated with the League of Nations (Clark, 1979). This merger was significant because it provided the Social Defence Section with an established international platform for bringing together an international network of experts and advocates to promote and expand the social defense movement.

For the IPCC, the merger was beneficial because it afforded its progressive proponents UN recognition for their agenda and access to an institutional platform for promoting their own norms and standards internationally. Thus, although López-Rey's (1954) account suggests that the social defense movement did not aspire to promote standardization, the incorporation of the IPPC directly contributed to the adoption of the *Standard Minimum Rules for the Treatment of Prisoners* at the First United Nations Congress on the Prevention of Crime and the Treatment of Offenders in 1955 (López-Rey, 1957; henceforth UN Crime Congresses). Subsequently, much of the work of the UN crime program's Secretariat during the Cold War focused on promoting international norms and standards that aligned with the IPCC's progressive agenda. This is not directly relevant to our historical analysis of the crime-development nexus, but it is worth briefly acknowledging for two reasons.

First, the promotion of norms and standards, often linked to the human rights pillar, reinforced the presumed universality and supremacy of the Western legal order that had been transposed upon the dependencies via colonization (Agozino 2014). Effectively, this was a progressive attempt to enhance its legitimacy rather than transform or abolish it. Second, norms and standards work highlights an enduring division within the UN crime program. Some, typically lawyers, see it as a vehicle for promoting human rights and criminal justice reforms. Others, typically criminologists, believe that its primary function is promoting crime prevention, domestically and, later, internationally. These perspectives are not necessarily conflicting, but they illustrate that the UN crime program has always occupied a space between the three pillars of the UN and that the ambiguous social defense doctrine never evolved into a coherent doctrine or agenda.

This suggests that the UN crime program has historically functioned as an institutional locus through which perspectives and agendas relating to crime, represented by a fairly diverse range of experts, could compete for recognition and attempt to shape the work of governments and practitioners around the world. As the custodian of these networks, it has also developed a vested organizational interest in maintaining and expanding them. At the same time, it would be inaccurate to reduce the UN crime program to an administrative actor or node, because the Secretariat and other UN actors, including secretary generals, have directly shaped the UN crime policy agenda. It is in relation to these contributions that we consider the initial construction crime-development nexus as a focus of international crime policy.

CONSTRUCTING THE CRIME-DEVELOPMENT NEXUS

Economic development was not an explicit focus of the UN crime policy agenda until 1953, when Secretary General Dag Hammarskjöld convened a meeting of the Advisory Committee and tasked it with discussing "the prevention of types of criminality resulting from social changes and accompanying economic development in less-developed countries" (UNDPA, 1953, p. 459). This prompted the commissioning of multiple studies that informed two reports submitted as preparatory material for the Second UN Crime Congress held in London in 1960. Before we review their content, it is worth examining the institutional conditions that elevated the significance of economic development as part of the wider UN agenda and Hammarskjöld's executive leadership.

Hammarskjöld was a leading proponent of the expansion of the UN as a development actor because he believed it could independently serve as the primary source of assistance and technical advice for the Third World. Hammarskjöld was also openly critical of attempts by former colonial powers to promote development aid through institutions like the OECD, which suggests that his interest in exploring the link between economic development and crime was driven by functional concerns and his liberal internationalist outlook, rather than the foreign policy interests of the United States or its European allies. Perhaps this explains why during the 1950s and 1960s, the work of the Social Defence Section in relation to crime prevention was poorly funded and relatively inconsequential, at least from a technical assistance standpoint (Ferracuti, 1963; Clifford, 1979).

The dominant understanding regarding the relationship between development and crime that emerged during the late 1950s and 1960s within the UN was later summarized by the late criminologist Franco Ferracuti in 1963:

> Quick economic change and development, accompanied by far-reaching social change, can easily result in a significant increase in criminality unless appropriate care is taken to minimize the extent of the resulting social and personal disorganizations. Also, those countries which are attempting to raise the levels of living of their populations must concentrate their not abundant material and personnel resources on the achievement of their development goals. In order not to strain their limited human and financial resources, every effort must be made to minimize the human loss and the financial drain involved in coping with the problems of crime prevention. (Ferracuti, 1963, p. 688)

Ferracuti's account is particularly useful because he served in the Social Defence Section in the late 1950s and 1960s, when the agenda was being formulated. This above statement makes explicit reference to "social disorganization," which, as noted in chapter 1, represented one of the dominant American sociological theories of crime since the 1920s and suggests that research and planning, à la social defense, could support the development of national strategies for managing these problems and mitigating their impacts.

In essence, it articulates an explicit theoretical link between economic development and crime that aligns with Rostow's (1960) modernization thesis and constructs an enhanced role for the Social Defence Section.

Ferracuti is one of several recurring characters in our story whose intellectual contributions to the wider UN crime program should not be overlooked. These individuals account for the agency of international organizations. As international civil servants, they act as translators who work to reconcile different agendas and interests in a manner that reflects their individual and institutional outlooks and aims (Blaustein, 2015; Murphy, 2006). Focusing on this agency in turn challenges the idea that the Secretariat is a purely administrative entity that does not shape policy, or does so in a manner that simply reproduces the interests of powerful states. Thus, as Barnett and Finnemore (1999, p. 699) argue, bureaucracies (or, perhaps more accurately, bureaucrats) "create social knowledge." A methodological challenge is that details concerning the individual contributions of international civil servants are often obscured by the aforementioned need for bureaucracies like the UN Secretariat to present themselves as apolitical and objective entities. Fortunately, in Ferracuti's case, insight into his formative influences and efforts to advance a universalist and international comparativist program of criminology through the UN Crime Program was provided by his contemporaries following his death.[5]

Ferracuti's story provides direct insight into how American criminological ideas came to shape the work of the Secretariat. Originally trained in the Italian positivist tradition of criminology, Ferracuti uncharacteristically took an interest in sociological approaches to criminality following a visit to the University of Wisconsin–Madison circa 1954 and his contact with prominent Swedish-American criminologist Thorsten Sellin, who chaired the 1953 Advisory Committee meeting convened by Hammarskjöld. Ferracuti applied this knowledge as the leader of the Section's work program on juvenile delinquency, which represented a significant focus of UN-commissioned research on modernization and crime in developing countries in the 1950s and 1960s. Our sense is that Ferracuti was directly involved with the production of at least one of the Secretariat reports that shaped the initial construction of the crime-development nexus development at the Second Crime Congress.

The 1960 Secretariat's report titled the *Prevention of Types of Criminality Resulting from Social Changes and Accompanying Economic Development in Less Developed Countries* provides direct insight into how the link between development and crime was framed at the time (UNDESA, 1960). Consistent with Ferracuti, quoted above, the key message was that economic development is criminogenic because it generates social disorganization in urban communities. The report also predictably emphasized that rapid urbanization via social disorganization increased juvenile delinquency in developing countries. Neither argument is surprising, but a deeper reading of the report reveals the complexity and sophistication of the Secretariat's analysis at the time. Notably, it acknowledged the criminogenic consequences of "punitive measures" employed by governments to address juvenile delinquency (p. 4); advocated for regulatory systems and investment in infrastructure to curb illicit enterprises and pollution in socially disorganized communities (p. 5); and emphasized the need for governments to understand "the social and cultural dynamics at work in countries undergoing rapid social and economic change" in order "to prescribe measures appropriate to the special social and cultural factors involved" (p. 5). Interestingly, the report also accounted for the problem of Mertonian anomie in rural communities that were increasingly being exposed to "materialistic views, with grossly altered conceptions of individual liberties and goals, [which disturb] the settled patterns of village authority and sow the seeds of discord and rejection of established norms of behavior" (p. 15).

The Secretariat's diagnosis was clearly grounded in the American tradition, but it also drew evidence from previously published UN reports (which were also anchored in this perspective.) These included a 1955 report titled *Problems of Social Disorganization Linked with the Industrialization and Urbanization of Countries Undergoing Rapid Economic Development*, a 1956 Secretariat report on *Urbanization and Crime and Delinquency in Asia and the Far East*, and a 1957 UN *Report on the World Social Situation*.[6] The issue has also previously been discussed at regional workshops and seminars in both Bangkok, Thailand (1956), and Santiago, Chile (1959), thereby illustrating that the work of the UN crime program as a coordinating node contributed to the diffusion of these ideas, and that this in turn served to reinforce their assumed universality.

Accordingly, two additional reports authored by criminologists from developing countries were prepared for the 1960 UN Crime Congress. The first report, by J. J. Panakal, an Indian criminologist, focused on Asia and observed that "all countries in the region are undergoing a metamorphosis in economic structure and way of life, accompanied by social tensions, which in turn contribute to an upward trend in criminality" (Panakal, 1960, p. 4). Panakal's analysis of these changes is largely consistent with that of the Secretariat report, but it was also seemingly ahead of its time insofar as it considered how rapid economic growth was impacting women and the criminological consequences of this in traditional societies. He argued that rapid industrialization and urbanization risked destabilizing traditional gender roles, and that increased participation in crime by women might be explained by new economic and social pressures that "forced [them] to seek employment and earn a living," particularly through prostitution (p. 31). This was hardly a radical take on gender and crime, but it is noteworthy because the contemporary Western criminological literature was either gender-blind or wedded to Lombrosian assumptions about female criminality (Heidehnson, 1968). At the same time, Panakal's analysis illustrates continuity with how women were represented as an element of the League of Nation's work program following the Great Depression. That is, women were constructed as being vulnerable to social change, and economic development was framed not as a source of their liberation but as a threat to traditional gender roles.

Similar themes were described in a second report authored by A. M. Khalifa (1960), an Egyptian criminologist, which examined recent statistical trends in different developing countries. These included Yugoslavia, Egypt, South Africa, Thailand, and South Korea. Khalifa's analysis evidenced a link between industrialization, urbanization, and crime; however, he also stressed that industrialization was not the cause of crime but rather an underlying condition that disrupts social structures and has the potential to generate "cultural shock" (p. 69). The report also included an extended discussion of the methodological challenges inherent to undertaking a comparative analysis of statistical trends in industrialization/crime between different developing countries. These challenges have long been acknowledged by criminologists, but their explicit discussion here is important because it framed the lack of standardization between criminal codes and data collection methods as an obstacle to the social defense movement. Specifically, it limited the movement's ability to establish a rigorous, scientific evidence base that could then be used to analyze trends and formulate universal principles that could be adapted for use in different contexts. There was no realistic prospect of achieving standardization at the time due to ideological divisions and the limited capabilities and resources of recently decolonized states, but promoting methodological standardization would long remain a priority for the UN crime program.

These early studies and those described in the following chapters highlight the important role of evidence when it comes to shaping the international crime policy agenda. At the same time, it must be noted that the policy development process cannot be reduced to either "evidence-based policy" or "policy-driven evidence." Rather, evidence and policies are mutually constructed through what Littoz-Monnet (2017) describes as an interactive process: The policy context influences knowledge production; this supplies evidence, which is selectively interpreted by policy actors and used to construct the policy agenda.

DEBATING THE CRIME-DEVELOPMENT NEXUS

The Secretariat report and those prepared by Panakal and Khalifa were discussed at a dedicated section of the Second Crime Congress in 1960 attended by delegates from different countries and representatives of non-governmental organizations. These deliberations, which are documented by the Secretariat, provide valuable insight into how these ideas were received by the wider international crime policy community. These political discussions would shape the agenda and work program for the Social Defence Section and promote recognition of the link between crime and development by ECOSOC and the UNGA.

During the dedicated panel discussions, various speakers noted that "too little information was available" to reach any concrete conclusions about the causal relationship between economic development and crime (UNDESA, 1961, p. 25). This suggests that the preparatory materials were not simply accepted as fact by the conference delegates but properly scrutinized. Their methodological limitations were acknowledged, particularly with respect to the lack of available statistical data and the challenges inherent to comparing statistics. The deliberations also called into question the universality of these trends, particularly in Latin America, where the Chilean representative observed rural to urban migration had not resulted in criminality and argued that further comparative research was needed to understand the specific conditions that rendered modernization criminogenic (p. 25).

The remarks of the Chilean representative evidence a nuanced discussion about the modernization paradigm, but their contribution along with those of delegates from the Soviet Bloc and non-aligned countries illustrates ideological contestation. For example, the delegates from both Yugoslavia and Chile maintained that economic development is not inherently criminogenic and argued, "The abolition of class oppression, of discrimination, and the exploitation of women and children, for example, could contribute to the elimination of serious social problems which had probably led to criminality" (p. 25). There was also resistance from Third World delegates to the term "less developed," which was insulting. These debates evidenced the growing influence of Third-Worldism and dependency theory, which, as noted above, aimed to shift attention to North-South divisions and establish a geopolitical movement to this effect.

Predictably, the most vocal critic of the orthodox position was the Soviet delegate, who argued that the revolution "brought great social and economic benefit to the population" and resulted in "decreases in crime" because the Soviet development model with its command economy and emphasis on social planning did not fuel mass urban migration (p. 26). Implicit in this assertion (which did not appear to receive affirmation from any of the other delegates in attendance) was the argument that the underlying structural cause of crime was not industrialization or its accompanying social changes. Rather, echoing what might be described as the Soviet tradition of criminology (Grygier, 1951), the problem was framed as capitalist development and its accompanying value system, which emphasized individualism and materialism. This highlights the epistemological incompatibility between the Western (positivist) philosophy of science, which had been adopted by the UN Secretariat, and the Soviet approach.

Whereas sociological positivism emphasizes the use of empirical methods to test and develop theories, scientific enquiry for the Soviets entailed using science to evidence the superiority of the Soviet system, advance this ideological project, or discredit Western institutions (Grygier, 1951; also Gouldner, 1970). In the criminological context, the Soviets simply argued that the criminogenic effects of modernization could be largely mitigated if countries adopted the Soviet model of development. Shelley's (1981) analysis, discussed in chapter 1, would later suggest there was limited truth to this in relation to property crime, but not when it came to violent crimes (and not necessarily for the reasons suggested by the Soviets). In any case, the Soviets were less concerned with evidence than ideology, so they maintained this position for the duration of the Cold War. This in turn limited their influence over the work of the Secretariat and the UN's crime policy agenda, but they nevertheless participated in political discussions and advisory panels, if for no other reason than to have their position formally recognized.[7] We also note that in the wider UN development system, their ideological commitment to the Soviet model also limited their influence and involvement with technical assistance, thereby ensuring that their voluntary contributions for multilateral development assistance would only support projects in Eastern Bloc countries (Browne, 2011).

The Soviet contribution predictably failed to influence the recommendations adopted by the 1960 Congress, but other criticisms and debates did. The recommendations therefore emphasized the need for the UN to adopt a more nuanced understanding of the relationship between development and crime; focus on general crime trends rather than specific or novel types of criminality; and undertake additional research on both international and local trends. The Congress also suggested that governments limit urban to rural migration and update their penal codes in light of social changes. Finally, it was agreed that the term "less developed" would only be used to refer to the economic status of Member States (pp. 27–28). Both the deliberations and the recommendations evidence that the early UN Congresses provided important institutional forums where the international crime policy agenda was negotiated and agreed upon, albeit within a particular ideological and epistemological paradigm that reproduced Western liberal hegemony through the institutionalization of a particular theoretical representation of the relationship between economic crime and development.

The crime-development nexus remained a prominent fixture of the UN crime policy agenda in the early 1960s, but this had limited impact on the capabilities or resources of the Social Defence Section. For example, a 1964 independent review of the social defense program concluded that the Social Defence Section was not in a position to provide "international leadership" due to financial constraints, its small Secretariat staff, and inadequate working arrangements. The assessment was endorsed by Secretary General U Thant, who reaffirmed the need for UN leadership on this issue by describing "the economic burden of criminality and the dissipation of gains from economic development . . . particularly in light of the major objectives set for the [First] Development Decade" (Thant, 1964, p. 2). At the same time, Thant emphasized that the funding required to expand the work of the Social Defence Section must come from "a system of joint financing" (p. 3) that included voluntary contributions from governments. Essentially, Thant recognized that the issue was important to developing countries, but the UN lacked the material resources to make a meaningful impact through the Social Defence Section without donor contributions.

In July 1965, ECOSOC adopted resolution 1086b in response to the secretary general's note. The resolution recognized the need for the UN to play a leadership role in relation to social defense; acknowledged that "the prevention of crime and control of juvenile delinquency should be undertaken as part of comprehensive economic and social development plans"; called for the strengthening of the UN's technical assistance capabilities in this area; made the Advisory Committee permanent while increasing its membership from seven to ten; and called upon the secretary general to establish a trust fund for social defense activities (ECOSOC 1086b). Less than two weeks later, the link between modernization and crime featured as the *first* agenda item of the Third UN Crime Congress in Stockholm, Sweden.

This time, the panel discussion was chaired by Marshall Clinard, the American criminologist who would later coauthor an influential book about crime and development in Uganda (see Clinard & Abbott, 1973; discussed in chapter 1). The deliberations, documented in the official Secretariat Report, albeit this time without reference to the identities or nationalities of individual speakers, once again illustrate critical engagement with the research produced by the Secretariat (UNDESA, 1966). Topics that had previously been discussed in 1960 were revisited, and objections to reductionist and universalistic assertions were raised. What is perhaps most interesting, however, is that the 1965 discussions were particularly concerned with what interventions should be prescribed to deal with criminogenic consequences of modernization and, specifically, what this implied for the role of the state.

Up to this point, the social defense paradigm presented the state as the primary vehicle for advancing social defense policies at the national level. This was consistent with the UN's emphasis on state planning, and it was also guided by the "development as efficiency" approach described above. The Section's emphasis had therefore been on using technical assistance to modernize state institutions (including those of the criminal justice system, but also social services), legal processes, and legislation.

During the 1965 panel discussion, participants started to question the viability of promoting a state-centric model of social defense in developing countries, and it was noted:

> [T]here was a need to involve ordinary persons rather than relying exclusively on governmental agencies and legal processes in coping with problems presented by social change.... This might involve more efforts at the local community level, responsibility for crime being assumed by smaller administrative units, and there should be greater involvement of persons in groups representing potential risks of crime and delinquency. (UNDESA, 1966, pp. 12–13)

This statement suggests that important techniques of liberal governance, later associated with neoliberal penal policies in the West, were already being advocated as a potential solution to the perceived inadequacy of a state-centric model of crime control, at least for governments lacking the resources or capabilities to emulate the ambitious (and expensive) Western prescriptions for social crime prevention (for example, the US proposals outlined by the 1967 President's Commission on Law Enforcement and the Administration of Justice). The contemporary appeal of enlisting non-state actors and institutions was therefore not a product of an ideologically-driven agenda to "hollow out" the Keynesian welfare state or a response to the social instabilities that neoliberal reforms generated (although for many developing countries, this would come later). Rather, in the 1960s it reflected a pragmatic acknowledgment that Western prescriptions were not viable in materially disadvantaged dependencies of the Third World. Their "less advanced" state institutions were therefore reimagined as vehicles for potentially mobilizing informal sources of social control and aligning their mentalities and efforts with "national objectives and values" (UN, 1966, p. 14). The emphasis given to education illustrates important continuities between these prescriptions and the governing techniques that had previously been developed to produce obedient, colonial subjects (Brown, 2006).

Another important element of the Stockholm discussions related to the Congress's support for integrating social defense into the "expanded program of technical assistance," which focused on wider economic and social issues (UNDESA, 1966, p. 29). The emphasis here was on developing links with UNDP, which was established three months later. The idea, therefore, was to increase the resources and capabilities of the Social Defence Section by integrating technical assistance experts into multiagency, country-based programs in order to develop comprehensive and contextually appropriate strategies for managing the criminogenic effects of development. For the Section, this was appealing because it seemingly provided an avenue for accessing additional resources and expanding its capabilities on the ground.

Integration was never realized for various reasons. For example, William Clifford, who served as chief of the Social Defence Section in the 1970s, later recalled that "many people inside and outside the United Nations" viewed "special problems like crime and rehabilitation as anachronistic and as better treated within the larger context of social improvement" (Clifford, 1979, p. 17). Another explanation links back to the competitive nature of the UN development system. In this regard, Clifford (1979, p. 6) noted that despite its recognition by the secretary general and ECOSOC, the Social Defence Section was "second class in a structure dominated by economics" and "could not even command priority within the social division." Thus, despite the establishment of a Social Defense Trust Fund and a Social Defense Research Institute (UNSDRI), the Secretariat failed to secure sufficient resources that would allow it to gain recognition as a development partner and expand its technical assistance work in the late 1960s. As discussed in the following chapter, this contributed to an important shift in the Section's work program and the decline of the social defense movement.

Chapter Five

International Crime in the Crisis Decades

Social historians, political economists, and Anglo-American criminologists have widely characterized the 1970s and 1980s as an important period of capitalist transformation. In *The Age of Extremes,* Hobsbawm (1994) described these as "the crisis decades" when the Keynesian model of embedded liberalism was gradually and unevenly supplanted by a neoliberal doctrine that emphasized free market capitalism, individualism, and the rejection of social democratic values. This ideological transformation was in part a response to the emergence of an increasingly unstable global economy, itself a product of the modernization project, and specifically America's advocacy of free trade in the 1950s and 1960s. The causes and dynamics of the economic crises of the 1970s and 1980s remain a subject of scholarly debate; however, like the Great Depression of the 1930s, their effects were felt by countries around the world. Both the onset and diverse experiences of the "crisis decades" illustrate the fallibility and failures of the modernization paradigm, specifically the idea that the dependencies would simply follow in the footsteps of their developed counterparts and benefit from integration with a global economy.

In the Anglophone West, the crises of capitalism are linked with the decline of manufacturing, structural unemployment, the dismantling of the welfare state, and rising levels of inequality (Harvey, 2005). In the Soviet Bloc, the economic crisis demonstrated that despite enduring ideological differences and its command economy, it was nevertheless part of a global economy (Strayver, 2016). For the Third World, the effects of this period, which has come to be associated with the early decades of economic globalization, were particularly pronounced, albeit uneven (Prashard, 2014). In Asia, there were "winners," countries that had successfully developed economic systems, social infrastructure, and technological capabilities that allowed them to attract foreign investment, increase manufacturing, and gain a competitive advantage on the West in a global marketplace.[1] For other parts of the developing world, particularly Latin America (Martins, 2020) and Sub-Saharan Africa (Hope, 1997), these decades were broadly characterized by rising debt, instability (economic, social, and political), and inequality.

The criminological implications of these crises are also well documented, at least the Anglo-American experiences. As the story goes, the economic crises of the 1970s that gave rise to neoliberalism contributed to the transformation of penal cultures and the hollowing out of the penal state (Garland, 2001; Wacquant, 2009). Whereas previously the state was seen as an important social crime prevention actor, the neoliberal penal assemblages that supplanted them became increasingly punitive and pragmatic in their focus. The rise of late modern penal cultures has therefore come to be associated with a range of factors and forces that have both contributed to and resulted from the economic and ideological shifts noted above (Garland, 2001). These include widespread disillusionment among criminological experts and practitioners with social crime prevention; rising public anxieties about crime; the politicization of crime (or, perhaps more accurately, insecurity) and growing disillusionment with experts themselves; criminogenic economic and social conflicts generated or exacerbated by neoliberal policies; fiscal conservatism and reduced expenditure on criminal justice agencies; privatization and the responsibilities or divestment of responsibility for social control (including self-control and regulation) to non-state actors, including communities and individuals; and the growing popularity of efficient and cost-effective neoclassical criminological approaches and theories, particularly those that emphasize situational crime prevention (O'Malley, 2018).

The Anglo-American experience is not the focus of this chapter, and various criminologists have questioned the generalizability of these narratives, noting, for example, the distinct penal cultures of former dependencies that were never in a structural position to emulate the economic or social development trajectories of the United States or Britain (for example, Steinberg, 2016). These criticisms are important, but it would be problematic to disregard the transformation of capitalism as a global phenomenon while accounting for the transformation of the international crime policy agenda during this period. Accordingly, we argue that the onset of neoliberal globalization and the crises that prompted it structured the work of the UN crime program and the reconstruction of the crime-development nexus during the 1970s and 1980s. We associate this with the perceived failure of social defense as a component of the modernization project, budgetary pressures within the UN system, and changing material, institutional, and ideological conditions that contributed to the internationalization and diversification of the international crime policy agenda. These conditions and shifts provided the UN crime program and its supporters with a narrative that helped justify not only its survival but also establish a foundation that supported expansion. Amid these changes, social defense did not immediately disappear from the agenda, but its prominence and significance were greatly diminished, while greater emphasis was afforded to the prevention of crime, human rights, and, perhaps most significantly, transnational crime. These institutional shifts, together with the economic and ideological changes that contributed to the global spread of neoliberalism in the 1980s, established the foundations of the discursive assumptions underpinning the crime-development nexus today. Whereas in the "Golden Age," the primary concern was managing the social instabilities and criminological consequences of modernization, this new paradigm has since been concerned with ensuring that problems that can be criminalized do not disrupt economic growth and free market capitalism.

FROM "SOCIAL DEFENSE" TO "CRIME AS BUSINESS"

By the late 1960s, social defense was not considered a development priority, at least within the wider UN development system. Notably, the Social Defence Section had failed to establish meaningful collaborations with other development agencies, particularly at the country-level, where the recently established United Nations Development Programme (UNDP) was responsible for promoting coordination and administering funds. Furthermore, despite the creation of a Social Defense Trust Fund in 1967, the Section had failed to secure sufficient funding to expand its reach and capabilities in relation to technical assistance (see Clifford, 1979, p. 17). It is noted in the Secretariat's Report for the Fourth Congress, for example, that additional money was required to convene additional preparatory meetings to support regional coordination (UN Secretariat, 1971). These financial constraints impacted not only the Section but also the activities of a wider epistemic community that connected these international nodes to regional, national, and local forums and actors.

This did not mean that the international community had altogether lost interest in the criminological consequences of development, and the theme featured prominently on the agenda of the Fourth (1970) UN Crime Congress in Kyoto, Japan. This was attended by a growing number of delegates from the Third World who had a direct interest in this problem. The point then is that the transformation of the UN crime program and the international crime policy agenda was triggered not by the disinterest or disillusionment of Third World countries but rather by institutional and material conditions that impacted the wider UN system. These were in turn being shaped by the growing divergence between the liberal internationalist outlook of the UN and the interests of Western capitalist nations.

Declining Western investment in the UN's development programs during the 1970s reflected the former's diminishing influence over the UN's budget and policy agenda. This was itself attributable to the growing numerical superiority of Third World countries in the UN General Assembly and ECOSOC (Murphy, 2006). Needless to say, the emergence of collective platforms that challenged Western hegemony (and Soviet imperialism) via the Non-Aligned Movement and, later, the New International Economic Order (NIEO) did not increase the UN's appeal to countries like the United States, which came to view it as an inefficient platform for advancing their foreign policy interests and, potentially, even an obstacle to its geopolitical aspirations. Clifford (1979, p. 36) would later recall that the financial impacts of this divestment were particularly disastrous for the UN crime program, which was already regarded as low priority:

> [W]henever, in a government or the United Nations, policies of economic restraint are being applied it is the less influential departments and sections which are likely to suffer. Those with status and position can usually defend themselves: crime prevention could not.

Deprived of material resources and institutional support, bureaucratic actors typically seek out opportunities to reinvent themselves to survive. Often this involves drawing attention to new or emerging problems that can be linked to the entity's existing portfolio or capabilities (Barnett & Finnemore, 1999). For example, in response to the funding challenges described above, UNDP accomplished this by reorienting itself toward the "development of freedom" model that prescribed collaboration and partnership with developing countries to address the issue that mattered to them (Murphy, 2006; Browne, 2011). This provided a useful strategy for developing new funding partnerships, and it was politically savvy because it signaled a symbolic break with the neocolonial, "development as efficiency" model and the "development as growth" model, which was being promoted by the West through bilateral aid and the Bretton Woods institutions.

UNDP's experience suggests that bureaucratic actors do not arbitrarily invent problems or craft new mandates to enhance their material position or institutional standing. Rather, adaptation is shaped by the entity's awareness of ideological, institutional, and material conditions and the opportunities they present. Further to this point, Cox (1969) argued that the quality of executive leadership is perhaps the most important determinant of whether an organization will recognize and respond to these opportunities. UNDP in the late 1960s was fortunate because its first administrator, Paul Hoffman, understood the political importance of maintaining the entity's status as an independent, multilateral development actor that was responsive to developing countries (Murphy, 2006). For the UN crime program, the process of reinvention was subtler and more gradual. This is perhaps attributable to the program's lack of executive leadership at the time.[2] Thus, its transformation exacerbated the divergence between its portfolio and the work of the wider UN development system during the 1970s and 1980s.

From a political economy standpoint, the most significant factor that indirectly influenced the transformation of the UN crime program is linked with the development of the global economy during the 1960s. This prompted greater awareness of, and concerns about, the economic interlinkages between different countries. The structural instabilities and uncertainties generated by the shift from the Inter Imperial Order to the Free World Order (Murphy, 1994, pp. 244–45) thus supplied the UN crime program with an intriguing and politically appealing narrative about the changing nature of crime and its international character. This narrative was seemingly born out of a meeting of the UN Consultative Group on the Prevention of Crime and the Treatment of Offenders in 1968 and later presented to delegates at the Fourth UN Congress in Kyoto in a UN Secretariat working paper (1970).

The working paper was primarily about social defense, and the first seven sections either echoed or expanded on many of the themes about economic development, social change, and crime that had been discussed in 1960 and 1965. However, the final section drew attention to "International Aspects" of social defense, thereby implying that crime may be changing, so the paradigm must evolve:

> Planning is no longer a purely national concern. The countries of the world are becoming progressively more interrelated, and the responsibility for achieving better standards of living for all is a burden shared by developed and developing nations alike. Equally, the problem of controlling and preventing crime has been recognized as international since nations first began to associate for their mutual advantage. In the days of the League of Nations there were commissions for white slavery and narcotics; and if the concept of crime be extended to cover "white collar" offences such as the exploitation of labor, tax evasions and the like, then more agencies than the United Nations itself are involved in crime prevention. Should political crimes be included as well, no area of international activity is really excluded. (UN Secretariat, 1970, p. 40)

This suggests that national planning and development are international issues, because the "burden" of uneven development is transnational and global. This position is consistent with an enduring, liberal humanist belief that the developed world has a responsibility to support its developing counterparts in the Third World. Conversely, it also suggests that governments of newly independent countries have a responsibility to engage with the international community to prevent and control crime. This was framed as a functional imperative.

The statement also demonstrates historical awareness by acknowledging that crime was previously addressed as an international problem by the League of Nations. This is particularly noteworthy because there is little evidence of institutional continuity between its work on trafficking and prostitution during the 1920s and that of the Social Defence Section in the1950s and 1960s. The Secretariat's (1970) observation that countries are "progressively more interrelated" further resonates with earlier concerns about the internationalization of crime during the Second Industrial Revolution and following the First World War (Knepper, 2009, 2011). Indeed, the earlier transformation of capitalism generated cultural anxieties about international crime, which moral and political entrepreneurs used to their advantage. A similar dynamic was evident from the 1980s onward, which we discuss in this and the following chapter. Most significantly, the working paper signposts the UN's embrace of a more expansive understanding of crime and its relevance to policy spheres that were of greater interest to donors and potential beneficiaries alike.

This discursive emphasis on change clearly resonated with these audiences and this narrative was incorporated into the Declaration of the Fourth Congress (UN Secretariat, 1971). The Declaration acknowledged the "increasing seriousness and proportions of crime"; reiterated "the need for the world community of nations to improve its planning for economic and social development"; and recognized "[the] many ramifications of crime" and "its new dimensions," which "saps the energies of a nation and undermines its efforts to achieve a more wholesome environment for the better life of its people" (UN Secretariat, 1971, p. iii). The following year, the increasingly complex and international character of crime was also acknowledged by ECOSOC (1584(L), and the Social Defence Section was rebranded the Crime Prevention and Criminal Justice Section (CPCJS).

In 1972 the UNGA endorsed the Declaration and established a special Working Group of the Committee on Crime Prevention and Control (CCPC) composed of experts who set out to develop an "International Plan of Action" for crime prevention (Redo, 2012, p. 152). William Clifford, who served as secretary of the Working Group, later reflected that one of its three foundational principles emphasized, "the world was shrinking and a common urban or industrial culture was spreading, making crime a distinctly international problem and even encouraging the evolution of new and special forms of crime deriving from the new styles of living" ("International Plan of Action," quoted by Clifford, 1979, p. 31). The Working Group also concluded that "the problems posed by transnational crime (in such forms as drug trafficking, the kidnapping or killing of diplomats, counterfeiting and the stealing of masterpieces, etc.) were of particular urgency and should therefore be the object of immediate action to develop common policies and programs among nations" (Clifford, 1979, p. 32).

In 1974 the CPCJS was "upgraded" to the Crime Prevention and Criminal Justice Branch (CPCJB; see Redo, 2012, p. 151), and the changing nature of crime and its transnational dimensions were discussed in a 1975 Secretariat working paper prepared for the Fifth Crime Congress (UN Secretariat, 1975). The topics covered in the working paper were diverse, but all of them aligned with the argument that new and emerging forms of criminality were potentially a cause for concern for developed and developing countries alike. The paper's emphasis on the vulnerability of developing countries to "crimes affecting the national economy" and transnational corporations "which appear to operate outside and above the law" is particularly noteworthy because it suggests that free market capitalism was contributing to, albeit not necessarily causing, these problems (p. 4). An explanation for this radical shift is provided in the following section, and we note that many of these themes featured prominently in the UN's crime policy agenda until the early 1980s.

Predictably, the Secretariat's narrative about the changing and transnational nature of crime as an international problem was endorsed by delegates at the 1975 Congress (UN Secretariat, 1976). The 1975 Congress Declaration itself is perhaps less pertinent to our analysis than the Congress's deliberations about the working paper and, specifically, its emphasis on organized crime, white collar crime, and corruption, which highlight heightened concern among a sizable Third World delegation about the threat these "relatively neglected" forms of crime pose to the economy. Summarizing these deliberations, the Secretariat (1976, p. 10) noted:

> It was agreed that the economic and social consequences of "crime as business" were typically much greater than the consequences of traditional forms of interpersonal violence and crimes against property. . . . Such crimes were, of course, a serious problem in many developed countries, but several representatives of developing countries emphasized that white collar crime, organized crime, and corruption posed especially severe problems for their countries—indeed, they might be virtually matters of life and death—since the national welfare and economic development of the whole society might be drastically affected by such criminal conduct as bribery, price-fixing, smuggling, and currency offences.

This signified an emerging consensus among developing countries that "crime as business" was a growing problem, albeit one that was poorly understood at the time.

Arguably, problems relating to corruption and organized crime did become more prevalent during the 1960s and 1970s as the economic development of newly independent countries of the Third World created new opportunities for these forms of criminality to occur. Indeed, wider concerns about the growth of illicit economies in the absence of legitimate opportunities, particularly in urban areas, had been raised at previous Congresses since 1960. However, due to the geopolitical changes described below, the political significance of these issues for developing countries in the 1970s is seemingly more relevant for explaining the transformation of the international crime policy agenda than the actual threat posed by these issues.

THE NEW INTERNATIONAL ECONOMIC ORDER

The diversification and internationalization of the UN crime policy agenda coincided with a broader ideological shift that redefined North-South relations within the UN system during the final decades of the Cold War (Rist, 2014; Prashad, 2007). The arguments of dependency theorists, including Raúl Prebisch and later Fernando Cordoso (1972), stimulated a critical dialogue among Third World states about the West's neocolonial approach to economic and social development. This intellectual tradition drew attention to the uneven nature of development and provided political elites in developing countries with a means of articulating their grievances by locating them in a critique of modernization theory. To this effect, Rist (2014, p. 110) argues that the fundamental tenets of dependency theory emerged as the antithesis of Rostow's (1960) paradigm. The NIEO ideology thus emerged in response to the perceived failures of the First Development Decade, the political momentum of Third-Worldism and the Non-Aligned Movement, the robust intellectual critique provided by dependency theorists, and the numerical superiority of countries in the UN's political organs. It was afforded even greater impetus by the economic crises of the 1970s, which primarily impacted the West, and coincided with a commodity price boom that increased the resources—and leverage—of many Third World countries (Hallwood & Sinclair, 2016).

NIEO was not, however, born out of an ideological critique of capitalist development. Rather, the main grievance was that "benevolent" modernization policies served to construct a system of capitalism that afforded Western states and transnational corporations privileged access to natural resources and emerging markets (Rist, 2014). Many of these issues were long documented within the UN system, initially by the UN Economic Commission for Latin America and subsequently by the UN Conference on Trade and Development, the secretary general of which from 1964 to 1969 was actually Raúl

Prebisch. A further grievance was that Western proponents of modernization eschewed their own prescriptions for promoting free market capitalism in the Third World by maintaining protectionist policies that insulated their growing manufacturing sectors from foreign competition. This limited scope for Third World countries to stimulate domestic production (Rist, 2014).

In 1974 the UNGA adopted the "Declaration on the Establishment of a New International Economic Order," which recognized "the remaining vestiges of alien and colonial domination, foreign occupation, racial discrimination, apartheid, and neocolonialism in all its forms" as "amongst the greatest obstacles to the full emancipation and progress of the developing countries and all the peoples involved" (UNGA 3201 (S-VI)). The Declaration then asserted that "even and balanced development of the international community under the existing international order" was "impossible" and that "the present economic order" had exacerbated "inequalities." Finally, it asserted that increased interdependence between developing and developed nations meant "the prosperity of the international community as a whole depends on the prosperity of its constituent parts."

To address these problems, the NIEO Declaration proposed a number of principles that were formulated to promote a more embedded model of capitalist development. The principles recognized the sovereign equality of every nation, called for international cooperation to address "the prevailing disparities," acknowledged the right of every country to select a model of economic and social development of their choosing, and asserted state sovereignty over natural resources and the right to nationalize them. Related to this final point about natural resources is the Declaration's call for the "[r]egulation and supervision of the activities of transnational corporations by taking measures of interest of the national economies of the countries where such transnational corporations operate on the basis of the full sovereignty of those countries" (UNGA 3201 (S-VI)).

The Declaration included no specific reference to crime or corruption, but the NIEO ideology "became an essential element in practically every [UN] discussion and was brought into criminal policy" (López-Rey, 1985, p. 93) because the work of the Secretariat and the international crime policy agenda became less insulated from the wider politics of the UN. These shifts provide insight into why, by the early 1970s, the UN crime program worked to expand its portfolio and align its work program with the political interests and concerns of the NIEO movement. For example, the authors of the 1975 working paper discussed above were almost certainly aware of these shifts. There is little evidence to suggest that influential members of the UN crime program actively subscribed to the dependency critique, but they would have at least recognized that the "crime as business" narrative was useful for linking their portfolio to the NIEO Declaration.

NIEO's influence on the UN crime policy agenda is probably most evident from the agenda of the Sixth UN Congress held in Caracas, Venezuela, in 1980. For the first time the Congress featured an agenda item that focused on "crime and abuse of power," the inclusion of which was a direct reflection of the growing influence of NIEO within the UN during the late 1970s (Redo, 2012, p. 68). The discussion centered on a working paper, which noted that the inclusion of this "potentially controversial topic" was "testimony to a changing climate" (UN Secretariat, 1980, p. 3). It also acknowledged "growing interdependence of the world" and that "abuses of economic and political power can transcend national frontiers." Most significantly, it explicitly acknowledged the developing world's preference for a shift away from the "development as growth" model toward a "development as freedom" approach that was oriented toward "promoting human dignity and a better quality of life."

The NIEO Declaration is remembered as a challenge to Western hegemony, with significant implications for global governance (Murphy, 1994). However, our sense is that the UN crime program paid lip service to it because it had to. In this regard, most of the agenda for the 1980 Congress continued to focus on more traditional issues relating to crime prevention and criminal justice reform (UN Secretariat, 1981). The Secretariat's working paper also noted that there was a lack of existing evidence concerning "crime and the abuse of power" and questioned whether these issues were best addressed through the machinery of the UN crime program (UN Secretariat, 1980). The program's conservative stance and reluctance to mobilize its bureaucratic authority to validate the NIEO agenda is also evident from the reflections of one of the chief architects of the UN crime program, who reflected that by the 1980s, "[crime prevention] had been frequently overlooked because of the importance attached to the badly defined concept of development" (López-Rey, 1985, p. 125).

For reasons discussed below, the NIEO movement was short-lived, but it had an enduring impact on the work of the UN crime program in two ways. First, its rise helps to account for the decline of the social defense movement and the concurrent expansion and internationalization of the UN's crime policy remit. As discussed below, "organized crime" and "corruption" subsequently became a mainstay of the international crime policy agenda, and much of the discussion at the 1985 Congress in Milan, Italy, centered on improving international cooperation to address transnational crime. Second, NIEO served to elevate the significance of human rights within the UN system, and this contributed to a number of important developments in relation to the UN crime program's normative work. For example, the CPCJB played an instrumental role in developing the 1984 United Nations Declaration of Basic Principles of Justice for Victims of Crime and Abuse of Power, which was adopted in 1984. While the progressive qualities of the Declaration have subsequently been scrutinized by scholars (Fattah, 1992), it was nevertheless made possible by the political climate. The growing influence of the human rights agenda on the UN crime program during the NIEO years is particularly noteworthy insofar as it would remain an enduring, albeit controversial, focus in the years ahead.

THE STATE AS AN OBSTACLE TO ECONOMIC DEVELOPMENT

During the 1980s, the West's growing interest in issues that later became associated with corruption and organized crime was not linked with NIEO's concerns about the unethical or harmful activities of transnational corporations. Nor was it inspired by a progressive belief in the need to promote economic and social justice at a global level in order to overcome the North-South divide. Rather, the structural adjustment agenda emerged in response to the transformation of the global economy and the West's desire to advance a free market ideology and protect transnational corporations from NIEO's calls for increased regulation and nationalization. The rise of "governance" as an element of the international development agenda is thus connected with what was ultimately a successful attempt by the West to neutralize the NIEO ideology and the dependency critique. Thus, from the West's perspective, the Third World's failure to make economic or social progress had not been impeded by the exploitative activities of transnational corporations or free market capitalism. Rather, underdevelopment was a consequence of the inability of Third World governments to adopt and successfully implement policies that advanced the public good. Part of this discourse specifically located responsibility in the "rent-seeking" behavior of Third World governments (Gould & Amaro-Reyes, 1983). Consequently, the state-led development model was reconstructed by the West as a barrier to economic growth, an obstacle to development, and antithetical to the advancement of the public good (Polzer, 2001).

Contextualizing the emergence of "corruption" as an international development issue and the "rule of law" revival of the 1990s necessitates consideration of the broader economic transformations that contributed to the collapse of NIEO and the rise of neoliberalism. These structural and ideological developments are also significant because they contributed to the growing influence of the "development as growth" model throughout the 1980s and 1990s, and because the economic, social, and political instabilities this model generated via structural adjustment policies seemingly served to exacerbate the issues of crime and corruption throughout the Global South (Currie, 2015, 2020), along with the "North's South" (Currie, 2017). The crime-development nexus today has been shaped by this neoliberal agenda and the international community's efforts to manage its structural and criminological consequences.

The rise of neoliberalism on a global scale is well rehearsed (Harvey, 2006), so our concern here is primarily with how this contributed to the collapse of NIEO and the rise of the governance agenda in the 1980s. A key point is that NIEO's emphasis on the increasingly interdependent nature of the transnational economy during the 1970s and the risks this posed for countries in the developing world whose economies had not diversified and were linked with primary commodity exports was fundamentally correct. This, together with the limitations of a state-led development model in an unfair and increasingly unstable global economy and easy access to private loans, contributed to the sovereign debt crisis in Latin America and Sub-Saharan Africa during the 1980s and 1990s (Devlin, 2014; Konadu-Agyemang, 2018).

The story goes that during the 1970s, governments of developing countries, particularly those in Latin America, borrowed a significant amount of money from Western commercial banks, which, thanks to an influx of oil money, lent at low interest rates. For developing countries, these commercial loans seemingly provided an attractive alternative to foreign aid when it came to stimulating state-led industrialization and renationalization. Essentially, commercial borrowing was viewed as a potential pathway to economic self-sufficiency, which would ultimately allow developing countries to compete in the global market. The debt crisis was quickly triggered by a decision by the US Federal Reserve to increase interest rates in an attempt to address the domestic problem of "stagflation." Commercial banks in turn increased their interest rates, and by the early 1980s, heavily indebted countries found themselves struggling to make their repayments, which, at an elevated interest rate, accounted for a growing proportion of their national GDP. This in turn deprived these governments of revenue required to sustain a rudimental welfare system and deliver core public services.

Western countries recognized that the sovereign debt crisis posed a threat to global capitalism. Fearing that commercial banks would collapse if the borrowing countries defaulted, the US put pressure on international financial institutions, including the International Monetary Fund and the World Bank, to step in and provide loans that would allow indebted countries to make their repayments and hopefully stimulate economic growth. The loans were made conditional upon borrowing governments adopting policies designed to open up their economies to foreign investment via liberalization, deregulation, and the privatization of state-owned industries and natural resources (Summers & Pritchett, 1993). These structural adjustment policies were grounded in a neoliberal doctrine, which signaled the demise of NIEO as a counter-hegemonic movement that aspired to create a more equitable capitalist order. Throughout the developing world, new divisions emerged between those who embraced neoliberalism as a vehicle for overcoming the deficiencies of state-led growth in the developing world and Marxists like Samir Amin (1982), who argued that NIEO had failed because its aspirations had not been radical enough. In any case, NIEO's failure implied the collapse of Third-Worldism as a collective ideology and a platform for contesting North-South relations. It also signaled a significant shift in how influential development economists would theorize the state and its relationship to the economy throughout the 1980s and 1990s.

The neoliberal model of capitalism rejected the assumption of modernization theory that the state was best positioned to promote economic and social development, but it retained a belief in the linear nature of development and the assumption that developing countries should adopt the policy prescriptions of their industrialized counterparts. Moreover, the end of the Cold War and the US-Soviet rivalry meant that—in Margaret Thatcher's words—"there [was] no alternative" to the neoliberal model, especially in the Third World (Hobsbawm, 1994). Structural adjustment policies in combination with the onset of globalization rendered developing countries increasingly reliant on foreign investors and transnational corporations, and it is here that the West's interest in corruption and rule of law as development issues emerged. This was most evident from the work of the World Bank in the 1990s following the collapse of the Soviet Union, but the importance of creating a "business friendly environment" was already recognized by the international development community during what economists have since come to refer to as the "lost decade" (Hayes, 1989).

It is important to note that corruption did not feature prominently in the first five World Development Reports (1978–1982), and there had been no reference to this problem in World Bank President Robert McNamara's 1971 address to ECOSOC (McNamara, 1971). It was only in the 1983 World Development Report that the issue was first identified by the World Bank as an obstacle to development. The emphasis was on corruption as a consequence of the state-led development model that had been widely embraced by developing countries—a model the World Bank associated with patronage networks, inflated bureaucracies, and rent-seeking behaviors. To this effect, the 1983 report specifically noted that "the particular circumstances of developing countries . . . may be peculiarly conducive to corruption" and that "it is the misuse of public funds and the failure of public trust that is of particular concern" (World Bank, 1983, p. 117). The World Bank's prescriptions for addressing corruption were therefore consistent with the structural adjustment policies it imposed upon developing countries. Specifically, it emphasized "reducing controls on international trade and payment" by having "fewer, better-paid officials controlling only what really needs to be (and can effectively be) controlled in the full light of public scrutiny" (p. 117).

Corruption received scant attention in the next three World Development Reports but reappeared in the 1987 publication titled "Barriers to Adjustment and Growth in the World Economy" (World Bank, 1987). Whereas the 1983 report put forth the case for developing countries to embrace structural adjustment policies to stimulate economic growth, the 1987 report focused on why the effects of these economic reforms had been uneven and had failed to address issues like poverty despite, in some contexts, stimulating economic growth (Summers & Pritchett, 1992). Thus, facing criticism and calls for debt relief, the 1987 report can be read as an attempt by the World Bank to defend its position by shifting responsibility for the failure of structural adjustment reforms to the governments tasked with implementing them. Once again, the problem of corruption was framed in relation to a neoliberal critique of protectionist policies, government interference with markets, and inflated bureaucracies. To this effect, the 1987 report noted that foreign investors increasingly came to associate corruption with "insecurity of economic rights" (p. 62) and a problem that "imposes high costs on doing business" (p. 75). The 1987 report included no specific reference to crime, but it described "black markets" and the "informal economy" as "tacitly tolerated . . . in most developing countries" and thus a threat to economic rights, economic growth, and free market capitalism (p. 74). This narrative would later resonate with the World Bank's efforts to raise the visibility of corruption as a threat to economic liberalization in the 1990s (see chapter 6), but it was once again de-emphasized in the 1988, 1989, and 1990 reports. Perhaps the explanation for this is that by the late 1980s, the World Bank had been forced to accept that its neoliberal shock therapy had not resolved the Latin American debt crisis and that this lack of progress represented a risk to both the global capitalist economy and the legitimacy of the neoliberal world order. Averting another economic crisis therefore necessitated both ideological and material concessions, so the World Bank and the IMF (with the support of the Bush administration) was forced to offer debt reduction plans to Latin American countries on the brink of crisis (Kenen, 1990).

Relatedly, in an effort to seemingly restore its legitimacy, the World Bank adopted what appeared to be a more palatable theme for its 1990

World Development Report: poverty (World Bank, 1990). The 1990 report acknowledged the uneven effects of development during the "lost decade," particularly for the poor in Latin America and Sub-Saharan Africa. It did not, however, suggest that poor countries abandon neoliberal prescriptions for economic liberalization but rather complement these with investment in "basic social services . . . to help those not able to benefit from these policies and, by safety nets, to protect those who are exposed to shocks" (p. iii). This signaled a softening of the neoliberal agenda—one that proved to be politically useful insofar as it later afforded proponents of "development as growth" with a means of aligning their aims with the emergent human development paradigm, which enjoyed greater legitimacy among developing countries of what would subsequently be referred to as the "Global South."

ECONOMIC DEVELOPMENT AND THE UN CRIME POLICY IN THE 1980s

Our final consideration in this chapter relates to how the collapse of NIEO and the rise of neoliberal globalization during the 1980s shaped the international crime policy agenda and, specifically, its framing of the relationship between crime and development. These are difficult questions to answer, because the range of issues that were being considered as part of this agenda had already expanded quite significantly by 1980, and much of this was in response to heightened awareness of the emergence of a global economy and its potential consequences for developing countries. It is clear, however, that the NIEO-inspired account of "crime as business," which referenced issues such as "corruption" and "organized crime," was at odds with the neoliberal diagnoses supplied by the World Bank. We believe it was NIEO rather than the World Bank that originally put these problems on the agenda, yet this progressive movement had a marginal effect on how these problems would subsequently be framed within the international crime policy agenda. Once again, official records of the UN crime policy agenda during the mid- to late 1980s provide valuable insight into how this framing shifted and evolved, albeit gradually and unevenly, with the rise of neoliberal globalization and neoconservatism in the United States. This in turn supplies insight into why organized crime emerged as a focal point of the UN crime policy agenda around this time.

The agenda for the 1985 Congress included several progressive issues relating to the rights of victims and human rights in the sphere of criminal justice, but social defense was noticeably absent (UN Secretariat, 1986). It was seemingly replaced by "economic development," which featured prominently in the discussions. This signified an important shift in how the relationship between crime and development would henceforth come to be understood by the international crime policy community. Insight is provided in the first instance by a working paper on "New Dimensions of Criminality and Crime Prevention in the Context of Development: Challenges for the Future" (UN Secretariat, 1985). The working paper was heavily influenced by the NIEO agenda, so it maintained an interest in the changing nature of crime, particularly organized crime and corruption. However, it also specifically acknowledged a "new dimension" of crime that relates to "the high degree of international coordination and extension characterizing certain criminal operations, such as a substantial part of the illicit activities of organized crime, particularly drug trafficking" (p. 5). It proceeded to acknowledge that "organized crime" was "certainly not a new phenomenon" but rather one that "has acquired an unprecedented geographical extension and international coordination in recent decades, as well as an effective diversification into all profitable economic activities" (p. 7). It further described criminal organizations as "generators of corruption" and suggested that this may "undermine the credibility of Governments" and result in their "inability to achieve a state of communal well-being and economic stability and prosperity" (pp. 7–8). The report did not explicitly suggest that public-sector corruption can be addressed through neoliberal reforms, but it can nevertheless be read as a discursive shift away from the NIEO agenda in favor of a narrative that aligned with the interests of prospective Western donors. The influence of the World Bank agenda on this framing is also evident from the fact that the 1985 Secretariat report references a 1983 working paper prepared by two World Bank economists for the 1983 World Development Report (see Gould & Amaro-Reyes, 1983).

The Secretariat's working paper also included a section that specifically accounted for the "Impact of crime upon development" (UN Secretariat, 1985, pp. 11–12). This was not the first reference by the Secretariat to crime as an obstacle to development, but it was certainly the most explicit and expansive discussion of this issue linkage to date. Again, there is no explicit reference to a neoliberal ideology or economic agenda, but elements of this section clearly resonated with the core assumptions of the "development as growth" mentality. To this effect, the report stated, "the sustained increases in criminality observed in many developing and developed countries in recent decades, are effectively undermining some of the most elementary pre-conditions of social life" (p. 11). It further suggested that rising levels of government expenditure toward crime prevention and criminal justice represented a drain on public resources. Corruption was again addressed in this section, this time described as a source of "economic inefficiency" (p. 12). Finally, it described "[i]llegal trafficking in narcotics [as] a source of great losses for many countries" (p. 12).

All of these issues were discussed at the Congress during a plenary session. The Secretariat's record suggests "[t]here was nearly complete agreement on the profoundly negative impact that criminality had on socio-economic development" (UN Secretariat, 1986, p. 113), but it also highlights important tensions between those developing countries that remained committed to the NIEO agenda and proponents of the emergent neoliberal orthodoxy, with its increasingly conservative prescriptions for controlling crime:

> [S]ome representatives pointed out that the economic situation facing the underdeveloped countries was currently deteriorating because of the effect of the external debt on their economies and reiterated the need for the establishment of a new international economic order. It was emphasized that there was a need to eliminate the ... [economic] causes of criminality [poverty, inequality, oppression, illiteracy and unemployment] and to promote social justice. (UN Secretariat, 1986, pp. 112–13)

This perspective is broadly consistent with many of the views expressed at the Third Annual Latin American Critical Criminology Conference, held the following year in Nicaragua (Dod, 1986).

In the following paragraph, the Secretariat report noted that other representatives "considered that social and economic conditions did not entirely determine behavior" and advocated what criminologists have since come to describe as a neoclassical or right-realist perspective on crime, which emphasized that "[i]ndividuals should, therefore, remain accountable for their offences" and that "emphasis should be increasingly placed upon the concept of duty, so as to provide proper balance to the affirmation of rights" (p. 113). The report did not identify who presented these arguments, but the conservative emphasis on "duty" and de-emphasis of "rights" clearly resonates with Reagan-era conservative thinking on crime (Vito, 1983), which was directly influenced by James Q. Wilson (1975). The Reagan administration's foreign policy legacy in Central America, including USAID-supported "public safety" projects (Salas, 2001), further indicates that advancing human rights was not a neoconservative priority.

A separate account of the proceedings also suggests that the US delegation was particularly active at this Congress and that their contributions were very much oriented toward promoting Reagan's policy agenda:

> The US representative asserted that there are no international laws, only treaties that become part of national law. Also, he had the temerity to comment that crime by a transnational corporation may affect a developing country, but if a developing country defaults on a loan, the banks and their depositors could become the victims of the developing country's action. (Colvin, 1986, p. 60)

The insinuation that "banks and their depositors could become the victims" clearly evidences the delegation's embrace of the emerging neoliberal orthodoxy, and the statement can thus be interpreted as an attempt to openly contest NIEO's framing of "crime as business."

The United States had previously sent a sizable delegation to Caracas, but its presence and visibility at the Milan Congress is particularly noteworthy because the country, together with Italy, later played the leading role in shaping the international crime policy agenda throughout the 1990s. The most obvious explanation for US interest in the Milan Congress is that organized crime was a hot political issue domestically in the 1980s, and it was no coincidence that this was the first UN Congress attended by the director of the Federal Bureau of Investigation. The domestic significance of this issue is evident from a lengthy article penned by President Reagan in the *New York Times Magazine* the following year, which described "organized crime in America in the 1980s [as] far more encompassing and wide-reaching than in the past" (Reagan, 1986). From this perspective, organized crime was a multiform threat to free market capitalism and traditional, conservative American values. With regard to its economic impacts, a 1986 report by the President's Commission on Organized Crime (1986) noted that "organized crime cost Americans 414,000 jobs and $6.5 billion in lost tax revenues [in 1985]" (quoting Hope & Skinner, 1986). These claims generated support for Reagan's war on organized crime, but they also drew attention to racketeering, corruption, unfair labor practices, and the links between unions and organized crime. From a political economy standpoint, this was significant because it suggests that Reagan's war against organized crime was, at least in part, a war on organized labor (Jacobs, 2007), which was perceived as an obstacle to economic growth.

Italy faced its own criminal issues, and the national government was also averse to radical, left-wing politics. But the need for functional cooperation also created opportunities for US agencies to collaborate with left-leaning politicians, including the mayor of Palermo, Leoluca Orlando, who later became a leading international proponent of the "culture of lawfulness" idea that proved popular with American neoconservatives (Godson, 2000). In the 1980s, Italy emerged as a natural ally of the United States, and there is evidence of bilateral cooperation between law enforcement agencies in the years preceding the Congress (Farber, 1985).

Fortuitously, the proceedings of the NIEO-influenced Caracas Congress positioned the nebulous problems of organized crime and corruption as elements of the UN crime policy agenda in the lead-up to the 1985 Congress. This afforded the United States and Italy a relevant political forum for reconstructing these problems as a threat to, rather than a consequence of, capitalist development. The most significant legacy of the 1985 Congress was therefore the adoption of the Milan Plan of Action, which explicitly acknowledged that "[c]rime is a major problem of national and, in some cases, international dimensions" that "demands a concerted response from the community of nations in reducing the opportunities to commit crime and address the relevant social-economic factors, such as poverty, inequality, and employment" (UN Secretariat, 1986, p. 2). It also asserted, "The universal forum of the United Nations has a significant role to play and its contribution to multilateral cooperation in this field should be made more effective" (p. 2). This signified a broad consensus that the focus and capabilities of the international crime policy community must evolve in response to the criminogenic impacts of globalization, and that these issues could not be addressed through the traditional model of national planning, which emphasized social defense.

The idea that the UN could play an important role in coordinating a US-led, multilateral response to international crime was most immediately realized with the adoption of the 1988 Vienna Convention Against Illicit Traffic in Narcotics, which included provisions relating to money laundering. Two years later, the importance of international cooperation to address international organized crime was also reaffirmed at the Eight UN Congress in Havana, Cuba, which the United States did not attend (UN Secretariat, 1991). For reasons considered in the following chapter, it took another ten years for the international community to provide the UN with a normative mandate to assume a leadership role in response to transnational organized crime and corruption.

Chapter Six

Securing the Global Capitalist Economy

The collapse of the Soviet Union signaled the end of the bipolar international system and the birth of a new global economic order grounded in neoliberal ideology, which presented free market capitalism as a recipe for international peace, prosperity, and progress. At the international level, this order was championed by the United States, which had already come to embrace neoliberalism during the previous decade and used its geopolitical and material influence to promote this doctrine internationally. The spread of this agenda was admittedly uneven throughout the 1980s, and neoliberal policies attracted a fair share of criticism, particularly in Latin America and, later, Sub-Saharan Africa, where structural adjustment was perceived to have destabilized economies and increased inequality. These criticisms were widely acknowledged, yet by the early 1990s there appeared to be no alternative. What one political scientist controversially described as "the end of history" (Fukuyama, 1992) was linked not only to the failure of the Soviet model but also the neutralization of the New International Economic Order (NIEO) and its emphasis on economic justice and embedded liberalism as the foundation for capitalist development.

Against this backdrop, the 1990s are widely remembered as a decade of American hegemony. Globalization, a process that is typically traced back to the 1970s, emerged as the dominant focus of global governance and a central theme of International Relations literature. The prospective benefits of globalization were thus widely celebrated, and it was hoped that increased economic linkages and a unipolar international system would establish a foundation for enhanced international cooperation and, most significantly, a lasting liberal peace.

At the same time, globalization as a process—which is perhaps best associated with the compression of time and space (Harvey, 1989)—would also emerge as a source of new challenges and problems that came to be recognized as a threat to this envisioned liberal order and, by extension, global capitalism. Key issues that attracted significant interest during this period included transnational organized crime, corruption, and crime and insecurity. The linkages between these problems and the emergence of the security-development nexus as an issue linkage would come to shape the work of international development actors, including the United Nations Development Programme (UNDP) and eventually, in the 2000s, United Nations Office on Drugs and Crime (UNODC).

This chapter sets out to account for the global governance initiatives that unfolded in each of these spheres for the purpose of contextualizing the construction of the crime-development nexus in the 2000s. In the first instance, we reflect on the emergence of transnational organized crime as a threat to international security and markets. Second, we examine the issue of corruption, which, together with criticisms of structural adjustment, contributed to the rise of the good governance agenda and the rule of law revival at the World Bank and other international financial institutions. Finally, the third sphere of governance we reflect on stemmed from the international community's acknowledgement of its failure not only to eradicate poverty and inequality but also to facilitate individual and human security. Indeed, as crime and violence skyrocketed across the developing world in the 1980s and 1990s, development actors came to admit that structural adjustment not only exacerbated these problems, but that this necessitated a more encompassing approach to development. For UNDP, this established the basis for the "human development" paradigm that became the cornerstone of the UN's development agenda throughout the 1990s and later gave rise to the concept of "human security." The rise of human security discourse is particularly important because it contributed to the international community's embrace of what Chandler (2012) refers to as the post-interventionist paradigm of global governance. This shift established important opportunities for UNODC to expand its operations and draw attention to the significance of its newly established portfolio in the 2000s.

TRANSNATIONAL ORGANIZED CRIME AND THE "DARK SIDE OF GLOBALIZATION"

"Transnational organized crime" emerged as the primary focus of the international crime policy agenda in the post–Cold War era, framed as one of the "new security threats" (Buzan, 1997) confronting the international community. The issue was for all intents and purposes invented in the early 1990s as an amalgamation of two long standing problems that emerged as focal points for the international crime policy agenda during the 1970s and 1980s: "transnational crime" and "organized crime" (Carrapiço, 2012; Sheptycki, 2003). Whereas critical scholars have come to associate the construction of this issue with a "governmentality project" (Edwards & Gill, 2002) designed to advance a US-driven security agenda (see also Woodiwiss, 2003b; Naylor, 1995), functionalist explanations have typically located the emergence of this phenomenon in relation to the accelerated nature and impacts of globalization (Shelley, 1995). Both perspectives are pertinent for making sense of how and why this agenda evolved in relation to wider political and economic forces.

From a functionalist perspective, globalization created new opportunities for organized criminal groups to not only expand their operations and power but enhance their transnational reach and influence by establishing fluid networks across borders (Findlay, 1999). Moreover, the growing permeability of borders meant that organized crime groups now found it easier to engage in illicit trade, just as demand for illicit substances and counterfeit goods was increasing in an era of growing consumption (Shelley, 1995, p. 465). Likewise, advances in global transport infrastructure and communications technology made it easier for criminal groups to operate beyond their countries of origin, and to plan and coordinate clandestine activities across multiple countries. Similarly, the growing role of the internet created new criminal opportunities (Findlay, 1999), as did increased levels of mobility and migration, which were argued to facilitate illicit activities such as smuggling and human trafficking (Hignett, 2012, p. 285). In short, while organized crime had always existed in "modern" societies, by the 1990s, globalization was seen to have established conditions for it to go global, with the increased economic, political, and cultural interconnectedness of the "upperworld" mirrored by an increasingly visible "underworld" (Hignett 2012, p. 283; Andreas & Nadelmann, 2006, ch. 4).

The expansion of this transnational underworld was also linked to the growing reality of state failure throughout the developing world. State institutions in the South—already lacking capacity due to legacies of colonialism and underdevelopment—were put under further stress by the "lost decade" of the 1980s, leading to weak border controls, ineffective rules and institutions, corruption, poverty and inequality, and failing criminal justice systems. This created lawless "gray zones" in which transnational organized crime operated with impunity (Williams & Baudin-O'Hayon, 2002, pp. 139–40). Moreover, criminal groups resorted to corruption, violence, and intimidation to penetrate the state and undermine its institutions while preying on marginalized segments of society and threatening the legitimacy of states (Mittelman & Johnston, 2011, p. 128). This was seemingly most pronounced in the post-Soviet sphere, where difficult transitions from socialism to free market capitalism via "shock therapy" decimated states and societies, creating an environment of corruption, lawlessness, poverty, and resentment in which criminals thrived (Hignett, 2012, p. 284). In this context, organized crime represented a growing "illegal power" within societies that posed a direct threat to the viability and sovereignty of states (Williams & Baudin-O'Hayon, 2002, p. 134).

Perhaps most significantly, the trans-nationalization of organized crime came to be seen as a threat to the global economy itself. From a liberal internationalist perspective, global economic integration required a rules-based multilateral system that would provide the stability and predictability necessary for capital to flow freely across borders (Williams & Beare, 2003, p. 101). The phenomenon of transnational organized crime thus created risk and uncertainty for corporations and investors, and this was framed as a barrier to economic growth insofar as it deterred investment (Shelley, 1995, pp. 482–83). Criminal activities like bribery and extortion were also seen by transnational corporations (TNC) as not only an unacceptable cost of doing business but also as a source of market distortions that undermined the continued expansion of the global economy (Mittelman & Johnston, 2011, pp. 133–34). Moreover, there were concerns about criminal groups laundering their ill-gotten gains through banks and financial institutions, enabling illicit money to enter the licit economy. This prospect undermined the confidence on which financial transactions depended, dampening financial flows and undermining the integrity of the global financial system as a whole (Helleiner, 1999, p. 59). As one former UN executive who was active during this period explained:

> Once organized crime got involved into money laundering and financial transactions . . . it became cross-border, it became alarming. Plus it was realized that it was not anymore only the Italian mafia and whatever mafias were in the US. With the fall of the Berlin Wall, first you had the Russian mafia that appeared . . . [then] the Chinese triads . . . [and] then you hear the revival of African mafias, the Nigerian mafia . . . mafias became an international phenomenon. There was a perceived risk of internationalization of organized crime, and therefore donors thought that it would be good to do something about it.

The functionalist agenda that emerged in the aftermath of the Cold War was therefore anchored in a Manichaean discourse that celebrated the "enormous possibility" of global integration while fretting about the "dark side of globalization," which threatened to undermine it (Sheptycki, 2007, p. 34; Kelly & Levy, 2012, p. 452).

In order to preserve the gains of globalization, combatting the "forces of darkness" required a coordinated response from the forces of "legitimate society" (Woodiwiss, 2003b, p. 30). Due to the global reach of transnational organized crime, such a response would necessarily involve the entire international community. This necessitated greater policy harmonization to ensure that members of transnational criminal networks could not exploit the differences between national laws or enforcement strategies, which represented potential vulnerabilities (Shelley, 1995, p. 487). As UN Secretary General Boutros Boutros-Ghali declared in 1994, "When the states decide to take effective, voluntary steps to combat transnational crime, and when they decide to cooperate with each other and harmonize their efforts, legitimate society regains all of its power and strength" (quoted in Woodiwiss, 2012, p. 98). Hyperbolic statements such as this were rarely backed up with credible evidence, and indeed, as we pointed out in chapter 2, scholars have subsequently questioned the veracity of alarmist claims about the extent of the phenomenon and the challenges inherent to actually measuring it (Andreas & Greenhill, 2010). Nevertheless, presenting transnational crime as an existential threat to the liberal world order in this manner served to establish a foundation for global cooperation while simultaneously deflecting attention away from unsavory linkages between licit and illicit economies, along with the structural and ideological conditions that contributed to these problems. From an institutional perspective, Boutros-Ghali's embrace of the functionalist discourse was particularly significant because it established a discursive foundation upon which the UN could work to position itself as an essential, multilateral actor when it came to facilitating cooperation and brokering the creation of a global regime that could support the transnational legal ordering of criminal justice (Shaffer & Aaronson, 2020). Indeed, the same former UN executive quoted above referred to the 1990s as "the golden age of international cooperation," and, as discussed below, it was against this backdrop that the UNODC was established and UNTOC and UNCAC negotiated.

It would however be misleading to suggest that the construction of transnational organized crime as a "new security threat" was the product of multilateral diplomacy that initially reflected universal concerns. Multilateral institutions like the UN certainly contributed to this constructive process, particularly in relation to the amplification and legitimation of the issue, but multiple participants acknowledged that the agenda was predominantly driven by the United States and its ally in the war on organized crime, Italy (Schneider & Schneider, 2011). The United States had long focused on combating organized crime domestically; however, from the 1970s onward the focus shifted to the international activities of organized criminal groups, which had become involved with drug trafficking (Carrapiço, 2012, p. 24). The US-led response to the nexus between organized crime and drug trafficking thus established a foundation for functional cooperation, which was afforded greater institutional recognition via the 1985 Milan Congress and the adoption of the 1988 UN Convention against Illicit Traffic in Narcotic Drugs (see chapter 5). However, what was previously an emergent but ultimately relatively marginal US foreign policy concern in the 1980s became, in the 1990s, an international policy priority.

Washington's interest in transnational organized crime reflected more than just a functionalist concern with the problems and threats described above. Many proponents of this agenda undoubtedly drank their own Kool-Aid, but the problem had strong political appeal to neoconservatives and liberal internationalists alike. Following the demise of the Soviet Union, neoconservatives sought to construct a new international threat that could sustain the American national security state (Andreas & Nadelmann, 2006). For example, one figure who seemingly played an important (or at least visible) role when it came to drawing attention to this issue was Roy Godson, director of the National Strategy Information Center, a neoconservative, Washington-based think tank that appeared to have close connections to the Pentagon and the State Department.[1] At a 1993 event at the National Press Club in Washington, DC, Godson and various government officials argued that the United States was confronted by a new security environment, which centered on the problem of "global ungovernability" (Godson in CSPAN, 1993). This referred to the perceived inability of weak states to control their territory, which in turn enabled transnational organized crime groups to thrive. This, Godson argued, contributed to a "dangerous neighborhood" for the United States and its allies. Godson's argument was that this was not a problem that could be dealt with "purely by law enforcement means alone." Rather, it necessitated the mobilization of the entire national security apparatus in search of a new mission—and new forms of cooperation involving counterparts in other countries. The following year, these sentiments were echoed by leaders from the US intelligence community at a conference on "Global Organized Crime: The New Empire of Evil," hosted by the Center for Strategic and International Studies. FBI Director Louis Freeh boldly asserted at this conference that transnational organized crime was "the greatest long-term threat to the security of the United States," while CIA director James Woolsey suggested that these issues "transcend traditional law enforcement concerns" and "affect critical natural security interests" (both quoted in Raine & Cillufo, 1994, p. ix). Thus, for neoconservatives who continued to occupy the upper echelons of the US intelligence community during Clinton's presidency, reorienting the national security state from "war fighting to crime fighting" offered a strategy for protecting its budgets and mandates at a time when conventional security problems, namely those associated with the Cold War, ceased to exist (Andreas & Price, 2001, p. 41).

It is important to stress, however, that for the United States, constructing transnational organized crime as a national security threat was not simply a neoconservative project. Indeed, there was strong support for this agenda from the liberal wing of the US foreign policy establishment because it afforded the country a rationale for maintaining its active international leadership at a time when this was being challenged by isolationist forces domestically (McLeod, 2010, pp. 103–4). A key player here was John Kerry, who was arguably the first US politician to take an active interest in the transnational dimensions of organized crime as chair of a 1987 Subcommittee on Terrorism, Narcotics and International Relations, which was established by the Senate Committee on Foreign Relations in the wake of the Iran-Contra scandal to investigate "the links between foreign policy, narcotics, and law enforcement in connection with drug trafficking" (Kerry, quoted in US Senate Committee on Foreign Relations, 1989, p. iii). What became known as the "Kerry Report" drew attention to issues that later came to be associated with transnational organized crime and corruption, namely laundering and the tendency of drug traffickers to move their profits "to any country which guarantees the fewest problems for the trafficker in handling the proceeds from illicit activities" (see US Senate Committee on Foreign Relations, 1989, pp. 113). The report is also notable because it explicitly frames these problems as a "continuing threat to national security at home and abroad" (p. iv), thereby establishing the foundations of the discourse that was later embraced by neoconservatives like Godson.

Throughout the 1990s, Kerry served as a leading liberal proponent of this issue, which he described as "the new communism, the new monolithic threat" (quoted in *Newsweek*, 1993). He even published a book on the topic in 1997 with the aptly hyperbolic title, *The New War: The Web of Crime That Threatens America's Security* (Kerry, 1997). In the preface to the book, Kerry openly reflects on how his interest in this problem was sparked by his involvement with the subcommittee:

> A decade ago I began to uncover portions of a common international infrastructure for transnational crime. I saw it created changes in the global marketplace, in computerization and globalization, in the realm of illicit arms and drug traffickers, in the world of covert action and espionage, in the networks of terrorism, in banking capitals and financial centers, in far-flung island resorts, and at ports and borders all over the world. I found that most people in government did not have a clue as to the existence of this infrastructure or how it operated (Kerry, 1997, p. 14).

Kerry's calls for the United States to "lead an international crusade" (1997, p. 32) against new security threats clearly appealed to the internationalist sensibilities of the Clinton administration and its interest in aligning the work of the UN with US foreign policy interests. In fact, two years prior to the publication of Kerry's book, President Clinton used his address at the UN's 50th anniversary ceremony as an opportunity to call for "[international] support through the United Nations for the fight against man-made and natural forces of disintegration, [including] crime syndicates and drug cartels . . . [which] cross borders at will . . . [and] require strong and international cooperation and mutual support" (Clinton, 1995). This would entail not only the enhanced forms of security and intelligence cooperation proposed by neoconservatives but also the harmonization of policies and institutions that would make the world safer for US capital. Clinton openly emphasized that the norms and standards that would shape the emergent transnational legal (and financial) order would be based on US designs when, in a subsequent speech, he declared:

> [N]ations should work together to bring their banks and financial systems into conformity with the international money laundering standards. We will work to help them do so. And, if they refuse, we will consider appropriate sanctions (Clinton, quoted in Woodiwiss, 2003b, p. 28).

In short, the US-led construction of transnational organized crime as a security threat in the 1990s was shaped by a combination of liberal internationalist and neoconservative interests domestically. These camps had somewhat distinctive agendas, but their proponents utilized similar language and ideas, which emerged (rather ironically) in the wake of the Iran-Contra scandal, to construct this threat and sustain US hegemony abroad.

Against this backdrop, the 1990s saw a flurry of bilateral and multilateral initiatives that were oriented toward exporting or otherwise transposing US legal and criminal justice models upon the rest of the world. This included US State Department audits of other countries' efforts to combat problems linked with drug and human trafficking and terrorism. The purpose of these audits was to "name and shame" governments into taking specific, US-prescribed actions to address these issues (Joutsen, 2018, p. 324). In essence, this provided the United States with a strategy for governing these problems from a distance, without the need for direct intervention, as had previously been the preferred neoconservative strategy during the Cold War. Countries that were deemed to have failed to meet "minimum standards" therefore faced economic sanctions, which could be imposed by American-dominated international financial institutions (IFIs), including the World Bank and the IMF (Friman, 2010). The United States also sought to use its hegemonic influence to internationalize the 1977 Foreign Corrupt Practices Act (FCPA), which criminalized the bribery of foreign officials by American corporations. Amid concerns that this disadvantaged US-based corporations abroad, the United

States first sought to advocate similar provisions through its engagement with the UN during the 1980s. However, its efforts to establish an international anti-corruption regime were largely derailed by Cold War–era, ideological debates about the meaning of "corruption." This prompted the United States to shift its focus to the Organization for Economic Co-Operation and Development (OECD), where it was able to pressure smaller Western countries to negotiate what would eventually become the 1997 OECD Anti-Bribery Convention, which mirrored most aspects of the FCPA (Sharman, 2017, pp. 36–37). This treaty, along with similar regional conventions, including the Inter-American Convention Against Corruption adopted in 1996, established the institutional foundations for a global anti-corruption regime.

Most of these initiatives were established beyond the UN system, through forums where the United States could more easily leverage its power and influence to shape the debates and discussions. Nevertheless, the United States ultimately recognized the value of institutionalizing this emerging regime through the UN. It was thought that this would not only serve to enhance the legitimacy of the regime but also to generate practical benefits by standardizing norms and processes through a single agreement. Beyond this, the United States recognized that the UN as a multilateral institution with an established Secretariat could provide technical assistance to developing countries to bring their legislation and criminal justice systems in line with global standards (Andreas & Nadelmann, 2006, p. 9; Romaniuk, 2018, p. 522). Again, this speaks to the idea of governing from a distance, in this case by reorienting the normative and technical capabilities of semiautonomous multilateral institutions with US foreign policy and security interests, which, in this context, were fundamentally oriented toward promoting and protecting the interests of American capital in an increasingly competitive, globalized economy.

The influence of the United States on the international crime policy agenda is readily evident from the transformation of the UN crime program and its governance during the 1990s. For starters, in 1991 the expert-led Committee on Crime Prevention and Control (CCPC), which had long shaped the international crime policy agenda, was replaced with the Commission on Crime prevention and Criminal Justice (CCPCJ). The newly established Commission was composed of diplomatic representatives of 40 governments, and the reform was initiated to encourage more direct Member State involvement in the crime program (Clark, 1994). It is unclear whether this reform was specifically advocated by the United States in anticipation of this shift (noting that the reform process preceded the collapse of the Soviet Union), but it nevertheless served to enhance the political legitimacy of the UN crime program, which had previously functioned as a technical organization, at an opportune moment. The CCPCJ's area of authority was broad, but transnational crime was quickly embraced as one of its priorities (Romaniuk, 2018, p. 519). Italy's involvement is particularly noteworthy here because the country had a long-standing interest in the problem of "organized crime," an established record of cooperation with US law enforcement and intelligence agencies (see chapter 5), and was regarded as an international leader when it came to addressing this problem domestically. At its behest, the CCPCJ organized the 1994 World Ministerial Conference on Organized Transnational Crime in Naples, which saw more than 2,000 participants and delegates from 142 countries convene to discuss the issue. The Conference's Political Declaration predictably called for global action against transnational organized crime, the need to harmonize legislation based on US standards, and an enhanced program of technical assistance to support these activities (Vlassis, 2002, pp. 84–85). The Declaration also set the stage for the UNTOC negotiations by directing the CCPCJ to "request the views of governments on the impact of an international convention on organized crime and the issues it might cover" (UN, 1994).

To accelerate the negotiation process, members of the Secretariat reportedly utilized back-channel diplomatic connections to encourage Poland, a country with no obvious political stake in this issue, to introduce a draft proposal for what would eventually become UNTOC into the UNGA in 1997. This resulted in a UNGA vote that formally established an intergovernmental group of experts to lead the negotiations (Vlassis, 2002, pp. 85–89). That same year, UNODC's predecessor, the UN Office for Drug Control and Crime Prevention (UN-ODCCP), was established through a merger of the UN Drug Control Program and the UN Center for International Crime Prevention. One of its initial responsibilities was to facilitate the UNTOC negotiations. Once these were adopted, the idea was that UNTOC would act as their custodian by monitoring their implementation and providing countries with technical assistance to accelerate harmonization.

UNTOC was adopted in November 2000, and it has since been signed by 147 countries. The following month, the UNGA instructed the secretary general to put together an expert group to begin the process of negotiating a follow-up convention that focused specifically on corruption. The need for this is attributed to the fact that during the UNTOC negotiations, many countries, including the United States, agreed that the problem of corruption was so significant and complex that it required a separate, universal agreement (Rose, 2015, p. 3). Building on the institutional and normative architecture established by the OECD Anti-Bribery Convention, regional anti-corruption treaties, and UNTOC, the UN Convention against Corruption (UNCAC) was negotiated in only three years. This suggests that an international consensus was already in place regarding the nature of this problem, and the need for a truly global regime to address it.

A detailed analysis of UNTOC and UNCAC is beyond the scope of this book, but two key points merit discussion. First, the definitions of "transnational organized crime" and "corruption" adopted in these treaties were overwhelmingly influenced by the United States. For example, the specific criminal activities defined in UNTOC—participation in an organized criminal group, money laundering, corruption, and obstruction of justice—were all US priorities at the time, and the notion of criminalizing membership of an organized crime group was directly influenced by the US Racketeer Influenced and Corrupt Organizations (RICO) Act of 1970, which is the basis for America's domestic approach to organized crime (Kelly & Levy, 2012, pp. 448–49). The provisions relating to the confiscation of proceeds from these criminal activities are also derived from the RICO Act. Other provisions regarding witness and victim protection are likewise modelled on the US programs. Similarly, many of the measures of UNCAC related to the detection and interdiction of corrupt money mirror the recommendations developed by the US-led Financial Action Task Force, and the whole chapter on asset recovery was based largely on a draft prepared by US negotiators (Sharman, 2017, pp. 48, 60). The degree of US influence over the Conventions is perhaps best described by the US State Department itself, which remarked that they "oblige other countries that have been slower to react legislatively to the threat of transnational organized crime to adopt new criminal laws in harmony with ours" (quoted in Woodiwiss, 2012, p. 98).

Consequently, the Conventions have served to reproduce definitions of transnational organized crime and corruption that align with US interests, and they omit or help de-emphasize references to other forms of harmful and illicit activities that might be of interest to developing countries (McLeod 2010, p. 110).[2] Indeed, as one of our participants observed, there was pushback during the negotiations from developing countries about the definition of transnational organized crime, with Latin American states in particular concerned that UNTOC "was actually not a convention against transnational organized crime, but it was more a mutual legal assistance convention that could be used for anything." The concern was hardly unfounded given the United States' track record in Latin America during the Cold War, but it was ultimately neutralized by proponents of the US agenda, who invoked the distinction between the "light" and "dark" sides of globalization to construct a universalist discourse about the problem. This was seemingly sufficient for brokering a consensus and establishing a normative mandate that would support the expansion of UN-ODCCP.

The second key point to stress is that the rise of transnational organized crime and corruption as focal points of the international crime policy agenda came at the expense of its development focus. Although the 1995 Crime

Congress did discuss the impact of transnational organized crime on development (see, for example, UN, 1995), the link between these two issues had yet to be clearly articulated and acknowledged in the post–Cold War context. As discussed in the following chapter, the lack of a coherent narrative about the relationship between crime and development was readily evident from the Millennium Development Goal (MDG) negotiations, and the omission of these issues from the MDGs directly contributed to UNODC's subsequent efforts to reconstruct this issue linkage. These efforts were also directly shaped by wider developments in the global governance system, particularly at the World Bank, which became a leading proponent of the rule-of-law revival in the late 1990s, and UNDP, which took an interest in the nexus between "human development" and "human security" from the mid-1990s onwards.

CORRUPTION, GOOD GOVERNANCE, AND THE RULE OF LAW

During the 1990s the issue of corruption emerged as a major policy concern for IFIs. As noted in the previous chapter, this issue first surfaced in the context of development policy in the 1980s, specifically in relation to the World Bank's argument that the developmental state bred corruption, by creating opportunities for rent seeking and giving government officials unaccountable discretion to intervene in the economy. This narrative built on new research in economics (e.g., Krueger, 1974; Rose-Ackerman, 1978) that challenged the previous orthodoxy that corruption aided development by helping overcome red tape and bureaucratic gridlock (Leff, 1964). Anti-corruption thus became part of the justification for structural adjustment reforms in the 1980s as privatization, deregulation, and liberalization were argued to reduce the state's role in managing the economy, thereby reducing opportunities for officials to engage in illicit activities (Brown & Cloke, 2004, p. 286). The emergence of corruption as a concern for IFIs during the 1980s is noteworthy, but the problem remained a relatively minor component of the World Bank's agenda until the end of the Cold War because legal and justice reform initiatives were considered a form of interference in the political affairs of sovereign states, and this was prohibited by the World Bank's Articles of Agreement (Messick, 1999, p. 119).

This attitude changed dramatically in the 1990s, with researchers at the Institute for International Economics (IIE)[3] noting that "this decade is the first to witness the emergence of corruption as a truly global political issue eliciting a global political response" (Glynn et al., 1997, p. 7). Just like transnational organized crime, corruption was seen to have dramatically increased due to globalization, with the OECD secretary general remarking that "the expansion and globalization of the world economy have given the problem a fresh dimension" (OECD, 1996, p. 9). The "fresh dimension" was attributable to the deregulation of financial markets and the spread of new information technologies, which not only increased opportunities for corruption but also made them harder to detect. There was a particular focus on bribery, which was seen as both an obstacle to doing business for transnational corporations and a deterrent to investors. This narrative was later supported by one prominent study, which claimed that the cost of investing in a corrupt country was equivalent to an additional tax of 20% (Wei, 1997).

For proponents of globalization, corruption was more than just an unacceptable cost of doing business abroad. As the IIE remarked, "[A] growing number of experts are beginning to recognize [that] widespread corruption threatens the very basis of an open, multilateral world economy" (Glynn et al., 1997, p. 13). This was due to the fact that corruption was seen as a source of risk and uncertainty, one thought to produce nontransparent and nonaccountable market processes that in turn deprived investors of clear and accurate information. The concern was that a lack of certainty about issues such as the enforceability of contracts and protection of property rights would undermine investor confidence and produce market volatility (Williams & Beare, 2003, pp. 108–09). As the OECD again remarked, corrupt practices "hamper the development of international trade by distorting competition, rising transaction costs, compromising the operation of free and open markets, and distorting the allocation of resources" (OECD, 1996, p. 9).

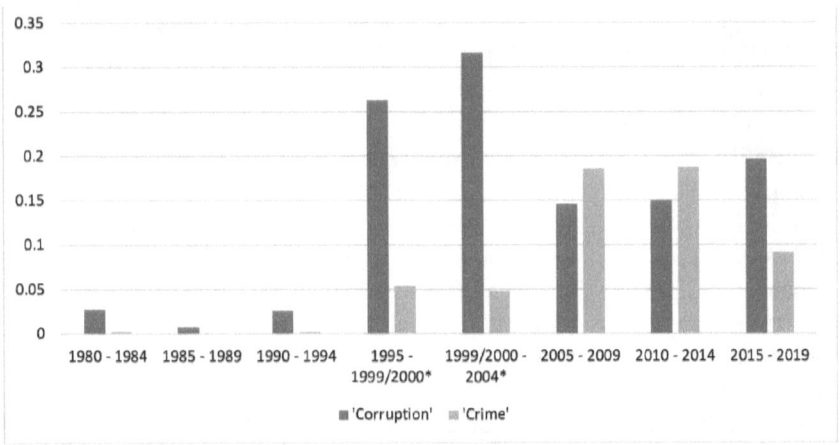

Figure 6.1. Mentions of "Corruption" and "Crime" per Page in World Development Reports (1980–2019)
Source: Author created from World Development Reports (See www.worldbank.org/en/publication/wdr/wdr-archive.)

During the 1990s, corruption also came to be seen as a major obstacle to development by neoliberal development actors, including the World Bank, whose newly appointed president, James D. Wolfensohn, made it the overriding priority for the organization in the mid- to late 1990s (see figure 6.1 above). In an influential speech to the World Bank's Board of Governors in 1996, Wolfensohn spoke about "the cancer of corruption" and the desire of citizens of the Global South to address this problem:

> In country after country, it is the people who are demanding action on this issue. They know that corruption diverts resources from the poor to the rich, increases the costs of running businesses, distorts public expenditures and deters foreign investors . . . and we all know that it is a major barrier to sound and equitable development (Wolfensohn, 2005, p. 50).

Following the speech, Wolfensohn established the Corruption Action Plan Working Group in 1996, which was tasked with articulating the World Bank's position on the issue. The result was a 1997 report titled *Helping Countries Combat Corruption: The Role of the World Bank*, which argued that "the Bank can take many actions within its Articles of Agreement to help countries fight corruption" because "sustainable development requires the control of corruption" (World Bank, 1997a, pp. 4–5). In constructing the problem as an obstacle to economic development, the report cited a growing body of empirical literature on the relationship between corruption and investment and growth, including a famous article by Mauro (1995), which claimed that high perceptions of corruption lowered private investment by almost 5%, resulting in a 0.5% reduction in GDP growth per year. Moreover, it suggested that corruption undermined the efficiency and competitiveness of economies in the Global South because it led to the misappropriation of domestic savings and foreign aid, diverting resources from pursuing development. Finally, the World Bank argued that corruption undermined the legitimacy of states because it violated public trust between states and citizens, threatening their viability and stability amid difficult transitions to free market democracy. As with the international community's interest in transnational organized crime (discussed above), the World Bank was particularly concerned about development in the post-Soviet sphere, where privatization came to be associated with the misappropriation of public wealth, weak or unstable infrastructure, and economic volatility that left many "transition" states on the verge of collapse (Shelley, 1998).

It would be misleading to suggest, however, that the heightened interest of the World Bank and other IFIs in corruption during the 1990s was benevolent. Rather, amplifying the visibility of this issue was strategically useful when it came to accounting for the underwhelming results of their structural adjustment policies, which had been championed throughout the developing world for more than a decade. Facing a growing chorus of criticism from non-governmental organizations (NGOs) about the failures of neoliberal reforms, constructing the problem of corruption as an obstacle to development thus enabled the IFIs to deflect the blame onto the governments of developing countries and their political elites (Sharman, 2017, p. 34). For example, IFIs attributed the 1997–1998 Asian Financial Crisis to the problem of "crony capitalism," which described an unholy alliance of state and business actors in East Asia that was said to have distorted markets and threatened the stability of the entire global financial system (World Bank, 1998; Krugman, 1998).

Moreover, drawing attention to the issue of corruption enabled proponents of neoliberal reforms to tap into widespread public anger about the issue in the Global South and present IFIs as key allies in the fight against corruption. To this effect, IFIs began to stress the need for "partnership" with civil society to enact anti-corruption measures and create domestic "ownership" of them. The rise of the anti-corruption agenda is therefore linked with the efforts of IFIs to bolster consent for their neoliberal reforms at a time when they faced not only a crisis of legitimacy (Taylor, 2003, p. 135) but also ideological and institutional competition from the emergent human development paradigm, which was anchored in the "development as freedom" tradition (discussed in the following section).

Accordingly, several international treaties and agreements to combat corruption were adopted in the mid- to late 1990s and early 2000s. Examples included the 1997 OECD Anti-Bribery Convention, the 1996 Inter-American Convention against Corruption, the Council of Europe's Group of States against Corruption (GRECO), established in 1999, and the 2003 African Union Convention on Preventing and Combatting Corruption. As noted in the previous section, these concerns also helped elevate the significance of this issue at the UN, and this contributed to the efficient negotiation and successful adoption of UNCAC in 2003. Many of these treaties outline measures for preventing corruption, and these were typically oriented toward increasing the transparency of government institutions and establishing legal and institutional frameworks to provide oversight of government decision making. These prescriptions thus reflected a wider shift in mainstream development thinking about both the causes of and solutions to corruption. Corruption, as the World Bank put it, "is a governance issue," meaning its prevalence was caused by badly constructed and functioning institutions (World Bank, 1997a, p. 5). Accordingly, the solution to this problem was "good governance," which the World Bank described as:

> a predictable and transparent framework of rules and institutions ... epitomized by predictable, open and enlightened policymaking ... a bureaucracy imbued

with a professional ethos; an executive arm of government accountable for its actions; and a strong civil society participating in public affairs; and all behaving under the rule of law. (World Bank, 1994, p. vii)

The emphasis on strengthening state institutions is noteworthy here because it highlights a significant departure from the orthodox neoliberal agenda of the 1980s, which prescribed a minimalist role for the state when it came to regulating economic activity. This was consistent with a broader ideological shift among the IFIs, which political economists associate with the post–Washington Consensus. The post–Washington Consensus refers to the concessions made by the proponents of the original neoliberal shock doctrine in response to their critics during the early 1990s. The key feature of this paradigm shift was an acknowledgment by IFIs that the state did have a role to play when it came to regulating the economy, and that this was essential for creating conditions that were conducive to the liberalization of markets. The good governance agenda thus aspired to encourage and enable states to create institutional environments that would support economic liberalization and successful integration of developing and transitional countries into the global capitalist economy (Kuczynski & Williamson, 2003). However, for the IFIs, including the World Bank, the "effective state" in the age of neoliberal globalization was not an interventionist state but rather a regulatory state that would "set rules underpinning private transactions" and also "play by the rules itself, acting reliably and predictability and controlling corruption" (World Bank, 1997b, p. iii).

A fundamental ingredient of an "effective state" was the "rule of law," which the World Bank described as "encompassing the collective importance of property rights, respect for legal institutions and the judiciary" (World Bank, 2002, p. 9), along with "transparent legislation, fair laws, predictable enforcement and accountable governments" (World Bank, 2004, p. 3). Accordingly, rule-of-law reform became a key feature of the good governance agenda during the 1990s as it aspired to "make the legal systems in developing countries and transition economies more market friendly" (Messick, 1999, p. 118). In practice, this meant that IFIs worked to promote institutional reforms, including those that enhanced judicial independence from the state in order to guarantee contracts and win the confidence of investors, and measures to increase the efficiency of judicial systems and develop alternative dispute resolution mechanisms to speed up commercial legal disputes (Trubek, 2006, p. 26).

There is clear evidence of continuity between this agenda and previous efforts by the United States to promote economic liberalization throughout Latin America in the 1980s, and by the 1990s USAID was spending around $200 million on law reform projects worldwide (Messick, 1999, p. 117). IFIs also got in on the act with the World Bank, the Inter-American Development Bank (IADB), and the Asian Development Bank (ADB), providing $500 million in loans for judicial reform projects in 26 countries between 1994 and 1999 (Messick, 1999). By the end of the decade, the majority of developing and post-Soviet countries were receiving financial and technical assistance to reform their legal systems. Accordingly, the structural and ideological conditions that prompted Western countries and IFIs to develop an interest in corruption also contributed to the "rule of law revival" of the late 1990s. This created further "pressure [for] governments to offer the stability, transparency and accountability that international investors demand" (Carothers, 1998, p. 98). Again, as part of the broader good governance agenda, the overarching aim was to renegotiate consent for a softer form of neoliberalism by reconstructing the sectional interests of capital as the common interests of society as a whole (Taylor, 2003, p. 134). Indeed, far from promoting the forms of social and economic justice that had been advocated by NIEO in the late 1970s, the agenda was fundamentally about "reforming" the institutional architecture of developing states in order to make them attractive to foreign capital and reduce the risks that domestic economic conditions posed to global financial markets (Williams & Beare, 2003, pp. 103–4). This led to criticisms that promoting the rule of law entailed more than securing commercial contracts and increasing judicial efficiency. Rather, critics argued that it necessitated the institutional protection of individual freedoms and human rights, as well as criminal justice reforms, to improve access to justice and security for the poor (Trubek & Santos, 2006, pp. 12–13). The World Bank itself acknowledged the narrow focus of its law reform programs, which devoted only limited attention to the criminal justice system and personal security. One issue was that in the late 1990s, the World Bank lacked the expertise to tackle such issues (Ayres, 1998, p. 22). As discussed below, other IFIs, including the IADB, were more proactive when it came to developing strategies for addressing issues like urban violence, but the primary driver of what became known as the human security paradigm was the World Bank's longtime competitor, UNDP.

THE "SECURITY-DEVELOPMENT NEXUS" AND POST-INTERVENTIONISM

The World Bank's growing interest in governance and the rule of law was also influenced by developments in the UN development community, at least indirectly. Specifically, we refer to the rise of human development discourse and UNDP's subsequent advocacy of a "human security" paradigm. The theorized interlinkages s between these concepts established the discursive foundations of the "security-development nexus" (see Krause, 2014), and, as discussed in the following chapters, this directly influenced UNODC's efforts to reconstruct the crime-development nexus following the adoption of the MDGs. Accordingly, the remainder of this chapter reflects on the emergence of "human development" and "human security" discourse along with their influence on the post-interventionist security paradigm (Chandler, 2012), which enabled UNODC to enhance its operational portfolio following the adoption of UNTOC and UNCAC. Finally, we reflect on the relationship between human security discourse and a growing interest in issues relating to urban violence and personal insecurity among IFIs around this time.

HUMAN DEVELOPMENT

The concept of "human development" became a staple of the international development community's lexicon following the publication of UNDP's first *Human Development Report* in 1990 (see UNDP, 1990). The concept was introduced as an alternative to the "development as growth" paradigm, which was predominant up to this point thanks to modernization theory, and, later, the growing influence of neoliberalism during the 1980s. Anchored in the established "development as freedom" model, which UNDP had embraced since the late 1960s (see Murphy, 2006; chapter 4), human development described "a process of enlarging people's choices . . . to lead a long and healthy life, to be educated, and to enjoy a decent standard of living" along with "political freedom, guaranteed human rights and self-respect" (UNDP, 1990, p. 10).

The emergence of human development discourse coincided with a broader neoliberal turn in global governance that first became apparent in the 1980s, and the appeal of human development in the age of globalization was linked with the fact that it emphasized agency-driven approaches (e.g., providing individuals and communities with basic capabilities and resources so that they could take responsibility for their own development) rather than top-down prescriptions for economic and social development (as prescribed by the "development as efficiency" model) or neoliberal structural adjustment policies that were championed by the IFIs but increasingly criticized by governments of heavily indebted development countries (Fukuda-Parr, 2003). Thus, human development discourse represented a lifeline for liberal internationalists at the UN, who retained a commitment to the "development as freedom" model yet found themselves confronted by a growing neoliberal orthodoxy and competition from bilateral agencies like USAID and the IFIs. As Murphy (2006, p.

232) reflects, "in mid-1989, it was easy to believe that [UNDP's] glory days were over."

UNDP's history is somewhat peripheral to our story, but it is worth reflecting on here because key developments during the 1980s and 1990s helped to establish a permissive climate that would later enable UNODC to champion its own agenda following the adoption of the MDGs. At the same time, these developments established UNDP as a potential competitor of UNODC within the development space. Both of these themes are revisited in the following chapters.

As Murphy (2006, p. 240) notes, UNDP underwent significant transformations during the 1980s under the leadership of its administrator, William Draper, a venture capitalist from the United States who challenged members of the organization to reflect on its values and justify the allocation of resources to different projects. These discussions prompted UNDP to think more strategically about how it engaged in development work, particularly in relation to opportunity costs, and this enabled the organization to establish a coherent cultural identity and ethos. This was seen as essential for differentiating UNDP from its competitors, who were perceived as more efficient and responsive by donors.

Human development not only served as the cornerstone of this identity but also provided the organization with "an extraordinary advocacy tool" together with a unique set of indicators for "benchmark[ing] progress" (quoting former UNDP administrator Mark Malloch Brown, in Murphy, 2006, p. 242). In Murphy's words (2006, p. 242), "This helped to turn UNDP from being an organization that increased the dependence of people on their governments to one that also helped to keep governments accountable to their citizens." This shift was naturally appealing to donors at a time when proponents of a neoliberal orthodoxy had already come to view the developmental state as an obstacle to economic and social progress rather than its driver. Human development also offered a potentially attractive alternative to the Washington Consensus, because while it moved beyond a narrow focus on economic growth, it remained grounded in liberal notions of human rights and the individual and did not challenge the overarching project of promoting global economic integration. Rather, it provided what might be described as a softer recipe for neoliberalism, which promoted a "globalization with a human face" (UNDP, 1999) that was largely compatible with the post–Washington Consensus.

The publication of the first *Human Development Report* (UNDP, 1990) received global attention, and this was particularly timely from a material perspective because its release directly preceded the collapse of the Soviet Union (Murphy, 2006, p. 245). Decreases in military spending at the end of the Cold

War thus freed up cash for development aid, and securing this funding from donors became a key strategic priority for UNDP (Browne, 2009). The annual publication of UNDP's *Human Development Reports* thus became an important element of its advocacy strategy, which was later emulated by other UN entities, including UNODC. Essentially, the *Human Development Reports* enabled UNDP to draw upon its research capabilities and bureaucratic authority to construct demand for its increasingly versatile portfolio of services by drawing attention to emerging issues and problems. The only requirement was that these could somehow be linked with the organization's development authority, and the expansive concept of "human development" created many possibilities in this regard. Over the last three decades, UNDP's use of this advocacy model has contributed to a growing reliance on voluntary contributions from donors to sustain and expand its expansive operational portfolio (Browne, 2009).

The fourth *Human Development Report*, published in 1994, is also particularly noteworthy from an advocacy standpoint because it introduced the concept of "human security" into the international development lexicon (UNDP, 1994). This in turn contributed to the construction of the narrative that human development and human security outcomes are interdependent—the "security-development nexus." Perhaps more significantly, the introduction of human security discourse is argued to have contributed to an important shift in the nature of global security governance, whereby the liberal interventionist paradigm that emerged in the 1990s was replaced by what Chandler (2012) describes as a post-interventionist paradigm, which remains dominant today. As discussed in the following chapter, it is within this post-interventionist paradigm that UNODC has expanded its own operational portfolio following the adoption of UNTOC and UNCAC.

HUMAN SECURITY AND POST-INTERVENTIONISM

The 1994 *Human Development Report* introduced the concept of human security as an alternative to the established, state-centric security paradigm that had previously dominated International Relations theory and the work of the UN (see Buzan, 1997). Human security was presented as a "universal," "people-centric" framework for conceptualizing and promoting security by creating conditions that would allow individuals and communities to access opportunities and make choices that would enhance their well-being, safety, and security (p. 22). Thus, much like human development, human security is oriented toward "facilitating or developing the self-securing agency—resilience—of those held to be most vulnerable" (Chandler, 2012, p. 213).

UNDP (1994, pp. 24–33) initially outlined seven dimensions of human security: economic security, food security, health security, environmental security, personal security, community security, and political security. It is beyond the scope of our discussion to reflect on each of these categories, but their diversity highlights an important critique of the concept that relates to its breadth and lack of definitional precision. To this effect, Paris (2001, p. 88) has argued that "[h]uman security is like 'sustainable development'—everyone is for it but few people have a clear idea of what it means." Although the vagueness of the concept has arguably limited its utility for scholarly research, Paris reflects that this has actually enhanced its utility as an advocacy tool. To this effect, he argues that the concept is in fact "slippery by design," and this helps to account for its appeal during the mid-1990s, particularly among "a jumbled coalition of 'middle power' states, development agencies, and NGOs—all of which [sought] to shift attention and resources away from conventional security issues and toward goals that have traditionally fallen under the rubric of international development" (p. 88).

It is unclear how one might attempt to demarcate the boundaries between this broad conceptualization of "human security" and "human development," and, again, this ambiguity appears to be intentional. For example, the *1994 Human Development Report* treats "freedom from fear" and "freedom from want" as mutually dependent and interrelated (UNDP, 1994, p. 24). This implies that "progress in one area enhances the chances of progress in the other. But failure in one area also heightens the risk of failure in the other" (p. 23). For UNDP and other development actors, constructing this issue linkage has been particularly advantageous because it has allowed the organization to expand its authority and position itself as a security actor. For reasons described above, this was materially advantageous for the agency at a time when it was becoming increasingly dependent on voluntary contributions from donors.

It is important to stress, however, that UNDP's approach to promoting human security was distinct from the dominant, liberal internationalist security paradigm of the 1990s. With regard to the latter, Western states, security coalitions, including the North Atlantic Treaty Organization (NATO) and the UN Security Council (UNSC), embraced their role of the guardians of a new global cosmopolitan order and viewed it as their responsibility to uphold its liberal norms, particularly in relation to the protection of human rights. This "protector" mentality was particularly evident in relation to the international community's responses to state failure, which often went hand in hand with what Kaldor (1998) famously described as the "new wars" of the post–Cold War era. These typically involved mass civilian casualties, ethnic cleansing, and genocide. From a liberal internationalist perspective then, the inability or unwillingness of states to protect their citizens and uphold human rights created both a justification and a moral obligation for humanitarian interventions. Chandler (2012) notes that these interventions typically involved the use of military force, and because they were initiated in response to crises, responsibility for addressing the conflict rested with the intervening powers.

By contrast, UNDP's approach to promoting human security focused on preventing conflict and instability through capacity building. This model effectively shifted responsibility for promoting human security to individuals, communities, and governments, albeit with the assistance (technical and material) of the international community. Thus, the human security paradigm features a strong rhetorical emphasis on empowerment, promoting local ownership, and sustainability (UNDP, 1994). Elements of the human security paradigm, specifically its emphasis on prevention and devolving responsibility (Chandler, 2012, p. 223), are seemingly consistent with prominent features of Anglo-American, late-modern crime control strategies, which also became popular at this time (Garland, 2001). In our view, these similarities are not coincidental but rather reflect the growing influence of, and interest in, neoliberal rationalities and technologies for improving the "art of governance"[4] at a time when the governing capabilities of modern, liberal institutions (including states and international organizations) were perceived to be increasingly limited in the face of new and emerging forms of risk (O'Malley, 2012). As Chandler (2014) and others have argued, the challenge of governing complexity at a time when ideological and structural forces were depriving modern institutions of material resources and regulatory authority gave rise to a new governmental paradigm that was oriented toward building resilience.

Chandler's (2012) analysis is particularly relevant here because it highlights that human security discourse was a direct precursor to the post-interventionist security paradigm that became dominant in the 2000s. By this time, the liberal internationalist doctrine, which focused on humanitarian interventions and state-building, had come to be seen as ineffective, costly, and politically unpopular (both domestically and internationally). The appeal of human security discourse was therefore linked with its preventative orientation and agency-centered approach, which offered liberal internationalists a new framework for promoting peace and security that relieved them of a moral obligation to directly intervene and commit resources to conflict prevention. Consequently, the international community's approach to promoting security shifted toward using aid and technical assistance to create resilient individuals, communities, and government institutions (including police) in order to supply them with the capabilities and the desire to reproduce and uphold conditions that were conducive to human development outcomes (Chandler, 2012). In essence, the rise of human security discourse allowed international donors to do their part by simply investing in security sector reform projects and rule-of-law promotion activities, which were seen as essential for building resilience, preventing conflict, and securing the global economy (Duffield, 2007). For bilateral and multilateral development agencies, this meant that more cash was available for capacity building projects if they could be linked with the security interests of donors.

URBAN VIOLENCE AND "CITIZEN SECURITY"

Preventing crime and corruption certainly fell within the scope of the human security paradigm, but these were not a major concern for UNDP (Murphy, 2006; Blaustein, 2015). For IFIs, however, these issues began to generate interest during the 1990s, when it became evident that structural adjustment policies had contributed to rising levels of recorded violent and property crimes throughout the Global South (Bourguignon, 2000, p. 203; Buvinić, Alda & Lamas, 2005, pp. 2–3).[5] Thus, the first references to "crime" in the World Bank's annual World Development Reports appeared in the mid- to late 1990s (see figure 6.1 on page 137). A 1998 World Bank report titled *Crime and Violence as Development Issues in Latin America and the Caribbean* would also explicitly acknowledge the impact of structural adjustment policies by describing how "the debt crisis of the early 1980s and the effects of the subsequent structural adjustment . . . led to severe shrinkages of real wages and job opportunities," as well as the "substantial decline in public expenditures on basic urban infrastructure and social services," which increased urban poverty and contributed to social breakdown as people turned to crime and violence as "ways out" (Ayres, 1998, p. 10). Similar narratives were also presented in a World Bank study, *Urban Poverty and Violence in Jamaica* (Moser & Holland, 1997), and the influential 1997 World Development Report, which asserted:

> High levels of crime and personal violence and an unpredictable judiciary combine to produce . . . the "lawlessness syndrome." Weak and arbitrary state institutions often compound the problem with unpredictable, inconsistent behavior. Far from assisting the growth of markets, such actions squander the state's credibility and hurt market development. To make development stable and sustainable, the state has to keep its eye on the social fundamentals. Lawlessness is often related to a sense of marginalization: indeed, breaking the law can seem the only way for the marginalized to get their voices heard. Public policies can ensure that growth is shared and that it contributes to reducing poverty and inequality, but only if governments put the social fundamentals high on their list of priorities. Too often, policies and programs divert resources and services from the people who need them most (World Bank, 1997, p. 4).

The excerpt quoted above openly recognizes inequality as a contributing factor to "lawlessness," but it also presents a characterization of "governments" as a potential impediment to developing and implementing public policies that address these issues. This is consistent with earlier World Bank narratives about public sector corruption and state capture (see chapter 5), and it reflected an overarching neoliberal discourse that predicted and prescribed a diminished role for the state when it came to matters relating to governance (Harvey, 2005).

Perhaps the most significant message in the excerpt quoted above was that personal insecurity had become a major concern for the international investors and domestic political and economic elites who occupied five-star hotels and gated communities and who relied on private security for protection in the rapidly expanding urban centers of the Global South (Mittelman & Johnston, 2011, p. 132). To this effect, the proponents and beneficiaries of neoliberal globalization throughout the developing world found themselves surrounded by slums, which emerged as the only "fully franchised solution to the problem of warehousing [the] century's surplus humanity" (Davis, 2017, pp. 200–201). Addressing the issue of "lawlessness" and creating safe (and attractive) business-friendly environments was therefore identified as a social development priority by IFIs, including the World Bank. In the absence of effective state institutions, a new approach to addressing the problem of urban violence in the Global South was required, and rule of law programming and anti-corruption initiatives offered little when it came to preventing or reducing urban violence.

By contrast, human security discourse—with its emphasis on local capacity building, empowerment, and resilience—provided IFIs with a framework for conceptualizing and establishing innovative crime prevention models that might help to activate local communities, individuals, and civil society as security actors. This idea of enlisting non-state actors as crime prevention partners was certainly a significant element of the "citizen security" model launched by the IADB in 1996.[6] We have not encountered any documentary evidence suggesting that the citizen security model that was later embraced by the World Bank and other IFIs was directly influenced by the human security paradigm or the work of UNDP, at least initially. To this effect, neither IADB documents nor the 1997 World Development Report quoted above makes reference to "human security," despite the obvious relevance and utility of this framework when it comes to conceptualizing the relationship between urban violence (as a source of personal and economic insecurity) and development.[7] The connection between these paradigms was therefore only later articulated (or at least acknowledged) by the World Bank in its influential 2011 World Development Report, *Conflict, Security and Development*, which included 51 references to "human security" and defined "citizen security" as:

Both freedom from physical violence and freedom from fear of violence. Applied to the lives of all members of a society (whether nationals of the country or otherwise), it encompasses security at home, in the workplace, and in political, social, and economic interactions with the state and other members of society. Similar to human security, "citizen security" places people at the center of efforts to prevent and recover from violence. (World Bank, 2011, p. xvi)

We can only speculate as to why there appears to have been an initial disconnect between the work of IFIs and the human security paradigm, but one possibility is that the IFIs viewed UNDP as a competitor and therefore were initially reluctant to anchor their work on violence reduction in the human development paradigm, which presented an alternative to its aggressive prescriptions for promoting economic growth through structural adjustment. From 1998 onward, however, the World Bank and other IFIs began to incorporate elements of human development discourse (specifically, its emphasis on poverty reduction) into their lexicons and lending strategies (Joshi & O'Dell, 2013, p. 252). This is attributable to the aforementioned shift to the post–Washington Consensus, and the influence of human development discourse on IFIs became particularly evident following adoption of the MDGs. IFIs have since adopted the position that human development and economic growth are fundamentally compatible and, indeed, mutually dependent. For example, the *2005 World Development Report* asserts that creating a better investment climate leads to better human development outcomes (World Bank, 2005, p. 24).

The *2005 World Development Report* also highlights the enduring interest of IFIs in crime and corruption and their belief that this represents a threat to neoliberal development (World Bank, 2005). We note, for example, that this report includes 117 references to "crime" and 136 references to "corruption" but, again, not a single reference to "human security." Instead, the concept of "security," which appears 77 times in this report, is primarily associated with the protection of property rights, which, from a neoliberal perspective, represents the cornerstone of a healthy, capitalist economy and a precondition for economic growth.

The *2005 World Development Report* is interesting for three reasons. First, it highlights that the security-development nexus has evolved into a contested sphere of liberal governance, albeit one that has become increasingly anchored in a centrist development agenda that reflects a compromise between proponents of the development as freedom model and those who advocate for development as growth. This analysis is supported by Joshi and O'Dell (2013, p. 255), who observe that following the adoption of the MDGs, the UN and the World Bank "appear to have adopted similar narratives and discourse arguing for a mix of neoliberalism and human development even if the World

Bank advocates more of the former than the UN." Further to this point, Joshi and O'Dell acknowledge that following the adoption of the MDGs, the World Bank and other IFIs have "become more state friendly while the UN has turned more market friendly" (p. 255). Along similar lines, Cammack (2017, p. 3) argues that today, "[t]he idea that the UNDP/HDR conception of human development represents an alternative to World Bank orthodoxy is a myth." The security-development nexus has inevitably been shaped by these shifts, but the convergence of these development models indicates that contestation occurs within a mutually agreeable ideological framework. Second, the reluctance of IFIs like the World Bank to explicitly adopt the language of human security does not imply that these organizations were in any way opposed to the post-interventionist paradigm described by Chandler (2012). To the contrary, their efforts to address the issue of "lawlessness" are consistent with its emphasis on enhancing the resilience of liberal subjects, including those governments that take an active interest in and creating business friendly environments. Finally, it evidences the World Bank's enduring interest in crime and corruption as obstacles to economic growth. This is important for reasons we discuss in the following chapter.

Chapter Seven

Reconstructing the Crime-Development Nexus

This chapter sets out to tell a story of how and why issues relating to crime and corruption came to be recognized as sustainable development issues following their omission from the Millennium Development Goals (MDGs) in 2000. The simple version of events is that the United Nations Office on Drugs and Crime (UNODC), an odd duck of the UN system, played an instrumental role in increasing the visibility of these problems for strategic reasons. Our discussion below therefore begins by reflecting on why UNODC made a concerted effort to "developmentalize" its portfolio and emphasize its links to the wider UN system following its tumultuous start as the United Nations Office on Drug Control and Crime Prevention (UN-ODCCP). Reflecting these formative years, we examine how UNODC worked to elevate the profile of its work during the 2000s using a combination of research and advocacy to emphasize its development credentials and link the problems of crime and corruption to the rule of law and human security agendas.

An institutionalist lens is particularly valuable here because we know that UNODC was actively involved with the construction of this agenda for bureaucratic reasons. However, international organizations like UNODC do not arbitrarily invent problems or create issue linkages. Rather, these are constructed through dialogues between the claims-maker (UNODC) and its various audiences. International Relations scholars associate these dialogues with "securitization" (Buzan et al., 1998), political scientists and criminologists with "legitimation" (Beetham, 1991; Bottoms & Tankebe, 2012), and sociologists with "dramaturgy" (Goffman, 1973). It is not our intention to rehash these perspectives; rather, we stress that understanding the dialogic construction of the crime-development nexus in the wake of the adoption of the MDGs necessitates consideration of *why* UNODC's claims were credible and appealed to various stakeholders. Returning to our Coxian framework, we therefore interpret the "developmentalization" of UNODC's portfolio in relation to the institutional, ideological, and material conditions that shaped the wider UN development agenda during this period.

THE FORMATIVE YEARS

In its early years, UN-ODCCP was not a cohesive entity. It lacked a unified culture, a clear sense of purpose, and a well-defined mandate. Staff from the UN Drug Control Program (UNDCP) continued work on drugs, while those from the Crime Prevention and Criminal Justice Branch (CPCJB) focused on norms and standards and the International Crime Victims Survey (ICVS). Whereas UNDCP had attracted significant interest and investment from Western donors since the 1980s, the CPCJB lacked a clear operational mandate until the United Nations Conventions against Transnational Crime and Corruption were adopted in 2000 and 2003. This in turn impacted their budget (see figure 7.1 below).

There had of course been various calls by UN bodies, including ECOSOC and the UN General Assembly, for Western donors to increase their support for the crime program during the 1990s, and it was widely acknowledged that this entity would potentially have an important role to play in facilitating international cooperation to address the growing threat of transnational organized crime. This recognition did not, however, translate into material resources or heightened status within an increasingly competitive UN system

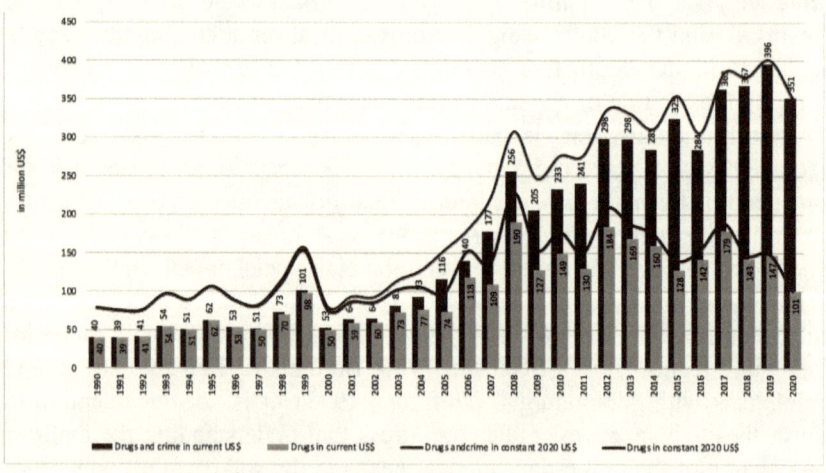

Fig. 7.1. UNODC Pledges from Donors (1990–2020)
Source: Created by UNODC

that by the late 1990s had become overwhelmingly dependent on voluntary contributions to fund its work (Murphy, 2006). Multiple participants reflected that the only things linking UNDCP and the CPCJB in the late 1990s were the name of this new organization, the office they cohabited in Vienna, and a new executive director.

The person selected to transform UN-ODCCP into a cohesive entity was Pino Arlacchi, who had previously served as vice president of Italy's Antimafia Commission and developed a reputation as an academic expert on the Mafia. Arlacchi was a curious choice for the role because he had no prior experience as an administrator within the UN system or at any international organization. His selection is perhaps best explained by the heightened importance attached to organized crime as an element of the international crime policy agenda in the 1990s. Arlacchi's nationality is also noteworthy because Italy had long been regarded as an international exemplar when it came to combating organized crime, and the country, together with the United States, had been instrumental in promoting international recognition of this problem and its transnational dimensions. While the United States was arguably the leading sovereign proponent of the global war on drugs and organized crime (Andreas & Nadelmann, 2006), appointing an American to the leadership position could have undermined UN-ODCCP's multilateral credentials and its ability to orchestrate the UNTOC (and later UNCAC) negotiations. Finally, his appointment seemingly reflected the secretary general's desire to position transnational crime at the center of UN-ODCCP's efforts to enhance international cooperation to combat "expanding global networks" of "uncivil society," which were already recognized as potential human security and human development issues around this time (Annan, 1998, p. 126).

It is worth reflecting on Arlacchi's legacy at UN-ODCCP because, as one of his former colleagues reflected, the executive director "sets the tone" for the organization. This is consistent with Cox's (1969) argument that executive leadership influences how international organizations navigate ideological, institutional, and material pressures. Unfortunately for UN-ODCCP, Arlacchi's tenure, which lasted from 1997 until 2002, was characterized by multiple former colleagues as a low point in the organization's history. He was particularly unpopular with the crime branch, which was (again) rebranded the Centre for International Crime Prevention (CHIC) in 1997. This was attributed by participants to his management style, personality, and efforts to shift the CICP's focus from norms and standards to preventing and combating organized crime. Some members of the CICP were resistant, and he reportedly dealt with these dissenters by involuntarily relocating them from Vienna to remote field offices around the world. One former colleague recalled, "It was sort of a political exile because I was actually kicked out, transferred against my will. . . . I was not the only one that it happened to that time." Arlacchi's arrival thus represented a significant turning point for the UN crime program, because these "exiles" had previously shaped its mentality and culture and functioned as an important source of institutional memory.

Arlacchi's aims and approach were divisive, but shifting the CICP's focus to transnational organized crime was arguably vital to the future success of UN-ODCCP in a hypercompetitive UN system. The most significant institutional development during the Arlacchi years was the successful adoption of UNTOC and the efficient diplomatic negotiation process, which CICP staff reportedly facilitated through both official and informal channels. This would later support the expansion of the crime program by supplying it with an operational mandate. It is debatable whether Arlacchi's leadership directly contributed to the successful drafting and negotiations of UNTOC, but its adoption clearly proved vital to the UN-ODCCP/UNODC's expansion over the next two decades. In the short term, however, the adoption of UNTOC created a challenge for UN-ODCCP, because fulfilling this operational mandate necessitated new sources of funding at a time when more than 90% of the CICP's funding still came from the UN's General Purpose Fund (Redo, 2012, p. 160; see figure 7.1 above).

UN-ODCCP AND THE CHANGING FUNDING LANDSCAPE

The UN's changing funding landscape during this period had a significant impact on the work of UN agencies, including UN-ODCCP/UNODC (Blaustein, 2015; Murphy, 2006).

There was a significant increase ($\approx$180%) in the overall UN budget between the years 1995 and 2010, which meant more resources were available (Naik, 2013). However, there was also a significant expansion in UN activities during this period, which meant greater interagency competition for these resources. A growing proportion of this funding was provided by donors in the form of "noncore" contributions, which accounted for approximately 71% of the UN budget in 2010, compared to only 36% in 1995 (Naik, 2013). This signified that countries were becoming increasingly selective about which multilateral activities and programs they would fund. Whereas contributions to the General Purpose Fund were administered by the UN General Assembly (UNGA), noncore contributions were typically benchmarked for projects or programs that aligned with donor interests. This provided donor countries from the Global North with a means of influencing the work of UN agencies, which of course was already overwhelmingly directed toward solving problems in the Global South. Although long regarded as an inefficient development actor, UN agencies nevertheless continued to play an important role in advancing the global liberal governance project because they enjoyed greater political legitimacy than international financial institutions (IFIs) and bilateral agencies in many parts of the Global South, particularly under the leadership of Secretary General Kofi Annan (Murphy, 2006).

One consequence of this changing funding landscape for UN agencies has been decreased autonomy over which aspects of their mandates and the work programs they prioritize. It has also undermined the ability of the UNGA and ECOSOC to steer the implementation of the international policy agenda by controlling the budget. The fact that noncore contributions typically come with strings attached has also prompted UN agencies to adopt "results-based management" (RBM) systems to demonstrate their efficiency and the impact of their work to donors (Blaustein, 2015). This managerial shift has reinforced the accountability of UN agencies to donors.

Reflecting on the UN's role in peacebuilding operations and international development assistance since the 1990s, critical scholars have previously come to associate the work of the UN with a post-liberal governance paradigm, whereby multilateral interventions and technical assistance programs are funded by Western donors to align the governing institutions of weak, failed, rogue, illiberal, and developing states with the ideological and material interests of Western capitalism (Chandler, 2010; Duffield, 2007). This critique implies that the envisioned function of the Secretariat as an international civil service has been compromised by material forces. This argument is well rehearsed, but the impact of these institutional changes on the work of UNODC has received little scholarly attention.

Arlacchi was undoubtedly aware of this funding climate, but UN-ODCCP was at a strategic disadvantage when it came to attracting donor support for the crime program, which did not have established capabilities it could market to donors, or a track record of successful projects to highlight. Accordingly, the strategic benefits of investing in the operational capabilities of the organization's crime program were not immediately obvious. Eventually, Western donors (at least European donors) came to recognize that providing voluntary support for programs and projects was a relatively cost-effective means of signaling their commitment to addressing transnational problems, without necessarily having to take meaningful action to address them domestically. For this reason, it is perhaps unsurprising that, as noted above, the vast majority of UNODC's work (both its monitoring efforts and technical assistance) has been directed at developing countries in the Global South. However, donors were not immediately throwing money at UN-ODCCP to address these problems, because neither UNTOC nor UNCAC was actually designed to be an effective regulatory instrument. The poorly designed review mechanism for UNCAC illustrates this,[1] as does the fact that an UNTOC review mechanism was only established in 2018.

Recognizing these problems was one thing, but enabling UN-ODCCP to tackle them by administering an effective audit system was undesirable for various reasons. Fundamentally, any review that portrayed a government in a negative light or drew attention to corruption or organized crime would signal risks to investors. In this respect, the rule of law revival inadvertently created a situation whereby international attempts to combat corruption and promote good governance were undermined by the need for governments to downplay these issues and present themselves as capable, law-abiding, and competent. More cynically, the very construction of these problems via Manichaean narratives about the "dark side of globalization" or "uncivil society" was itself problematic. Evocative language and imagery is certainly useful for consensus-building (what government could afford to be seen as a supporter of corruption and organized crime?), but these narratives constructed a false dichotomy between licit and illicit activities and enterprises. In this regard, many political elites in both the developed and the developing world recognized that corruption and transnational organized crime were not simply a threat to global capitalism but an integral part of it. Establishing effective review mechanisms risked drawing attention to these linkages, as did providing UN-ODCCP with material resources that would allow it to function autonomously. UN-ODCCP needed to be controlled, and the budget, together with its conservative governing bodies, provided Member States with the ability to do so.

A MISSED OPPORTUNITY AND A SERIES OF SCANDALS

Two additional factors complicated UN-ODCCP's financial situation during its formative years. The first links back to the omission of crime and corruption from the MDGs. The second relates to a series of scandals that tarnished the reputation of the organization. Both are worth reflecting on insofar as they provide insight into why the organization attempted to reinvent itself as an international development partner following Arlacchi's departure in 2002.

The MDGs were developed to function as an "effective method of global mobilization to achieve a set of important social priorities worldwide" (Sachs, 2012, p. 5). The rationale was to "generate incentives to improve performance" and focus international investment toward measurable objectives that would help address the most significant global development challenges (Sachs, 2012, p. 5). As one former UN-ODCCP executive recalled:

The negotiations for the Millennium Development Goals had already started by 1998. By 1999, crime and drugs didn't feature highly on the agenda. The agenda was still very much about poverty reduction and crime was not given a place on it.

According to this participant, UN-ODCCP made a "last chance effort to get the Viennese agenda a place in the Millennium Goals, but it was too late." In their view, part of the problem was that Arlacchi "was not a person with any prior interest in development aid," so he did not recognize the strategic importance of this issue linkage. Another colleague described this as a "missed opportunity."

This "last chance effort" is evident from the proceedings of the Tenth UN Crime Congress, in April 2000. UNTOC was the main focus of the Congress, but references to the complex relationship between crime prevention, rule of law promotion, and human security featured in both the preparatory materials and high-level discussions. For example, the Secretary General's Report acknowledged the links between crime and globalization, which it described as "a new phase of development that has the potential to benefit millions of people" but also "to create fertile ground for illegal activities" (Annan, 1999, p. 1). A working paper by the Secretariat also suggested that crime control measures should be integrated into comprehensive rule of law projects, particularly those that target organized crime, terrorism, and corruption. These problems were described as "a direct threat to rule of law elements such as equality, judicial independence and basic legality" and "erode[d] the credibility of criminal justice systems" (UN Secretariat, 2000a, pp. 8–9). The Discussion Guide for the Congress further noted, "many developing countries and States with economies in transition are in need of technical assistance in building or reforming their crime-prevention and criminal justice systems" (UN Secretariat, 2000b, p. 3).

These examples illustrate that development remained an enduring element of the UN crime policy agenda, albeit one that had become subordinate to more pressing issues, such as organized crime and corruption. For this reason, there was only a single vague reference to the crime-development nexus in the Vienna Declaration adopted at the Congress, which stated:

> 10. We undertake to strengthen international cooperation in order to create an environment conducive to the fight against organized crime, promoting growth and sustainable development and eradicating poverty and unemployment (UN Secretariat, 2001, p. 2).

Despite the relative neglect of these issues in the Vienna Declaration, they were explicitly referenced in the Millennium Declaration adopted by the

UNGA in September 2000 (UNGA, 2000). It is unclear whether Arlacchi, his colleagues at UN-ODCCP, or the organization's American or Italian supporters advocated for their inclusion, but this seemingly served as a wake-up call for Arlacchi, who addressed the Third Committee of the UNGA three weeks later.

In his speech, Arlacchi stated:

> We are encouraged that the Summit included in the Declaration a series of commitments to strengthen respect for the rule of law and to act against the drug problem, terrorism, the arms trade, economic crime and transnational crime in general. . . . I am absolutely certain that we can defeat the uncivil society. The linkages between poverty and the areas of responsibility given to ODCCP are perhaps one of the least understood aspects of our work. Yet it is one of the most important. . . . We are working in some of the poorest areas of the world. This is not by chance. We are also working in some of the most violent locations. Again, this is not by chance. Poverty alleviation without the rule of law is not an option. It will simply not work (Arlacchi, 2000).

Arlacchi's reference to "uncivil society" paid homage to how Secretary General Kofi Annan had previously framed these problems. This is also, to our knowledge, the first explicit reference Arlacchi made to this issue linkage in a public statement. The narrative later became an important element of UNODC's "developmentalization" strategy, but in the lead-up to the MDGs, it was too little too late.

None of the problems that had been identified in the section of the Millennium Declaration relating to "Peace, security and disarmament" (Section II) were included in the MDGs. The reason for their omission remains a matter of speculation, but one of Arlacchi's former colleagues suggested that the leading architects of the MDGs "thought the idea that you can promote sustainable development through fighting crime was bullshit." This explanation is seemingly credible, because it is well known that the MDGs were drafted by a small group of development economists and UN administrators who were keen to "avoid a Christmas list of goals with every interest group racing to get in their goals."[2]

According to the same former UN-ODCCP executive, another issue was that, at this time, "the evidence that crime control or drug control could make a contribution to sustainable development was not so strong, it was more a hypothesis." This observation is interesting because it highlights recognition by staff at UN-ODCCP that the relationship between crime and development was fundamentally different in the age of globalization than it was in the era of modernization. Consequently, the previous evidence base, which focused on the relationship between industrialization, urbanization, and crime, was of limited relevance when it came to evidencing or theorizing the crime-development nexus circa 2000. Scholarly research on the link between crime and development also remained fairly limited at the time, and much of this work was descriptive or conceptually focused, so it supplied limited scientific evidence or theoretical insight into the issue linkage.[3] This in turn limited UN-ODCCP's advocacy capabilities, so the adoption of the MDGs created an immediate need for the organization to align its expanded portfolio with development issues.

The second complication was linked with a series of scandals that came to light in December 2000 (the same month the MDGs were adopted). A resignation letter penned by one of UN-ODCCP's directors, Michael von der Schulenburg, accused Arlacchi of mismanaging the organization's resources and criticized his management style. The letter also included allegations of financial misconduct and claimed that UN-ODCCP under Arlacchi is "an organization that has increased its international visibility" yet "crumbling under the weight of promises that it is unable to meet under a management style that has demoralized, intimidated and paralyzed its staff" (Michael von der Schulenburg, quoted in Transnational Institute, 2005). The letter was leaked to the press and attracted significant international media attention.

In 2001 UN-ODCCP was subjected to an inspection and a formal investigation by the UN Office of Internal Oversight Services (OIOS). The inspection, conducted in February, presented a damning assessment of Arlacchi's leadership (UN OIOS, 2001a, p. 2). The subsequent investigation later cleared him of misconduct but concluded that "multiple incidents of mismanagement of project operations and waste of ODCCP funds occurred" (UN OIOS, 2001b, p. 2). UN-ODCCP's reputation and credibility with donors had been tarnished at a time when the organization had several strengths, including "clear mandates, its high priority on the intergovernmental policy agenda and its broad range of expertise in the mandated areas" (UN OIOS, 2001a, p. 2).[4] Repairing this reputational damage, securing voluntary contributions, and developing the entity's operational capabilities thus became an immediate priority for the secretary general. Arlacchi's tenure was not renewed, and in 2002 he was succeeded by Antonio Maria Costa. Under Costa, UN-ODCCP enhanced its credentials as an international development partner and its appeal to donors.

MAKING CRIME A DEVELOPMENT ISSUE ... AGAIN

Antonio Maria Costa was an eccentric leader with a strong personality. He was a competent administrator and highly skilled when it came to advocacy, but at times he appeared indifferent to or disinterested in UN protocols and diplomatic niceties. For reasons discussed below, this would ultimately cost him his job.

Like Arlacchi, he was a curious choice for the Executive Directorship. A fellow Italian, his nationality undoubtedly factored into his selection, but Costa was not a crime fighter or an expert in organized crime. Nor did he have a background in drug policy or public health. Rather, Costa was an economist who had served as secretary general of the European Bank of Reconstruction and Development (EBRD), which had been established following the collapse of the Soviet Union "to foster the transition towards open market-oriented economies and to promote private and entrepreneurial initiative in the Central and Eastern European countries" (EBRD, 1990, p. 4). A former UNODC executive explained that Costa's leadership experience at the EBRD directly factored into his appointment because the secretary general "wanted someone with an understanding of development."

Recognizing the significant problems he had inherited, Costa's first priority was to restructure the organization and repair the reputational damage. "UN-ODCCP" was rebadged "UNODC," and UNDCP was merged with the CICP to create the managerial structure that exists today (see figure 1.1). The rationale was to create a more cohesive culture that would allow members of the crime program to benefit from the experience and expertise of colleagues from the drug control program. It was hoped that this would enable them to develop operational capabilities and donor relationships. As noted above, accessing voluntary funding was crucial for fulfilling UNODC's obligations as the custodian of UNTOC and, later, UNCAC.

Embracing Development

Organizational reforms represented an important starting point for rebuilding UNODC, but Costa faced another significant challenge in the wake of the 9/11 attacks that prompted the United States to initiate its "global war on terror." The problem was that the Bush administration, staffed by Reagan-era neoconservatives, did not share Clinton's enthusiasm for multilateralism or liberal internationalism. Their interest in development was limited, and when it came to international security, the Bush administration viewed the UN as either inconsequential or an obstacle to its foreign policy interests. Although UNTOC explicitly recognized the link between transnational organized crime and terrorism (UNGA, 2000, p. 3), and the United States was an important financial benefactor of the drugs program, there was no immediate prospect of positioning UNODC as an instrumental partner in the global war on terror. For starters, one former executive explained that none of the influential governments trusted UNODC with intelligence because "the UN is completely incapable of keeping secrets." Enlisting UNODC's support would only increase the risk of leaks, scandals, and geopolitical backlash and offer little in terms of legitimizing the global war on terror through the guise of multilateralism. Second, Kofi Annan was a vocal critic of the global war on terror and remained committed to the liberal internationalist agenda. He was intent on positioning the UN as a political counterforce to American unilateralism and as an institutional safeguard against breaches of international law (Annan, 2003). This divergence of agendas added further impetus to the need for UNODC to clearly articulate a narrative about its portfolio that would appeal to donors who remained committed to the liberal internationalist project. Emphasizing the links between crime and development offered a logical starting point because the MDGs were a central focus of the UN's work, which was materially supported by European governments. The secretary general also remained committed to the idea that economic and social development were the building blocks of international security (Annan, 2005), and, as noted in the previous chapter, other UN entities and IFIs were interested in these links. By 2002 everyone acknowledged that these issues were somehow related, but the nature of these relationships and, specifically, the relevance of crime had yet to be clearly articulated.

Costa did not simply invent the narrative that crime represents an obstacle to development. The previous chapters have demonstrated that variations of this idea had been a fixture of the UN crime program since the late 1950s. It appears, therefore, that Costa's attempts to draw attention to this issue linkage was directly influenced by the work of the CICP, which had undertaken research to examine this empirically in the lead-up to the MDGs. Specifically, we refer to an article published in the journal *Forum on Crime and Society* by criminologist and then-Officer-in-Charge of the CICP, Jan van Dijk.

Van Dijk's (2001) paper examined several different dimensions of the macro-relationship between crime, rule of law, and economic development using various cross-national data sets. These included statistics from four sweeps of the International Crime Victims Survey (ICVS), police-recorded homicide statistics, and perception-based measures sourced from three waves of the Executive Opinion Survey, which was administered by the World Economic Forum. The statistical analysis was then supplemented with a qualitative trends analysis of organized crime. Several findings are pertinent to our discussion. First, rates of conventional crime, street-level corruption, and homicides were found to be significantly higher throughout the developing world than in developed countries. The paper emphasized that developing countries featured higher levels of poverty, unemployment, and inequality and this provided a "breeding ground" for crime by creating "large pools of motivated offenders" (p. 5). By implication, promoting economic and social development were deemed essential for addressing the root causes of crime. Second, van Dijk observed that "the perceived extent of organized crime is inversely related to national income per capita" (p. 7) and argued that developing countries (but not the poorest countries) were most likely to be impacted by, and a source of, this global threat. Third, the paper appears to evidence the impact of organized crime and corruption on rule of law in developing countries by noting that rule of law was "strongly correlated to national income per capita" and that "organized crime is perceived to be much more problematic in countries where the rule of law is not assured" (pp. 9–10). Finally, the paper found high levels of formal and informal social control, described as "lawfulness," to be "an important predictor of economic growth" and concluded "that countries of all levels of development can experience thirty per cent more economic growth if crime and corruption problems are tackled more effectively" (p. 12).

The analysis presented by van Dijk appears to resonate most closely with the "development as growth" mentality, which remained popular with neoliberal IFIs until the late 1990s. This was perhaps inevitable insofar as van Dijk used country-level indicators, which offered little insight into individual-level, human development outcomes. At the same time, the paper adopts a somewhat critical perspective toward the neoliberal growth model in stating:

> [E]conomic liberalization alone does not present a way out [of the poverty trap]. The serious crime-related economic problems of several transitional countries bear testimony to the limitations of market mechanisms based on economic freedoms. (van Dijk, 2001, p. 14)

The paper was not particularly impactful in terms of its scholarly citations, but it provides valuable insight into how UN-ODCCP's understanding of these issues evolved after the Tenth Congress. Despite its methodological limitations and the challenges inherent to quantifying the relationships between three nebulous concepts (crime, rule of law, and development), the paper illustrates how the organization's unique research capabilities would later support and legitimize its advocacy work in this space. UNODC's research would henceforth influence, and be influenced by, the organization's efforts to "developmentalize" its portfolio in the lead-up to the SDGs. This iterative process is worth examining in detail because it provides insight into how expert knowledge is produced and deployed by UNODC, thus illustrating that in this policy context, "science and politics are irreducible" (Littoz-Monnet, 2017, p. 11).

In August 2002 Costa made his first public reference to the crime-development nexus at the World Summit on Sustainable Development. He described the potential consequences of globalization and illustrated the scale of this problem and its economic impact by claiming "illegal profits may be as high as 3 to 4 percent of global GDP annually" (Costa, 2002). He then referenced the link between terrorism and organized crime before articulating how UN-ODCCP contributed to sustainable development:

> [W]e are not dealing with the "hardware" of development—building roads, schools, electrification, or irrigation systems. Rather, UN-ODCCP is heavily committed to strengthening the "software" aspects of development—the ingredients being good governance, honest and open markets, absence of corruption, human safety, and the rule of law . . . let there be no doubt—unless they are present in society, development can never become sustainable. (Costa, 2002)

Much of the address was derivative of Arlacchi's speech to the UNGA and themes from van Dijk's paper. The difference, however, was that Costa seemingly believed that establishing strategic partnerships with members of the wider international development community was an institutional priority for UNODC. Thus, in an effort to position UNODC as both a development and a security actor, Costa mobilized the organization's research section and tasked its members with preparing a series of reports to highlight the relationship between crime, rule of law, and development throughout the Global South. In this sense, Costa's emphasis on this issue linkage went beyond what Littoz-Monnet (2017, p. 9) describes as "minimizing institutional insecurity." Rather, it was indicative of a mode of knowledge mobilization that sought to actively shape the international policy agenda and reconstruct UNODC's identity in the process.

Building a Positive Identity

The first influential report elaborated on a particular element of UNODC's portfolio that directly resonated with the wider development agenda and the global war on terror: "alternative development." Specifically, it synthesized data from UNODC's annual opium poppy surveys with economic data provided by the Asian Development Bank and the World Bank to analyze Afghanistan's opium economy. This was constructed as a threat to international security because it reportedly provided a source of financial revenue for international terrorist networks. It was also framed as a global public health threat. The report then presented the findings of a series of UNDCP country-level evaluation studies to evidence that its alternative development projects that "create the economic and social environment in which households can attain an acceptable standard of living, without the need for drug crop cultivation" (Mansfield, 1999) had contributed to a significant reduction in the country's annual opium production between 1997 and 2000 (UNODC, 2003,

p. 103). Costa certainly did not invent alternative development, but it immediately resonated with his interest in addressing the underlying economic and social causes of crime. His preface to the report therefore attempted to position UNODC as a key development partner who could contribute to a global reduction in narcotics production and terrorist finance, rather than as a security actor:

> Although counterterrorism is the key battleground, the enemy has to be confronted on other fronts as well, first and foremost in the struggle against illicit drugs. This challenge can be faced: Thailand, Pakistan, and Turkey (on the opium front), Bolivia and Peru (on the cocaine front) have shown that legally and commercially viable crops can replace illicit cultivation. (Costa in UNODC, 2003, p. 103)

Alternative development has been criticized by drug policy researchers, but this messaging was politically compelling, so the report attracted international media attention and interest from the IFIs.

Later in 2003, Costa was interviewed for a *New York Times* article, which claimed that "huge opium and heroin crops are being used by militants to finance their activities" and that "Afghanistan was still in danger of falling into the hands of drug traders" (Gall, 2003). The article, which parroted Costa, argued that military intervention alone would not establish conditions that would serve to address this problem. Rather, as Costa previously wrote in his preface to the report: "Dismantling the opium economy ... must be done with the instruments of democracy, the rule of law, and development" (Costa in UNODC, 2003, p. 1).

A former colleague of Costa's recalled that this article caught the attention of the World Bank's President James Wolfensohn, who contacted UNODC, saying, "we need to do something, this is unacceptable." To this effect, another former colleague reflected, "Afghanistan for a number of years was hugely important for UNODC ... because of the interest in state building in Afghanistan post the intervention there." Ironically, although UNODC could not position itself as a counterterrorism organization or an international security actor, the global war on terror and the US occupation of Afghanistan nevertheless established a valuable opportunity for the organization to showcase its credentials as a social development actor.

Almost immediately, other IFIs began to take an interest in UNODC as a potential partner with unique expertise and capabilities when it came to developing the aforementioned "software" aspects of development, especially given their own lack of expertise in matters relating to crime, as noted in the previous chapter. As one former UNODC executive explained:

We had wonderful relations with World Bank, IMF, the African Development Bank, the Asian Development Bank, the European Union, because the message we were pushing through was not one of repression and security but rather, "let us change the world together."

The above quote highlights another important distinction between Costa's approach to developmentalizing UNODC and Arlacchi's earlier focus on crime fighting. Specifically, Costa set out to create a positive identity for the organization that emphasized what it was for rather than what it was against.

Several former employees of UNODC suggested this was quite important, because up to this point UNODC had always been seen as anathema by other UN entities that did not understand the value of its work and considered its conservative mandate and values to be at odds with their own progressive agendas. One former UNODC executive recalled:

In Afghanistan, we're talking with [the Food and Agricultural Organization of the UN] about how to integrate development but apparently they preferred to create a Frankenstein—an abstract schizophrenic farmer which in daylight is a matter for FAO and at night time is a matter of drug control. That is a far-fetched picture away from any reality. A poor Afghan farmer thinks integrated on revenue to feed his family—not in abstract disintegrated terms. Also, in Myanmar we faced problems in getting development actors involved, such as UNDP. So, the reciprocity was not always as easy as it seems today.

The concept of "rule of law" and to a lesser extent "good governance" thus supplied UNODC with a relevant vocabulary that allowed it to emphasize its positive contributions to development and link these to the interests of IFIs, other UN agencies, and, most significantly, donors.

The significance of this language was described by multiple members of Costa's inner circle:

The concept of the "rule of law" is fundamental, and it has advantages compared to talking about fighting criminality or fighting corruption. The "rule of law" is always, it sounds very noble. So, if you talk about "rule of law" and you sit in a meeting with people who are promoting education, promoting food, promoting health, well they feel comfortable that this guy is promoting justice.

This positive framing was also important because IFIs were reluctant to talk about crime. Not only could this be considered interference in a state's internal affairs, but implying that recipient states had a crime problem might create a perception of a risk for investors and thus undermine the bank's aims. As one participant reflected:

[Y]ou will never find the word "crime" in these World Bank reports, [rather] it's "governance" they refer to. Crime was a very scary concept for them because if you say, "Your government has a crime problem," meaning they are infiltrated by the Mafia, that was way too much for the World Bank.

As noted in the previous chapter, IFIs including the World Bank embraced the rule of law agenda as a recipe for taming the final frontiers of economic globalization and establishing free and stable markets in the Global South and former Soviet Bloc. The fact that it took so long for the link between UNODC's portfolio and the rule of law agenda to be recognized is probably a testament to the primacy of transnational organized crime and illicit drug trafficking as the focal points of the organization's work during the Arlacchi years. Due perhaps to his background as a development economist, Costa seemingly recognized the importance of strategically deploying more palatable language to emphasize how multilateral efforts to prevent crime at the national, regional, and international levels would support good governance and, by extension, economic growth.

Following the success of the Afghanistan report, UNODC's research division was tasked with preparing a series of regional follow-up studies that explored the impacts of crime on development in the Global South. The Southern focus highlights the enduring influence of the "development as efficiency" model, which is rooted in the "benevolent colonialism" of the Mandate System discussed in chapter 3. In this regard, UNODC's interest in crime in "developing" as opposed to "developed" countries highlights that this research agenda was shaped by the material and ideological legacy of European colonialism. This is obvious in relation to the political economy of the UN system, because donor countries, typically those who benefited from colonialism, have historically used their geopolitical influence and material resources to shape the institutional agenda of the UN. It is therefore exceedingly rare, perhaps even unheard of, for a Western donor country to provide funding to the UN to address a domestic problem or to provide technical assistance to another "developed" country, because this would signal a crisis of governance. Aid and assistance is therefore oriented toward addressing problems in the Global South, which, in the age of globalization, are also perceived to be problems, risks, or threats to donor interests in the Global North. From a strategic standpoint, it is therefore unsurprising that UNODC's next three reports focused on Africa, Central America, and the Caribbean.

At the same time, we do not wish to suggest that the geographical focus of this research was entirely unjustified. All three regions faced elevated levels of crime, violence, and corruption, and this was convincingly evidenced in the reports. The point to emphasize, however, is that the Global South's crime problems today are at least in part a consequence of the structural violence associated with "development" in its various guises, notably colonialism, modernization, and neoliberalization (Blaustein et al., 2018). Acknowledging these continuities and the economic, social, political, and cultural instabilities they have generated is crucial for developing contextually appropriate strategies for reducing the harms of crime and the criminal justice system. Reflecting on the legacy of European colonialism and its influence on development theory and practice is also important because it highlights that the development of the South has been shaped by enduring institutional, ideological, and material linkages with the North. These arguments are well rehearsed by dependency theorists and postcolonial scholars, but we reference them here to emphasize that framing the crime-development nexus as an ahistorical, Southern phenomenon is inherently problematic.

Costa, together with the researchers at UNODC who produced the reports discussed below, recognized the political sensitivities surrounding these issues, and they paid lip service to the legacy of colonialism and the role of Northern countries in stimulating demand for illicit commodities, which contributed to undesirable forms of economic activities in developing countries. Ultimately, however, UNODC's research and advocacy has overwhelmingly reproduced a reductionist narrative about a complex problem that appeals to donors and IFIs who remain committed to growth, efficiency, and freedom but have little interest in addressing the structural causes of global inequality.

The Development Game

For Costa, this issue linkage represented an important opportunity for UNODC to further establish its development credentials, build new partnerships, and access new sources of funding. As a former colleague explained:

> Costa, the executive director, said, "We know there's a lot of money in development, so if you can tie our topic to development then there's lots of access to development funds." As a matter of fact, that's the truth with all of this. Most of the money we tapped into is bilateral aid to developing countries.

Research produced by UNODC and funded by Northern donors supplied evidence that enabled it to secure finance for its projects and programs throughout the developing world. While the impact of this research and Costa's advocacy on UNODC's budget is difficult to assess, we note that donor pledges for the UN crime program increased by more than tenfold between 2003 and 2010 (see figure 7.1 above).

The first of three follow-up reports focused on *Crime and Development in Africa*. The 2005 report was prepared by UNODC and financed by France and the UK (UNODC, 2005). The preface, written by Costa, diplomatically acknowledges that exploitation, colonization, economic dependence, "crippling debt burdens," and "health conditions" contributed to "Africa's failure to develop," but adds, "there is more that holds back Africa's economic performance":

> These additional impediments are mostly disregarded by development aid providers and humanitarian agencies, though they are mostly well known to African leaders: "[C]ross-border crime, illicit proliferation, circulation and trafficking of small arms and light weapons, drug trafficking, corruption and terrorism constitute serious threats to security and stability. They hamper the harmonious economic and social development of the Continent." (Lome Declaration of the African Union Assembly, 12 July 2000) (UNODC, 2005, pp. v, vii)

Costa did not attempt to discredit the radical "underdevelopment" narrative inspired by dependency theorists. Rather, he shifted the focus to more proximate obstacles linked with criminality. Asserting that these issues have been "mostly disregarded" implies a need for new interventions, and referencing the Lome Declaration signaled that there was political support "internationally-endorsed preventative measures" (Chandler, 2004, p. 67). Costa's statement thus framed African governments as willing, liberal subjects who, unlike donors, recognized that addressing crime, violence, and corruption was essential for realizing their economic potential.

This politically astute report did not simply reduce the concept of development to economic growth. Rather, it linked economic growth to the human development paradigm and invoked Amartya Sen's (1999) influential ideas to legitimize its agenda:

> Sen has touched on an idea that is often underappreciated by development experts: that freedom from crime and violence are key components of development. Freedom from fear is as important as freedom from want. It is impossible to enjoy one of these rights without the other. (UNODC, 2005, p. 101)

Linking "freedom from fear" with "freedom from want" implied that human security and human development were mutually dependent. As noted in the previous chapter, this idea gained prominence following the publication of the *1994 Human Development Report* (UNDP, 1994) in the 1990s. Three months prior to the publication of UNODC's report, it was also referenced by the secretary general in his 2005 progress report on the MDGs when he stated, "we will not enjoy development without security, we will not enjoy security without development, and we will not enjoy either without respect for human rights" (Annan, 2005, p. 6). By this point then, the security-development nexus was already an established dogma within the international development community, and this was beneficial for UNODC.

It is also important to note that by 2005, the liberal interventionist paradigm that originally sparked the international community's interest in the security-development nexus had fallen out of favor due in part to the UN's perceived failures during the 1990s. What emerged in its wake was a "post-interventionist" paradigm of global liberal governance, which shifted the UN's focus away from direct intervention (peacekeeping operations) "towards a concern with facilitating or developing the self-securing agency—resilience—of those held to be the most vulnerable" (Chandler, 2012, p. 213). UNODC's portfolio and mandate aligned perfectly with this post-interventionist paradigm, which aspired to promote human security at a distance through multilateral capacity building projects, including rule of law promotion. The evidence and analysis supplied in the 2005 report and UNODC's advocacy thus proved influential, and two years later the African Union adopted its Revised Plan of Action on Drug Control and Crime Prevention (African Union, 2008).

UNODC published two additional reports that addressed development in 2007. *Crime and Development in Central America* echoed the 2005 report's emphasis on the link between human development and human security and proceeded to describe the consequences of crime in economic terms, stating: "Crime and corruption are derailing attempts to address the global polarization of wealth, as people choose not to invest their lives or their money where they are insecure (UNODC, 2007, p. 11)."[5] This statement constructed crime and corruption as contributing factors to economic inequality of the region. Once again this implied that they must be addressed in order for economic growth and human development outcomes to be realized. Interestingly, the report presented a nuanced account of the various factors that contributed to the region's problems (illicit drug production/trafficking and homicides) and at least tacitly acknowledged the influence of US support for authoritarian governments during the Reagan years. This particular report is a testament to the quality of the in-house research produced by UNODC. Its contextualization of Central America's crime problems, rigorous use of empirical data and trends analysis, and engagement with the wider scholarly and gray literature illustrates this rigor.

The conclusion is also noteworthy because it highlighted a "false dichotomy" between crime prevention and social development and argued that both must be pursued in tandem (UNODC, 2007, p. 88). The emphasis here was that economic and social problems cannot be addressed by law enforcement or crime prevention measures alone. At the same time, it acknowledged that there was an immediate need to develop practical and efficient interventions that would alleviate the effects of crime for residents of the region. This pragmatic argument was both compelling and politically useful because it highlighted that UNODC, a pseudo-development actor, could make an immediate impact by sidestepping complex and contentious debates about the merits or consequences of different development models and strategies. UNODC acknowledged that these debates were important; but, more immediately, an apolitical, technocratic approach to crime prevention was required to promote citizen security and create economic, social, and political conditions necessary for supporting any model of development.

The final report set out to account for the costs of crime in the Caribbean, and this was produced by UNODC in collaboration with the World Bank. Again, the report explicitly stated, "Crime and violence are a *development issue*," and emphasized the impact of crime and violence on "economic growth and social development" (UNODC and World Bank, 2007, p. i; original emphasis). It also suggested that "there is a trade-off between resources spent on combating drug trafficking and those spent on other forms of crime and violence prevention" (p. i). This is interesting and potentially controversial, because it drew attention to the complexity of crime as a regional phenomenon and acknowledged that internationally driven efforts to combat drug trafficking were potentially counterproductive. Like the Central America report, it also acknowledged that crime and violence prevention could be achieved through investment in law enforcement alone and thus advocated a three-tiered model consisting of crime prevention through environmental design (CPTED), citizen security approaches, and public health–based measures. These prescriptions were oriented toward shifting responsibility for crime and violence prevention away from states, and these were clearly influenced by research and policy developments in the Anglo-American context (Blaustein, 2016; Ituralde, 2019, 2020). The fundamental aspiration was therefore to establish efficient assemblages of social control that required minimal public investment, public sector involvement, and oversight from Central American governments and police that were under-resourced, unreliable, and, in some countries, a major source of violence (Cruz, 2011; Cruz & Vorobyeva, 2021). CPTED was well established by this point and had been advocated since the 1980s, so it does not warrant further discussion. The "citizen security" model is noteworthy, however, because it occupied a space between the post–Washington Consensus, promoted by IFIs, and enduring subaltern critiques of structural adjustment policies and neocolonialism.

As noted in the previous chapter, the citizen security model emerged in Latin America during the late 1990s and was advocated by the Inter-American Development Bank (IADB) and other IFIs as part of their tool kit for addressing the problems of crime and corruption as threats to economic growth. Ironically, the model's popularity throughout the region has been attributed to the desire of "emboldened" Latin American governments in the 2000s to distance themselves from the economic and foreign policy prescriptions of the West (Muggah & Carvalho, 2014, p. 2). This push for autonomy was enabled by the relative economic prosperity of many Latin American countries during the 2000s following a commodity super cycle that enabled left-leaning governments to implement economic and social policies geared toward addressing the problems of poverty and inequality. This "Pink Tide" also prompted Latin American governments to establish and fund networks that supported greater regional cooperation in relation to policy matters, in the hope that this would help them collectively assert their autonomy and reduce dependence on the United States and Europe (Chodor, 2015). The citizen security model benefited from these developments, and it also continued to attract investment from IFIs and the West because it provided a platform for indirectly promoting evidence-based crime prevention strategies (IADB, 2012). The ill-defined nature of "citizen security" rendered it universally appealing (Muggah, 2017), so embracing this model was strategically advantageous for UNODC because it already aligned with its existing portfolio.

Drawing on the evidence and analyses presented in all three reports, Costa addressed the CCPCJ in 2008 and emphasized that "rule of law" should be recognized as a precondition for achieving progress with the MDGs:

> [T]he rule of law is not only a goal in itself, it is also a means. It is a crosscutting issue, the foundation upon which most other MDGs can be built. This point is easy to prove.
>
> Economic analysis has consistently shown the clear correlation between weak rule of law and weak socioeconomic performance. Clear correlation, I said, though some people actually see strong causality: in countries ravaged by crime and corruption, and where governments lost control of their land, the poor suffer the most, and the services provided to them get delayed, or never arrive. They—the so-called "bottom billion"—have no access to justice, health and education and face rising food prices: how can such countries meet the MDGs?" (Costa, 2008)

Costa then asked the CCPCJ to participate in the UNGA's midterm review of the MDGs and to "undertak[e] measures so as to facilitate the realization of the MDGs in the next half period" using a "three-pronged approach," which involved using *evidence* to shape *policy*, which would in turn guide UNODC's *assistance* to governments. Costa was effectively advocating for a model of evidence-based policy making that would enable UNODC, as both a producer and a curator of evidence, to exert greater influence over the international crime policy agenda. The fact that UNODC was governed by the conservative CCPCJ posed an obstacle to Costa's "developmentalization" agenda, along with UNODC's ability to establish sustainable partnerships with more-progressive UN agencies. Adopting an evidence-based approach would therefore afford UNODC greater autonomy. Its technocratic expertise could then be deployed to shape the wider development agenda and secure voluntary funding from donor countries (Littoz-Monnet, 2017).

Costa's address had no immediate impact on the CCPCJ, which did not appear to participate in the midterm review of the MDGs. Nevertheless, during his final two years as executive director of UNODC, Costa persisted in his efforts to highlight the link between crime and development, and he found a receptive audience with the UN Security Council (UNSC) and the new secretary general, Ban Ki-moon. The significance of Costa's engagement with the UNSC during his final years cannot be overstated. For example, Costa addressed the UNSC in July 2009 and argued that trafficking and rule of law deficiencies were undermining progress toward the MDGs in West Africa. UNODC was at the time already active in the region, so his UNSC statement drew upon a threat assessment prepared by UNODC's Policy Analysis and Research Branch to evidence his claims (UNODC, 2009a). The meeting was attended by the secretary general and senior representatives of other influential UN agencies (UNODC, 2009b), and his message was seemingly well received. It not only led to greater cooperation between UNODC and UN peacekeeping agencies in West Africa but, more significantly, it prompted the UNSC to "hold periodic debates on the threat posed by organized crime to stability" (Costa, 2010, p. 5).

In February 2010 Costa was invited back to address the UNSC, and his speech explicitly emphasized the link between crime and the MDGs:

> Development is the best prevention. Throughout the world, prosperity and good governance are vaccines against violence. The Millennium Development Goals (MDGs) are the most effective antidote to crime, while crime prevention helps to reach the MDGs. (Costa, 2010, p. 2)

Costa concluded by praising the UNSC for "supporting growing cooperation" between UN agencies in its efforts to address the "crosscutting nature of organized crime" and its intersections with conflict and development (p. 5). At the same event, the president of the UNSC issued a statement acknowledging that transnational organized crime was an international security threat and called for "the coordination of United Nations actions, including those of its agencies, funds and programs, in order to enhance the effectiveness of appropriate international efforts" (Araud, 2010).

Addressing the UNSC was a power play by Costa, who was reportedly fed up with the inaction of the Vienna commissions and the political constraints they imposed on UNODC. He had by this point fallen out of favor with many influential donors who felt that his "strong moral conviction"[6] was a liability, and that he could not be controlled. Costa's willingness to push boundaries, name and shame countries, and draw attention to problems that directly threatened the economic interests of elites from developed and developing countries was described by several of his former colleagues. This was also evident from both his advocacy and engagement during his final years. For example, in his preface to the 2009 West Africa report, Costa called upon developed countries to take responsibility for the fact that demand for illicit goods originated with them (Costa in UNODC, 2009a, p. 1). He also called attention to the harmful activities of private transnational corporations that "use[d] West Africa as a dumping ground for weapons, waste, and fake medicines." Most controversially, he argued, "Private companies that are complicit in this illegal business should be named, shamed, and banned, and codes of conduct more rigorously enforced."

Later that year, Costa told the *Observer* (a British newspaper) that following the 2008 Global Financial Crisis (GFC), $352 billion USD in criminal proceeds was laundered by commercial banks that faced a major liquidity crisis and needed a quick cash injection. His argument was that banks were not only complicit in illicit activities but that these illicit transactions actually rescued some banks (Syal, 2009). The British Bankers Association, also quoted in the article, challenged this claim and questioned its evidence base. Costa provided this evidence in a 2010 report titled *The Globalization of Crime*, for which he penned a particularly controversial foreword that openly criticized the global capitalist order:

> In the past two decades, insufficient regulation and unchecked growth, together with the internet and free trade zones, have enabled abuse of the economic and financial systems. (Costa in UNODC, 2010, p. iii)

This statement directly challenged the Manichaean construction of transnational organized crime and corruption as threats to the neoliberal global economy by suggesting that illicit financial activities were in fact an integral element of it. Furthermore, the emphasis on "insufficient regulation and unchecked growth" implied that leading architects and proponents of the neoliberal growth model were responsible for creating conditions that enabled, and perhaps even encouraged, "abuse[s]" to occur. This represented a significant, albeit temporary, departure from the traditional construction of the crime-development nexus as a Southern problem.

In light of Costa's controversial statements and advocacy methods, it is understandable why the conservative CCPCJ did not support greater autonomy for UNODC. Costa was a threat to an already fragile consensus, and adopting an evidence-based approach to policy making meant the CCPCJ would need to acknowledge and discuss these structural and institutional issues. This risked causing reputational damage for both donor and recipient countries, particularly if UNODC's evidence-based assessments implicated powerful elites and institutions in illicit activities. Drawing attention to problems such as "insufficient regulation" or "abuse[s] of the economic and financial systems" at the national and regional level could also potentially deter investors and therefore impede economic growth. In a global capitalist economy, this serves nobody's interests. Perhaps most significantly, drawing attention to the links between licit and illicit markets threatened the legitimacy of a global economic order that, thanks to the GFC, was already in a fragile state.

Costa's second term concluded in 2010, and to nobody's surprise, he was not reappointed. By this point, however, the UNSC and the secretary general had already come to embrace the idea that combating crime and corruption was essential for promoting the rule of law, and that this was the cornerstone of sustainable development. As discussed in the following chapter, this provided UNODC with a platform to expand its regional programs, attract voluntary contributions, and contribute to the negotiation of Sustainable Development Goal 16.

Chapter Eight

Global Crime Governance, Rule of Law, and the Sustainable Development Goals

By 2010 the success of the Millennium Development Goals (MDGs) was widely debated. There had certainly been some demonstrable achievements, but critics argued these were uneven (Fehling, Nelson, & Venkatapuram, 2013), slow (Gwatkin, 2005), and immeasurable (James, 2006). The process by which the final list of MDGs had been formulated was also criticized, and dependency theorists argued that a liberal development framework could not address historically-rooted structural inequities (Amin, 2006). It was clear that the MDGs faced a crisis of legitimacy and a fresh approach was needed to revitalize the post-2015 development agenda (Wilkinson & Hulme, 2012). The successor to the MDGs was the Sustainable Development Goals (SDGs), which, as noted at the beginning of this book, include SDG 16 and several other targets that relate to crime, corruption, and violence. These issues had not previously featured in the MDGs, so this chapter sets out to account for the institutionalization of the crime-development nexus as a fixture of the United Nations (UN) system and the SDGs between 2010 and 2015. As discussed in the first part of this chapter, UNODC's research and advocacy under Costa created opportunities for the agency to expand its network of regional- and country-based operations, establish new donor relationships and partnerships, and ultimately mainstream these issues into the SDG negotiations. All of these activities evidence the institutionalization of the crime-development nexus and UNODC's ascent within the UN development community. At the same time, our analysis suggests that during this period, UNODC's efforts to expand its operational portfolio reinforced the depoliticization of the crime-development nexus and reverted to a "Southern" as opposed to a "global" framing of the problem. The second part of the chapter then proceeds to reflect on how the crime-development nexus was shaped by the wider SDG negotiations, along with UNODC's behind-the-scenes contributions to this process.

"DELIVERING AS ONE"

According to Robert Cox (1969, p. 205) "executive leadership may prove to be the most critical single determinant of the growth in scope and authority of international organization." This had certainly been the case in UNODC's early years. Pino Arlacchi's leadership put the organization in a precarious position during its formative years. Antonio Maria Costa's advocacy was seemingly impactful, but also provocative. Both directors were large personalities who actively attempted to shape the organization's identity and align its strategic focus with their interests, while negotiating institutional developments within the UN system and the ideological and material conditions of their times. Costa's successor, Yury Fedotov (2010–2018), was, by contrast, a muted personality, and his legacy at UNODC suggests that the importance of executive leadership as a determinant of an organization's success or failure should not be overstated.

Fedotov is remembered as a conservative director who played by the rules and prioritized diplomacy over advocacy. A career-long Russian diplomat, Fedotov was risk-averse and politically astute. He was regarded by former colleagues as more of an administrator than a leader, and few could articulate his overall strategic vision for the organization or his personal views on crime, corruption, or drug control. One of his former colleagues described his leadership as "not visible." His appointment (and reappointment) can therefore be interpreted as an attempt by the Commission on Crime Prevention and Criminal Justice (CCPCJ) to reestablish its control over UNODC and realign its research and advocacy with the Manichaean distinction between licit and illicit economies, and an international crime policy agenda that framed transnational organized crime and corruption as Southern problems with global implications.

None of this is to suggest, however, that the Fedotov years were a dark period in UNODC's history. Between 2010 and 2018, the organization continued to elevate its profile in the UN system, expanded its operations, and increased its voluntary contributions from donors for crime-related activities by 166% (see figure 7.1 on p. 152). Depoliticizing UNODC's portfolio and shifting the focus exclusively to the South was probably a contributing factor, but these successes were also greatly facilitated by two key interrelated factors. The first links back to the UN Security Council's (UNSC's) formal recognition of the need for enhanced cooperation between UN agencies to address the problem of transnational organized crime. The second relates to the efforts of senior managers at UNODC to champion organizational reforms and promote greater alignment between UNODC and other UN agencies.

In 2010 UNODC's portfolio gained visibility due to the significant international attention that maritime piracy in the Horn of Africa was receiving (UNSC, 2010). There was certainly a political dimension to this problem that resonated with the dominant "dark side of globalization" narrative, but this was not simply a "moral panic" (Cohen, 1972). From a political economy standpoint, this was "the single greatest maritime threat since the Second World War" (Murphy, 2011, p. 6) because it disrupted international trade and commerce. UNODC's analysis of this problem, outlined in chapter 8 of its controversial 2010 report, *The Globalization of Crime*, highlighted its complexity and its economic and political roots. Notably, it associated the causes of piracy with a lack of legitimate opportunities, which rendered it "a rational vocational choice" (UNODC, 2010, p. 200). The report further argued that it could not be addressed through "target hardening" or naval interventions. Rather a comprehensive strategy that combined state-building, rule of law promotion, economic development, and "specific [domestic] measures aimed at enhancing law enforcement effectiveness" was required (p. 200). The report offered no concrete prescriptions for how this might be achieved, but this analysis reinforced the UNSC's recognition of the need to enhance cooperation between UNODC and UN agencies responsible for peacekeeping and development. This suggests that UNODC was not only instrumental in amplifying the visibility and significance of its portfolio but that its efforts aligned with the ongoing aspiration of the UN to "deliver [the MDGs] as one" (quoting Annan, 2006).

In March 2011 Secretary General Ban Ki-Moon established a UN System Task Force on Transnational Organized Crime and Drug Trafficking (henceforth "Task Force"). A small group of senior managers at UNODC reportedly advocated for the creation of the Task Force because they recognized that a lack of coordination with other UN agencies impeded UNODC's ability to secure funding for regional and national-level activities. The aims of the Task Force were therefore "to integrate responses to TOC into the peacekeeping, security, and development activities of the UN" and "to raise awareness and mobilize collective action against the growing and multifaceted threat of TOC and drug trafficking" (UN Task Force, 2012, p. 3).

The creation of the Task Force was a symbolic victory for UNODC, which co-chaired it alongside the Department of Political Affairs (UNDPA), which by this point had developed an interest in organized crime in the context of peacebuilding and transitional societies (McMullin, 2009). Several other UN agencies were also represented, including, most notably, the United Nations

Development Programme (UNDP). Cooperation between UNODC and these other actors had previously been patchy at best, and, with the exception of the World Bank, we encountered little prior evidence of sustained partnerships, particularly at the regional and country levels, where UNDP viewed UNODC as a competitor in the human security space. For the secretary general, part of the impetus for organizing the Task Force was to develop a model of partnership that would support comprehensive, multiagency approaches to addressing crime and corruption within the context of core UN activities linked with peacebuilding and development.

From UNODC's perspective, the problem was that UNDP managed regional and country-level development coordination and donor relations. Previously, this had limited UNODC's ability to develop its operational capabilities on the ground, so field representatives reportedly bypassed UN resident coordinators and approached donors directly to secure funding for specific projects. UNODC was not the only UN agency doing this, but UNDP's gatekeeping was regarded by multiple participants as an obstacle to interagency cooperation and UNODC's ability to develop, finance, and coordinate effective regional programs. Much of UNODC's work on the ground therefore consisted of patchwork attempts to address specific issues that responded to local needs or aligned with donor interests. In other cases, projects were simply developed in relation to specific funding opportunities of which UNODC's country- and regional-based staff became aware. The UNODC managers who pushed for the Task Force recognized this to be problematic, and they hoped that mainstreaming the UNODC's portfolio throughout the wider UN development system would support a more strategic and results-oriented approach.

The Task Force convened multiple times in 2011, yet documentary sources provide little insight into the nature of its deliberations. One participant did note that members of the Task Force had "widely divergent views and strategies and approaches to these issues," so it is unclear how productive these meetings were. For example, Fedotov's briefing on the Task Force to the UNSC in June 2011 provides no substantive details of the discussions or of any actual progress toward establishing a framework for enhanced cooperation (Fedotov in UNSC, 2011a). However, three months later, Helen Clark, chair of the UN Development Group (UNDG) and also the administrator of UNDP, together with Burton Lynn Pascoe (undersecretary general for UN-DPA) and Yury Fedotov, sent a jointly-authored letter to all of the Regional UNDG Teams and resident coordinators "invit[ing]" them "to integrate strategies for tackling transnational organized crime and illicit trafficking into their tools and policies" (Clark, Pascoe & Fedotov, 2011). This was to occur through:

Inviting members of the Task Force to provide briefings at the UNDG Regional Team meetings . . . ; Inviting representatives of the Task Force to Regional meetings of Resident Coordinators to explore ways in which the Task Force could support the efforts of country teams . . . ; Utilizing Task Force members" assessments (including the UNODC Regional Transnational Organized Crime Threat Assessments (TOCTA) to inform the upcoming [Common Country Analysis] and [UN Development Assistance Framework] processes; Adopting into your presentations on human security and development the relevant messages on organized crime as endorsed by the Secretary-General . . . ; Assisting in making Member States aware of the capacities that exist in the system to support their efforts to combat transnational organized crime. (Clark, Pascoe, & Fedotov, 2011)

This signaled that crime was now a UN development priority for regional and national stakeholders. It also validated the UNODC's status as a development partner with unique organizational capabilities that would support regional cooperation to address transnational criminal threats. The precise impacts of this letter are difficult to gauge, but in the months and years that followed, UNODC established or expanded multiple regional programs that contributed to its growth and increased its budget for crime-related activities.

THE REGIONAL PROGRAMS

Over the next few years, UNODC produced several threat assessment reports to illustrate the need for UNDG resident coordinators and governments to work with the organization to develop regional strategies for addressing transnational criminal problems. From our reading, the analyses presented in the reports are fairly compelling and well-evidenced, with multiple participants noting that UNODC's research capabilities had evolved quite significantly by this point. It is not our intention to scrutinize the data or analyses presented in these reports, but we note that they all focused on the Global South, or regions in transition. The reports were predictably funded by Western donors, both countries and IFIs, who had an ongoing, strategic interest in addressing specific criminal threats that were understood to originate in these regions. For example, a 2012 threat assessment, *Transnational Organized Crime in Central America and the Caribbean*, was funded by the Inter-American Development Bank, which was actively promoting and financing citizen security projects throughout the region (UNODC, 2012a; see also IADB, 2012). *Opiate Flows through Northern Afghanistan and Central Asia* was paid for by the United States,[1] Germany, and Turkey (UNODC, 2012b); *Transnational Organized Crime in East Asia and the Pacific* by Australia and

New Zealand (UNODC, 2013a); and *Transnational Organized Crime in West Africa* by France (UNODC, 2013b).

Collectively, these reports reinforced the idea that problems associated with transnational organized crime and corruption should be addressed through interventions that focus on the Global South. As noted above, this represented an important shift away from Costa's emphasis on the transnational and structural dimensions of these problems, both in relation to the legacy of colonialism (Costa in UNODC, 2005) and in the wake of the Global Financial Crisis (Costa in UNODC, 2010). These critical narratives were unappealing to Northern donors because they implied that transnational organized crime and corruption were endemic features of the current capitalist and transnational legal order, which they worked to construct and sustain. Furthermore, addressing the problems highlighted by Costa would necessitate following the money and shifting the focus of law enforcement and regulatory bodies from illicit to licit enterprises and sectors. This represented a significant risk to industry along with its political backers, including US President Barack Obama, who, in response to the Global Financial Crisis (GFC), provided taxpayer funded bailouts to banks, financial institutions, and transnational corporations in an attempt to stave off its consequences. European governments faced similar concerns, and it is reasonable to assume that other powerful Member States, including Russia and China, were more than happy to shift the attention of the international crime policy community, the media, regulators, and law enforcement agencies away from lucrative enterprises, industries, and financial flows.

Shifting the focus back to the Global South therefore neutralized a progressive, potentially even radical agenda for global crime governance that conflicted with the interests of global capital during a period of material and ideological crisis.

UNODC regional programs have since been established in Afghanistan/Central Asia, South East Asia and the Pacific, Central America and the Caribbean, West Africa, East Africa, and Southeastern Europe. In 2010 there was also an ill-fated attempt to develop a regional program on Drug Control, Crime Prevention, and Criminal Justice Reform in the Arab States. Each of the programs was/is led by a regional representative responsible for developing and implementing a regional strategy for addressing specific criminal threats that had been identified in the threat assessment reports in partnership with a range of actors, including donors (countries and IFIs), other international and regional organizations, governments, law enforcement agencies, and civil society. Each regional program has distinct modes of operating, funding models, and priorities, but the general approach is as follows: UNODC generates and collates *information* about regional threats, trends, and their causes.

The information informs regional and national *advocacy* to amplify awareness and generate political will to confront the threats. UNODC then works with governments to develop consistent *legal frameworks*, which ensure the issues are uniformly recognized and that states have a statutory obligation and authority to address them. Finally, UNODC supports *capacity building* to support enforcement and implementation through technical assistance work. Operational links provide UNODC with opportunities to *network* with agencies on the ground, identify new problems, and the cycle repeats itself (Douglas, 2013, slide 15).

Unsurprisingly, much of the documentation produced by UNODC's regional programs since 2011 references "development." For example, "sustainable development" is referenced in the opening paragraphs of the proposals for both the regional program in the Arab States and Central America and the Caribbean (see UNODC, 2011, p. 1; UNODC, 2012a, p. 7). There is rarely much substance to these references, and the documents provide little if any theoretical insight into exactly how specific criminal problems and threats in these regions conflict with "sustainable development" or "growth" (noting that the two issues are frequently linked and conflated). Our sense is that providing such detail was probably unnecessary, because by 2011 the issue linkage was already established and widely accepted. Furthermore, it was not in UNODC's interest to define "development" or engage with wider political debates, because combating transnational organized crime and corruption, promoting human security, and upholding the rule of law could simply be presented as technical matters that benefited all countries, regardless of their political and ideological leanings.

UNODC's efforts to depoliticize its work under Fedotov were seemingly effective because the newly established regional programs appealed to Northern and Southern governments alike. From 2011 onward, UNODC's pool of potential donors began to expand and diversify. For example, UNODC's work in Afghanistan and Central Asia between 2011 and 2014 was financed by a diverse group of countries, including Canada, Denmark, France, Germany, Italy, Japan, Norway, Russia, Sweden, the UK, and the United States (UNODC, 2012b, p. 5). In Southeast Asia, the regional program managed to secure financial contributions from the Association of Southeast Asian Nations (ASEAN), Australia, Canada, China, the EU, Germany, Japan, Republic of Korea, New Zealand, Norway, Sweden, Thailand, the UK, the United States, and Vietnam (UNODC, 2013a). Here the major concern was the production and trafficking of opium and methamphetamine in the Golden Triangle, which bordered Myanmar, Laos, and Thailand. Suppressing these activities was a priority for Northern donor countries where these illicit commodities were sold, but also for governments throughout the region, which had adopted their own draconian drug policies and viewed the drug trade as a source of violence and corruption. The impetus for Southeast Asian countries to invest resources in a UNODC-led regional strategy was therefore a product of their desire to maintain their reputations as stable, safe, and investor-friendly business environments. From a security standpoint, many of these governments also recognized that the illicit drug trade provided dissident groups with a source of revenue, thereby highlighting the potential link between organized crime, terrorism, and conflict. All of these potential consequences were (and continue to be) evidenced by UNODC's research and advocacy activities to attract funding from governments in both the core and the periphery. For example, the current regional coordinator in Southeast Asia has been particularly successful in such advocacy, publishing several articles in international media outlets, including CNN, about the threat of transnational organized crime in the region (e.g., Douglas, 2018).

Cooperation between UNODC and regional associations like ASEAN has also created political pressure on governments to at least participate in these partnerships, and this helps legitimize internationally-driven law reform initiatives and create pressure for policy harmonization. This appears to be consistent with what Shaffer and Aaronson (2020) have characterized as the transnational legal ordering of criminal justice. More significantly, from a political economy standpoint, it also speaks to the hegemonic influence of the free market ideology in countries like Vietnam that have undergone (economic) liberalization and actively participate in multilateral governance in the region. It also highlights that, as a consequence of their rapid economic growth, developing countries like Thailand and Vietnam are now in a position to make a financial contribution toward UNODC's work, and are expected to do so. It would, however, be incorrect to simply reduce the UNODC's regional programs to a strategy of "responsibilizing" developing countries and convincing them to pay for projects that simply advance Northern interests. This may occur in certain instances, but participants stressed that this model affords developing countries greater influence over regional priorities, and Northern countries remain willing to contribute funds so long as the programs are deemed successful and broadly align with their strategic interests.

There are of course governments that do not wish to be the "beneficiaries" of Northern aid or participate in North-South partnerships. UNODC has therefore developed alternative models for establishing and financing operations in these contexts. For example, UNODC's proposal for the ill-fated regional program in the Arab States emphasized the benefits of South-South cooperation when it came to addressing transnational criminal problems (UNODC, 2010, p. 5). This implied that Arab States could develop a regional framework for cooperation that preserved their cultural autonomy, as long as they were able and willing to pay for it. The anticipated involvement of wealthy countries like Qatar, Saudi Arabia, and the United Arab Emirates meant that this was, in principle, materially viable, and UNODC stood to benefit from its position as an intermediary between the West and the Arab world, particularly because of its ability to strategically de-emphasize certain issues or aspects of its portfolio that were potentially controversial in this context (for example, human rights). The regional program of Arab States never transpired due to the Arab Spring, but UNODC has since established a presence in the region.

UNODC's relationship with Qatar is probably most significant in this regard because it highlights the diversification of the donor pool and the influence that non-Western donors can potentially have on the international crime policy agenda. Notably, Qatar hosted the 2015 UN Crime Congress and subsequently provided financial support for UNODC's Global Education 4 Justice Programme (E4J), which "seeks to prevent crime and promote a culture of lawfulness through education activities designed for primary, secondary and tertiary levels" (UNODC, n.d.). The reference to a "culture of lawfulness" is particularly noteworthy here because this idea, which can be traced back to Palermo's war on organized crime in the 1980s, was later embraced by American neoconservatives in the 2000s, who advocated mobilizing civic and religious education to promote "law-abiding, values-oriented citizenship" (Godson, 2000, p. 97). Its inclusion in the E4J Programme and the Doha Declaration adopted at the 2015 Congress signifies its universal appeal, but some of the "old-timers" we interviewed expressed concerns about the concept, noting that it did not include an explicit emphasis on "human rights" or other values that aligned with the UN's liberal internationalist outlook. From UNODC's perspective, however, the concept is strategically useful because it avoids politically contentious debates about the meaning of the "rule of law" by simply promoting a world where "the average person believes that legal norms are either a fundamental part of justice or provide the gateway to attain justice and that such a system enhances the quality of life of individuals and society as a whole" (Godson, 2000, p. 93; also quoted in Watson et al., 2020). The ascent of this concept as a staple of the international crime policy agenda is significant because it speaks to the fragility of the transnational legal order and, by extension, UNODC's ability to provide *global* leadership.

For countries like Qatar, the benefits of providing political and material support to UNODC are primarily symbolic rather than strategic. In other words, publicly supporting international efforts to address transnational organized crime and promote a "culture of lawfulness" offers a simple and relatively cost-effective way of signaling that the state is part of the solution rather than the problem. Functional cooperation (real or symbolic) is of course welcomed by organizations like UNODC and the West, even if countries like Qatar are less willing to embrace a thick definition of the rule of law. From a global governance standpoint, "cultural differences" are generally tolerable so long as countries are willing to participate in the global capitalist economy and do not represent a risk to regional or international stability. The increasingly flexible nature of the transnational legal order, together with the need for liberal actors to make concessions in order to sustain multilateral institutions that fundamentally serve their interests, is also evident in relation to the negotiation of SDG 16, discussed below.

NEGOTIATING SUSTAINABLE DEVELOPMENT GOAL 16

The SDG negotiation process was one of the most ambitious, inclusive, and successful exercises of deliberative agenda setting and consensus building in the history of global governance (Dodds, Donoghue, & Leiva Roesch, 2016; Browne, 2017; Kamau, Chasek, & O'Connor, 2018). It was particularly remarkable because the negotiations took place at a time when multilateralism was in a state of crisis due to the enduring effects of the GFC, a growing international backlash against neoliberal globalization, and the fragmentation of traditional political alliances within the UNGA (Kamau, Chasek, & O'Connor, 2018, pp. 20–27). Negotiating a consensus-based, post-2015 development agenda that was "action–oriented, concise and easy to communicate, limited in number, aspirational, global in nature and universally applicable to all countries, while simultaneously taking into account different national realities, capacities and levels of development and respecting national policies and priorities" (Rio+20, 2012, p. 63) was a monumental challenge.

Several issues generated significant debate, but the most controversial goal was probably SDG 16 (Bergling & Jin, 2015). As noted in the previous chapter, the Millennium Declaration had acknowledged the link between security and development, but this was not reflected in the MDGs. Throughout the 2000s, the UN's interest in the link between the rule of law and development grew, particularly following the publication of *In Larger Freedom* by then–secretary general Kofi Annan (Annan, 2005). Subsequently, the idea that "the advancement of the rule of law at the national and international levels is essential for the realization of sustained economic growth, sustainable development, the eradication of poverty and hunger" (UNGA, 2006, p. 1) was reaffirmed annually by UNGA resolutions.

UNODC benefited from and advanced to the rule of law agenda at the UN, but other agencies, including UNDP, the UN DPKO, World Bank, and civil society organizations, were also instrumental in driving this. Member states, particularly donor countries from the Global North, also came to embrace the idea that peace, security, and the rule of law were obstacles to the realization of the MDGs. The point is that by the early 2010s, there was nothing particularly novel or radical about these issue linkages. Nevertheless, matters relating to security and the rule of law were seemingly de-emphasized in the early deliberations concerning the legacy of the MDGs that shaped the formulation of the post-2015 development agenda. This is evident from the content of the 2009 UNGA resolution that established the Rio+20 Conference (UNGA, 2009), the agenda for the 2010 UN Summit on the MDGs (UNDPI, 2010), and the *2010 MDG Report* (UN, 2010). This suggests that circa 2010, there was limited consensus that issues associated with security and rule of law should feature within a post-2015 development agenda. So how did SDG 16 find its place on the menu?

The answer is complicated because the SDG negotiations were shaped by multiple processes and inputs over a three-year period (2012–2015).[2] These influences included a UN System Task Team (2012); the Rio+20 Conference (2012); a UNGA resolution recognizing the link between rule of law and sustainable development (2012); a High-Level Panel established by the secretary general (2013); an international survey (2013–2014); and an Open Working Group (OWG) consisting of 70 countries (sharing 30 seats), with input from civil society and briefings provided by a UN Technical Support Team (UN TST). These formal activities were also shaped by informal advocacy and diplomatic interventions that took place behind the scenes and are thus poorly documented. It is beyond the scope of this book to detail the SDG negotiations, but the brief overview presented below highlights how the UN Secretariat, including UNODC, helped facilitate them. It also illuminates the wider significance of SDG 16 and the political debates to which it gave rise.

KEY INFLUENCES

Following the 2010 MDG Summit, the secretary general established a UN Task Team composed of more than 50 UN agencies and other international organizations "to support UN system-wide preparations for the post-2015 UN development agenda, in consultation with all stakeholders" (UN Task Team, 2012, front matter). This included several agencies with a long-standing interest in bridging the gap between security, human rights, and development. The Task Team was co-chaired by UNDP, but UNODC was also involved. The Task Team produced thematic think pieces on a range of issues, including "Peace and security" and "Governance and development."[3] Its final report, published in June 2012, concluded, "The MDGs also did not adequately address issues of . . . peace and security, governance, the rule of law and human rights" (p. 7) and that "peace and security" represented a key component of an "integrated framework for realizing the 'future we want for all' in the post-2015 UN development agenda" (p. 24). Crime was not a major focus of the report, but UNODC's portfolio is explicitly acknowledged in paragraph 91, which references the idea that crime (framed as a threat to human security) is an obstacle to development (p. 32).

Later that month, more than 45,000 people representing 188 countries and 3 observers, plus representatives from civil society organizations, attended the Rio+20 Conference to develop a universal vision for a post-2015 sustainable development agenda (Rio+20, 2012). As noted above, one of the major criticisms of the MDGs was that they had been drafted by a group of UN elites, behind closed doors. Several issues that had been included in the UNGA's Millennium Declaration had therefore been omitted, without consultation or explanation. Enhancing the legitimacy of the post-2015 development agenda was seen as an imperative for the UN, and this necessitated an inclusive, transparent, and participatory process for articulating the post-2015 agenda (Dodds, Donoghue & Leiva Roesch, 2016). Rio+20 kickstarted this process and its outcome document, *The Future We Want*, identified a list of focus areas to guide the OWG negotiations and provide a framework for formulating specific sustainable development goals and targets (Kamau, Chasek & O'Connor, 2018).

The Rio+20 outcome document acknowledged that "democracy, good governance and the rule of law, at the national and international levels, as well as an enabling environment, are essential for sustainable development" (Rio+20, 2012, p. 2). However, it did not explicitly identify peace and security or the rule of law as a sustainable development focus areas in their own right. The decision to create a stand-alone focus area on "Conflict prevention, post-conflict peacebuilding and the promotion of durable peace, rule of law and governance" was therefore an afterthought, and it was initially opposed by some members of the OWG, as discussed below.

In response to a recommendation put forth in the Rio+20 report, the secretary general also convened a 27-member High-Level Panel in July 2012 "to advise on the global development agenda beyond 2015" (UN, 2012). The Panel met three times in 2012–2013 and submitted its own recommendations to the secretary general in a May 2013 report titled *A New Global Partnership* (High-Level Panel, 2013). The High-Level Panel concluded that issues relating to the rule of law and security should be incorporated into the post-2015 development agenda and proposed two stand-alone goals to "10. Ensure Good Governance and Effective Institutions" and "11. Ensure Stable and Peaceful Societies" (High-Level Panel, 2013, pp. 50–53). The High-Level Panel also recommended that "justice- and security-related targets should be cross-applied to several other goals" (Bergling & Jin, 2015, p. 438), thereby emphasizing the intersecting nature of security and development issues.

The UNGA also convened a High-Level Meeting on the Rule of Law in September 2012. The key outcome of this meeting was the adoption of a declaration that formally acknowledged "that the rule of law and development are strongly interrelated and mutually reinforcing, that the advancement of the rule of law at the national and international levels is essential for sustained and inclusive economic growth, sustainable development" (UNGA, 2012, p. 2). There was nothing particularly novel about this statement, which echoed previous UNGA resolutions concerning the rule of law, but its timing is noteworthy because it coincided with the work of the High-Level Panel and preparations for the OWG sessions. It is safe to assume that this political statement from the UNGA helped to further legitimize the ex post facto decision to include a thematic discussion area on these issues in the OWG negotiations, and multiple supporters of the High-Level Panel's recommendations would reference the "Declaration" in their OWG statements.

A final factor that seemingly validated the decision to include this stand-alone focus area was the preliminary results of the UN's MY World Global Survey, launched in January 2013. The survey asked people around the world to select the six issues that mattered most to them and their families from 16 different options.[4] A summary of preliminary results based on more than one million responses was published in May 2013, and this was cited as strong evidence that people around the world wanted "an honest and responsive government" (third) and "protection against crime and violence" (seventh; see UN, 2013b, p. 8). The preliminary results were formally recognized during the High-Level Session of a Global Dialogue on Rule of Law and Post-2015 Development Agenda, held in September 2013, where the UN's deputy secretary stated, "Delivering the rule of law through strong institutions is paramount to development" (Eliasson, 2013). They were also presented to members of the OWG in an issue brief prepared by the UNDG (2014), which argued that the MY World Survey highlighted global demand for "a stand-alone goal to reduce violence, promote freedom from fear, and encourage sustainable peace—one that goes beyond the absence of violence to address prevention and the drivers of peace." The survey is particularly significant because it supplied empirical evidence that these were universal concerns. This was politically significant because it made it difficult for developing countries that were resistant to the inclusion of this focus area to deny that there was a problem, and it also framed the problem as a *global* issue, which helped to preemptively deflect the critique that this was just another attempt by the North to securitize development in the South.

THE POLITICS OF SDG 16

Collectively, these processes established a fundamental consensus that the interlinkages between security, governance, and sustainable development were important. Countries that participated in the OWG sessions would therefore, at the very least, need to acknowledge this. Nevertheless, there was still initial disagreement about whether issues relating to security and governance should be formally incorporated into the post-2015 development agenda. Issues that aligned with UNODC's portfolio clearly sat within this focus area, but they were rarely the focus of these debates. Rather, much of the debate centered on broader issues, such as defining or operationalizing the "rule of law," and whether peace and security should be framed as the foundation for sustainable development or vice versa. Any bureaucratic entity is "organizationally bound to try and get try as much of my organization or its issues onto the agenda,"[5] but there was never any prospect of establishing a stand-alone goal that directly aligned with UNODC's mandates. For this reason, it focused its energy on advocating for explicit recognition of issues relating to governance and security in the SDGs, which it could then latch on to.

Recognizing the controversy surrounding these issues, the co-chairs of the OWG and their support team scheduled "Conflict prevention, post-conflict peacebuilding and the promotion of durable peace, rule of law and governance" as the final thematic discussion at the eighth OWG session in February 2014 (Kamau, Chasek & O'Connor, 2018, p. 81). Our content analysis of country statements presented at this session suggests three positions were evident from this discussion.[6] First, donor countries from the Global North overwhelmingly endorsed the High-Level Panel's recommendations to create stand-alone goals relating to peace and security and governance. Their statements emphasized that conflict, violence, and weak institutions represented significant impediments to sustainable development and they referenced the 2012 UNGA Declaration and MY World Survey results to evidence that a mandate already existed to address these issues within the SDG framework. Most of their statements centered primarily on the link between conflict and poverty, which implied that these issues were particularly pronounced in the Global South. This was not coincidental, because for years Northern donors had become increasingly frustrated about the misuse of aid funds and the failure of their investment to deliver results. Conflict was obviously a significant problem in this regard, but one UN executive we interviewed explained that corruption and weak institutions were also perceived as major obstacles to delivering results:

[T]he necessity of including SDG16 was to have aid become more efficient. You can drop loads of money in a country and see that only 10%–15% perhaps is reaching the most vulnerable . . . if you're an international donor and you're in an austerity crisis, you're asking, "How can I make my aid more efficient? How can I stop illicit financial flows? How can I deal with the corruption issues in those conduits?"

From the perspective of Northern donors, who remained committed to the liberal internationalist project, this suggests there was a functional imperative to include these issues in the post-2015 development agenda.

At the same time, Northern donors recognized that they could not explicitly frame these problems as exclusive to developing countries, so they described "violence" as a universal issue that also affected people in developed countries, particularly women and children. The statement from the United States (also on behalf of Canada and Israel) provides an excellent illustration of this (Cousens, 2014). It starts by asserting that "countries affected by conflict have been the most trapped by persistent poverty and the most impeded from reaching the Millennium Development Goals." It then describes the cross-border dimension of these problems and suggests they are exacerbated by "external stresses like illicit flows, organized crime, and trafficking," which also "impede progress in otherwise peaceful societies." It then proceeds to qualify this by suggesting, "this is a universal issue," and evidences this by stating:

[A]ccording to UNODC, the United States has a higher homicide rate not only than our two teammates but than half the countries in the United Nations, and cities and communities with higher homicide rates are generally also economically disadvantaged.

This message was consistent with the liberal internationalist outlook of the Obama administration: We are all in this together. Politically, this framing was important because it provided Northern donors with a means of neutralizing the argument that they were attempting to create an agenda *for* developing countries, rather than a set of *global* goals, which they would also be accountable for implementing (as prescribed by the Rio+20 outcome document).

The second camp was composed of those countries that resisted the High-Level Panel's recommendations to create stand-alone goals for political and ideological reasons. The overarching concern among these countries, which included the G77 and China and what remained of the Non-Aligned Movement (represented by Iran), was preserving sovereignty and resisting the securitization of the sustainable development agenda. Whereas Northern countries framed peace and the rule of law as the foundation of sustainable development, dissenting countries emphasized that economic and social development was a prerequisite for peace and security (e.g., China, Indonesia, and Kazakhstan; see Murniningtyas, 2014). Accordingly, these countries used their statements to call attention to structural problems that impeded progress with the MDGs, and they described inequality as the primary cause of instability and violence. Several countries, including Bangladesh, also argued at this meeting that the "democratization of the global financial architecture" was crucial for addressing inequality and creating conditions conducive to peace and stability (Rahman, 2014). Others emphasized that the rule of law was not just a domestic issue and argued that its international dimensions must also be acknowledged and respected by powerful countries if it was going to be incorporated into the post-2015 agenda. Contrary to the messaging of the first camp, the argument here was that structural and systemic reforms were necessary for promoting sustainable development in the Global South. Reducing the shortcomings of the MDGs to issues relating to conflict or corruption was therefore framed as an attempt to deflect attention away from the issues that really mattered. It was also seen as an attempt by the Global North to advance the neoliberal project through the post-2015 development framework. As discussed below, there is a degree of truth to both critiques, at least from a political economy perspective.

Finally, a third camp of countries expressed skepticism about how these issues were framed in the preparatory materials and questioned how abstract ideas like the "rule of law" could be translated into targets and indicators. The nature and degree of their skepticism varied, as did their political orientations. For example, countries like Nicaragua and Brazil (which initially vehemently opposed the inclusion of these issues on political grounds) argued that "conflict" and "violence" were distinct phenomena, and cultural differences between member states meant there was no basis for developing universal indicators to measure the "rule of law" or "good governance." Similar concerns were also raised by the troika of Argentina, Bolivia, and Ecuador. However, countries like Romania and Poland, which were politically aligned more closely with the Northern proponents of what would become SDG16, suggested that the question was not *if* these issues should be included, but *how*.

THE ROLE OF THE SECRETARIAT

Several countries referred to the Secretariat's briefing materials in their statements at the eighth OWG session, so it is worth considering how the TST, composed of different UN entities, contributed to the negotiations. In relation to SDG 16, the work of the TST was seemingly led by the Peacebuilding Support Office (UN PBSO) and the Rule of Law Unit with support from various agencies, including UNDP and UNODC. For example, in the lead-up to the

OWG sessions, UNDP produced an initial concept note (UNDP, 2013) and organized workshops about rule of law and development in 2013, including a Global Dialogue on Rule of Law and the Post-2015 Development Agenda in September 2013. UNODC participated and later organized a follow-up workshop, which generated a report that accounted for possibilities for developing SDG 16 indicators (UNODC, 2013c). This report once again highlights how UNODC's research capabilities supported its advocacy, this time by allowing it to demonstrate that it was in fact possible to operationalize and measure concepts like violence and corruption. This argument was incorporated into the final TST briefing paper and repeatedly referenced by Northern proponents. UNODC's technical expertise and research capabilities also explain why the agency was ultimately appointed as the UN "Custodian" for SDG 16 and several crosscutting targets, despite its diminutive size.

Behind the scenes, UN agencies also used their diplomacy and their advocacy skills to help generate support for including these issues. One participant explained that this had to be done very carefully, because "the one thing which Secretary General Ban was very clear on was this was a member state owned process." Therefore, UNODC and other UN agencies involved with the TST actively supported countries from the OWG that advocated for the inclusion of what would ultimately become SDG 16. The same participant explained:

> [W]e would reach out to [key influencers in the OWG], you know, to sort of inject some of our arguments. And then we also kept track of the states that were kind of opposed to including any of these concerns into the new agenda and look at the arguments they were making and provide responses. . . . So there was a lot of overt input that we provided into the negotiation process and there was also a lot of, shall we say, informal inputs that went through individual level consultations with certain missions and at all levels . . . there was obviously no reason to expect that our health related mandates . . . would not make the agenda because these are classical development concerns. . . . So we looked at the rule of law related issues and within that there was the substantive sort of aspect of it, which was making the arguments about why working within a framework of the rule of law, looking at issues related to security and justice and corruption are all, in one sense, preconditions for sustainable well-being but also components of sustainable well-being. . . . So there was a substantive line of argumentation. And then there was more research statistics driven, to sort of, a stream of work, where we were engaged in showing that these issues can be measured, that we have been measuring these issues in the past, that we have developed standard methodologies.

These activities illustrate how international organizations shape the international policy agenda in ways that reflect their technical capabilities and advance their bureaucratic interests (Barnett & Finnemore, 1999). This is well established, but rarely acknowledged by the UN itself for reasons that are hopefully obvious by now. The influence of the Secretariat as a knowledge producer, advocate, and diplomat cannot be ignored, and without the UN's leadership, it seems unlikely that negotiating a global development agenda with any semblance of legitimacy would have been possible. This is readily acknowledged by scholars of global governance, who argue that despite, and perhaps even because of, the current crises of multilateralism, the UN remains more relevant than ever when it comes to sustaining a liberal order (Browne & Weiss, 2014).

BUSINESS AND INDUSTRY

At the same time, it would be misleading to suggest that the SDG negotiations were fundamentally responsive to the bureaucratic interests of the UN Secretariat. Indeed, political economists and global governance scholars have long argued that the work of international organizations typically aligns with the interests of powerful state actors, at least when those powerful actors are committed to advancing the liberal internationalist project. It is therefore no coincidence that the bureaucratic interests of the UN agencies, including UNODC, were more closely aligned with those of Northern donors, who were in favor of SDG 16 and financed their operations, than developing countries, which questioned and opposed it.

From a political economy standpoint, Northern proponents of SDG 16 remained fundamentally committed to preserving the post–Washington Consensus and rebuilding a global economy that would support their recovery from the GFC. As longtime subscribers to the "development as growth" model, their argument remained that a healthy global economy would generate material benefits for countries and people in the Global South. From a liberal internationalist perspective, nation-states would therefore remain the building blocks of a healthy global economy, but they must use their sovereign authority to create conditions that support economic and social development. In a global capitalist economy, the argument is that this necessitates the creation of a business-friendly environment, the cornerstones of which are liberal economic policies, effective legal and regulatory systems that support international commerce and ensure predictability, and strong institutions that serve to minimize perceptions of risk for investors (see chapter 6). These assumptions were made explicit by the US delegate at the eighth OWG session, who stated, "[V]iolence and conflict, in addition to physical damage and the toll on human and social capital, create uncertainty about the future and undermine precisely the confidence that is necessary for economic activity and social support" (Cousens, 2014).

Similar arguments were subsequently presented by representatives from the Major Group for Business and Industry and Global Business Alliance. For example, during the 12th OWG session, the speaker for the Major Group for Business and Industry stated:

> Goal 16 . . . should be among the top two or three goals. Countries can only develop and grow in a sustainable fashion if there is a solid foundation of peace, rule of law, and good governance. This is a crucial enabler of many of the other goals listed in this document, and thus moving it towards the top of the list reflects its critical importance. (Kantrow, 2014)

At the same meeting, the Major Group for Business and Industry also presented a list of proposed (tracked) changes to the OWG's provisional list of sustainable development goals and targets (Major Group: Business and Industry, 2014). This document is particularly revealing because it illustrates how the provisional list of goals and targets, negotiated through a deliberative process, were received by the interests of global capital. We note for example that the Major Group opposed the inclusion of a stand-alone goal to "Reduce inequality among social groups within and among countries" (SDG 10; see Major Group: Business and Industry, 2014, p. 14), and the only suggested edit to the basic wording of the other goals was in relation to SDG 16, where it proposed that the word "stable" should replace "peaceful" (p. 4). The wording of several individual targets was also scrutinized and the proposed changes were overwhelmingly oriented toward minimizing the potential impact of regulation, conservation, or social justice initiatives on free market capitalism. This is evident from the proposed changes to the provisional SDG 16 targets, which the Major Group hoped would fundamentally contribute to stable, business friendly environments (pp. 21–22). For example, it proposed adding the word "efficient" to the wording of Target 16.1; rewording Target 16.3 to focus specifically on "corruption," "bribery," and "illicit financial flows" (thereby omitting specific references to "money laundering and all forms of organized crime"); deleting Target 16.4 ("increase inclusive, participatory and representative decision making"); amalgamating several targets into a new target that linked access to justice with "independent and responsive justice systems including relating to property and tenure rights, employment, business, taxation, trade and finance"; and the deletion of provisional target 16.16, which called for the "establish[ment] and implement[ation] [of] effective regimes to decrease and provide accountability for corruption and bribery in all of its forms and at all levels."

It does not appear that the Major Group's suggestions had an impact on the final SDGs (see table I.1 on page 16), but the document highlights that the relationship between the interests of global capital and the rule of law is rather complex, particularly in the context of the sustainable development agenda. In other words, several elements of the OWG's negotiated vision for a more equitable and sustainable model of capitalist development were clearly perceived as a threat or inconvenience to business and industry, and the Major Group's proposals for SDG 16 were oriented toward constructing an unobstructive transnational legal order. From their perspective, this was necessary not only for achieving stability and managing risk but also for ensuring that the emergent capitalist order did not call attention to illicit, unethical, undemocratic, or otherwise harmful/lucrative activities that could be linked to transnational corporations or financial investors. This was particularly important because by 2014, the Manichaean distinction between the licit and illicit economies was already becoming increasingly difficult to uphold following high-profile scandals, including HSBC's involvement with money laundering activities for Mexican drug cartels, which attracted global media attention in 2012 (see Permanent Subcommittee on Investigations, 2012). Subsequent scandals, including the Volkswagen emission scandal and the Panama Papers leak, would seemingly confirm that "noble" concepts like the rule of law and good governance actually represent a double-edged sword for the interests of global capital.[7]

After the OWG sessions concluded, civil society organizations were also afforded a final opportunity to provide feedback on a revised list of SDG targets at the Stakeholder Preparatory Forum in January 2015. At this event, the interests of global capital were represented by the Global Business Alliance (GBA), which reaffirmed its position that rule of law is the "bedrock of our economies and societies" (Kennedy, 2015). The GBA further emphasized the role that business and industry must play as a "partner" when it came to actually implementing the SDG agenda, and described this as "an untapped resource pool, not only for technology and investment but also for successful approaches and know-hows." To this effect, it reiterated the importance of creating "enabling environments for economic growth [which] go hand in hand with the ideal conditions for productive partnerships that will be needed at all levels—national, regional, and global, i.e., at the UN level—to achieve the SDGs."

The GBA's statement reflects a growing emphasis on "partnership" between the UN and the private sector in global governance initiatives that had been encouraged by the Cardoso Report, published in 2004 (Panel of Eminent Persons, 2004). This was in turn reflective of an earlier shift from "government" to "governance" during the 1990s, which coincided with the rise of a neoliberal ideology that advocated that public institutions, namely the state, should do the "steering" while non-state actors, particularly the private sector, mobilizes its efficiencies to do the "rowing" (Osbourne & Gaebler, 1992). In the context of the SDGs, this partnership model was seen as beneficial for both sides. For the UN, it meant buy-in from the business sector for mandated initiatives, programs, and projects. It also afforded them access to a wealth of expertise, operational efficiencies, and potentially even capital, all of which were necessary for implementing this ambitious agenda.

For business and industry, the potential benefits extended beyond the prospect of securing lucrative contracts as "rowers." Indeed, the reality of the neoliberal partnership model is that the "rowers" actually play a role in shaping the policy agenda. In many instances, this enables them to influence the actual steering. In the SDG context, the emphasis on partnerships that is explicitly recognized in SDG 17 meant that business and industry (along with other civil society actors) would have a seat at the table. Insofar as the 20 million businesses around the world that were represented by the GBA controlled a vast amount of capital, their involvement would help ensure that various initiatives would be developed and implemented in such a way that would further entrench market-friendly governance in the developing world. Whether such initiatives would actually prove effective or advance the public good is of course a separate matter, and other civil society actors, including the Global Initiative Against Transnational Organized Crime, have subsequently complained that the opportunities for civil society engagement have in fact become more restricted following the adoption of the SDGs. We explore these, and other limitations of the crime-development nexus in the Conclusion.

Conclusion
Reimagining the Crime-Development Nexus

The crime-development nexus is an important element of Sustainable Development Goal (SDG) 16 with its focus on "Peace, justice and strong institutions." The assumption that crime represents an obstacle to economic growth and sustainability is also reflected in several other targets (see table I.1 on page 16). This represents a significant departure from the Millennium Development Goals (MDGs), which did not address these issues. As discussed in the previous chapters, the earlier omission helps to account for why the United Nations Office on Drugs and Crime (UNODC), other UN agencies, civil society actors, and Northern donors advocated for greater recognition of the link between the rule of law and development in the lead-up to the SDGs. More significantly, these advocacy efforts and the SDG negotiations illustrate that several issues that sit within SDG 16+ remain politically and ideologically contested. Thus, while there is broad recognition that crime and corruption threaten the rule of law and represent obstacles to economic growth and sustainable development, there is limited consensus about how, or even if, these issues should be addressed through international cooperation. Even today, one UN executive we interviewed acknowledged that SDG 16 is "still not fully accepted by many."

Historically, UNODC has attempted to negotiate these tensions by using its bureaucratic authority to frame crime and corruption as a universal threat. Its ability to generate, collate, and present evidence to support this issue linkage has benefitted these efforts greatly, and, with the exception of a momentary blip during the final years of Antonio Maria Costa's tenure as Executive Director, this has overwhelmingly reproduced an ahistorical and largely uncritical narrative about the origins of the global crime problem, which is rooted in colonialism and was later exacerbated by the structural and cultural effects of modernization and neoliberal globalization. Depoliticizing these issues and constructing transnational organized crime and corruption as Southern problems using narratives that reference the "dark side of globalization" or "uncivil society" has therefore enabled UNODC and its governing bodies, partners, competitors, and financial supporters to preserve a transnational legal order that is fundamentally oriented toward sustaining a global capitalist economy. This is consistent with Robert Cox's (1987, 1994) argument that international organizations and global governance networks fundamentally exist to preserve the status quo and shore up hegemony by evidencing the need for functional cooperation and deflecting attention away from the political economy of global problems.

At the same time, institutions like the United Nations (UN) may offer subordinate actors opportunities to actively contest and negotiate the status quo, albeit within a liberal ideological framework. As evident from our discussion of the New International Economic Order (NIEO) in chapter 5 and the negotiation of the SDGs in chapter 8, political negotiations and the compromises that are enabled and brokered by international organizations may help advance progressive agendas (Murphy, 1994). However, only rarely does contestation within these political spheres lead to radical change. Again from a Coxian perspective, this is attributable to the fact that the global governance project and the various institutions and organizations established to support it remain fundamentally wedded to international political economic structures that supply the architecture of our global capitalist system today.

The post–Washington Consensus continues to privilege the "development as growth" model above all else. Critical development scholars have therefore argued that a "growth" agenda is embedded in the SDGs, which are, at best, a compromise between the interests of global capital and its discontents. From this perspective, the 2030 Agenda is not a significant departure from our current, unsustainable economic and ecological trajectory, and the carefully formulated, politically palatable SDGs will not allow us to address the most significant challenges facing our species: inequality and climate change (Spangenberg, 2017). Criticisms have also been leveled against dominant constructions of "sustainable development," which some suggest does not provide a framework for transforming the historically-rooted economic structures that generate these problems (Carvalho, 2001). Critical criminologists have even gone as far as to argue that existing political institutions, both national and international, are not only incapable of addressing these structural issues but also fundamentally disinclined to do so insofar as this conflicts with corporate interests (Whyte, 2020). From this perspective, weak and ineffective regulatory regimes are a defining feature of the capitalist political economy, which is inherently susceptible to what some would consider as high-level corruption. Elites who enable and exploit these conditions have therefore been labeled "carbon criminals" (White, 2017).

Unfortunately, UNODC as an international organization currently offers little when it comes to addressing the institutional or structural drivers of the criminological dimensions of these problems in the Global North, where the capabilities of governments, their intentions, and rule of law credentials are either left unquestioned or above scrutiny. When US governments embrace the liberal international agenda (for example, the Clinton and Obama administrations), the capabilities of their criminal justice institutions and their commitment to a thick definition of the rule of law are rarely, if ever, questioned because they pay the bills. When US governments deviate from the liberal internationalist agenda (for example, the Bush and Trump administrations), the UN works to preserve multilateralism and the transnational legal order, but its efforts are mainly symbolic. For example, we did not see UN Peacekeepers deployed to Ferguson, Portland, or Minneapolis, nor is it conceivable that UNODC would approach the US attorney general to propose a EU-funded technical assistance project to improve regulation or high-level anti-corruption monitoring, even in the wake of the Trump administration.

Even mundane activities are seemingly designed exclusively for developing countries. For example, it is unlikely that UNODC would view the United States or even Australia as a natural partner for piloting its Qatari-funded, Education 4 Justice curriculum to promote a "culture of lawfulness." Put bluntly, the UN, and by extension UNODC, was never established to solve *global* problems through its development pillar unless responsibility for addressing them could be located in the Global South. "Development" in this institutional context does not describe an ongoing process experienced by all nations, but rather the ongoing experience of former dependencies that are expected to participate in a global economy and contribute to the maintenance of a transnational legal order that was established by their former colonizers (Amin, 2011; Rist, 2014). It is therefore no coincidence that UNODC has never developed regional programs in North America, Western Europe, or even East Asia, where issues relating to crime and corruption are either treated as domestic issues or selectively addressed through bilateral or multilateral cooperation (if necessary and politically desirable).

This is not to suggest that staff at UNODC see it as their fundamental mission to create conditions that will advance the interests of corporations or Northern donors. Rather, they are prone to negotiating the institutional, ideological, and material conditions of their field through a dominant, cultural lens that emphasizes the importance of functional cooperation and promotes a Manichaean distinction between licit and illicit activities. Like police officers, these international civil servants often see themselves and their partners as "good guys" working to stop "bad guys" (Bowling & Sheptycki, 2012). This dominant worldview is further validated by the evidence UNODC produces and collates, much of which demonstrates that crime, violence, and corruption are legitimate issues (and they are) that are often concentrated, or at least most visible, in the Global South.[1]

For International Relations scholars, the argument that global governance is geopolitically imbalanced is hardly groundbreaking, but this must be openly acknowledged and confronted by the international crime policy community if it is going to generate meaningful impact through its efforts to promote *sustainable* development. In our view, the institutional architecture of global crime governance needs to be radically reconfigured so that the international crime policy community can work to address those activities that generate the greatest economic, social, and ecological harm. *At a minimum*, institutional reforms are necessary to ensure that global crime governance does not become an obstacle to the realization of some of the most ambitious, and important, elements of the 2030 Agenda. Reforming UNODC, transforming the global governance of crime, and reframing the focus of its work is therefore essential for constructing a more inclusive and authentic transnational legal order that *might* prove consequential when it comes to creating conditions that support a more equitable and sustainable future (Dryzek, 2009).

REFORMING UNODC

In our view, the UN still has an important role to play when it comes to coordinating international efforts to "[p]romote just, peaceful, and inclusive societies," but it cannot provide effective issue leadership if its mandate and strategic priorities remain beholden to the Commissions in Vienna. In the absence of significant institutional reforms, UNODC's contributions to the SDG agenda may at best prove inconsequential and out of sync with the wider UN system, and this will continue to undermine the long-standing aim of promoting system-wide coherence. At worst, it may simply serve to reproduce a transnational legal order that is fundamentally designed to preserve an unsustainable and inequitable model of global capitalism, which would represent an obstacle to the realization of the most ambitious and progressive aspirations of the 2030 Agenda.

The enduring aspiration to promote system-wide coherence within the UN provides an important starting point for promoting better alignment between the work of UNODC and more progressive agencies based in New York and Geneva. It is undeniable that issues relating to crime and corruption intersect, and have significant implications for, other spheres of global governance, but criminological issues must be framed in ways that will actually support "multidimensional approaches" (as prescribed by the 2021 Kyoto Declaration) that target their underlying structural drivers. As it stands, UNODC's governance structure is fundamentally designed to ensure that the agency works to reproduce an innocuous international crime policy agenda, so abolishing the Commissions and replacing them with a majoritarian model might help stimulate actual policy debates and discussions, which are necessary for advancing a progressive agenda. In our view, this is essential for governing these problems as *global* as opposed to *Southern* issues, and there is even precedent for this within the UN system. Indeed, as we note in chapter 5, the UN crime policy agenda was influenced by the political agenda of the New International Economic Order (NIEO), which dominated the UNGA and ECOSOC and helped shift the focus from social defense to transnational crime. The NIEO agenda was seemingly neutralized and appropriated by the West in the 1980s, but there is still scope for meaningful contestation and negotiation to occur within the UN system. This is evident from the proceedings of the Open Working Group (OWG) for the SDGs, described in chapter 8.

There are of course institutional risks inherent to re-politicizing the international crime policy agenda, but fostering uncomfortable conversations about the causes and consequences of crime in different parts of the world (as discussed in chapter 1), transnational crime in particular, is necessary for developing multidimensional strategies for addressing these issues. In some instances, this means calling attention to those actors, state and non-state, who stand in the way. Political economy must also be an explicit part of these dialogues. A contestation-based model of global governance is thus, in our view, preferable to a consensus-based one, because it treats the transnational legal order as a site of negotiation rather than uncritically accepting it as an ahistorical, universal public good.

As a bureaucratic actor with established capabilities in terms of both research and advocacy, UNODC must be empowered to actively and visibly contribute to such an agenda-setting process. It is not UNODC's role to dictate the international crime policy agenda, but as the custodian of SDG16+, UNODC can draw upon its bureaucratic authority, research capabilities, and diplomatic skills to moderate discussions and structure deliberations in a manner that promotes inclusive and authentic dialogues. One possibility for realizing this moderator function might be to revisit Costa's prescriptions for promoting an evidence-based model for international crime policy making, which were discussed in chapter 7.

Of course there are other bureaucratic pathologies UNODC must overcome if it is to perform this role in a manner that advances the global public good, as opposed to the interests of powerful donors or its own organizational agenda. For example, UNODC's material dependence on voluntary contributions from donors must be reduced, even if this means scaling back operational capabilities. Some of the innovative funding models described in chapter 8 are potentially promising in terms of aligning programs and projects with regional and local needs, but Northern donors continue to play a disproportionate role in influencing international crime policy agenda in Vienna, along with normative agendas and operational priorities in regions of concern. Perhaps it is time to question whether some of UNODC's expansive portfolio of global programs and projects could in fact be undertaken by civil society actors. This would potentially enhance UNODC's autonomy while leveraging the capabilities of regional and local civil society networks, thus extending its capabilities as the custodian of SDG16+.

At the same time, simply opening up the international crime policy agenda to broad-stroke, politically-motivated critiques of Western or capitalist hegemony offers little when it comes to improving the quality of the deliberations about specific global or transnational issues. This was evident during the Cold War in relation to the Soviet Union's ideological arguments about the nature of crime and the inherent superiority of its own system. These perspectives should be recognized, but a Manichaean discussion of "development" or "capitalism" that lacks nuance is just as unhelpful as reductionist narratives about problems like crime and corruption or denying the overlap that exists between licit and illicit economies. As discussed in the following section, opening up these policy deliberations to civil society actors may therefore offer a possibility not only for democratizing the international crime policy agenda but also for improving the quality of critical dialogues and debates. This is essential for promoting a better global politics of crime and, by extension, more impactful approaches to global crime governance.

From a practical standpoint, institutional reforms could be initiated by the UNGA, but the support of the secretary general would also likely be required. As of 2021, the current secretary general, António Guterres, is a progressive figure with strong global leadership credentials, so this is not unimaginable, although perhaps unlikely, given that global crime governance does not appear to be a major concern of his. Some countries would also undoubtedly resist such proposals, and resistance might also come from the undersecretary in Vienna, who happens to be the executive director of UNODC. The current executive director, Ghada Fathi Waly, is seemingly more active, visible, and progressive than her predecessor, but even if she were inclined to champion a reformist agenda, her capacity to do so would likely be constrained by the same institutional and structural conditions that need to be addressed. Costa's leadership, particularly his controversial engagement with the UNSC, demonstrated that even at this level, executive leadership can have a significant impact on institutional politics, although it seemingly cost him his career. The significant impact that strong, executive leadership can have is also evident in relation to other UN agencies, notably UNDP and UN Women, which have managed to increase their profile and influence in recent decades. Their governance structures are arguably less restrictive than UNODC's, but it would be inaccurate to suggest that the issues they deal with, development and gender, respectively, are uncontroversial. UNODC's portfolio is arguably more politically sensitive, insofar as the transnational legal order it works to sustain is framed as the cornerstone of a global capitalist economy, but, at least in our view, this only strengthens the case for reform.

TRANSFORMING GLOBAL CRIME GOVERNANCE

Reforming the UN will achieve little unless this creates greater scope for civil society engagement when it comes to both shaping and implementing the international crime policy agenda. While the prospect of UNODC assuming the role of moderator of a deliberative forum and facilitating regional dialogues (as it has done for decades) is appealing, enhancing the quality of political discussions about transnational crime and corruption ultimately necessitates input from other non-state actors. Carayannis and Weiss (2020, p. 2) refer to this as the "Third UN," or:

> the ecology of supportive non-state actors—intellectuals, scholars, consultants, think tanks, non-governmental organizations (NGOs), the for-profit private sector, and the media—that interacts with the intergovernmental machinery of the First UN [member states]and the Second UN [the Secretariat] to formulate and refine ideas and decision making at key junctures in policy processes.

As it stands, several participants noted that civil society actors are excluded from key meetings and negotiation processes where the international crime policy agenda is crafted. This is in part a reflection of how the Vienna-based Commissions operate and, by extension, the aforementioned political sensitivities associated with UNODC's portfolio. At the same time, it also signifies the enduring primacy accorded to states as legitimate actors within the UN system. From the perspective of one leading civil society network, this was all but confirmed by the negotiation process and content of the Kyoto Declaration, which was adopted unanimously at the 14th UN Crime Congress in 2021:

> [T]he Kyoto Declaration represents an enhanced focus on state responses. It conceptualizes law enforcement and criminal justice as the "central components of the rule of law," and affirms the "primary role and responsibility" of

states and governments to implement responses. The role of civil society is consequently sidelined and mentioned only in reference to the establishment of partnerships with the state, "as appropriate" (Tennant, 2021).

This is not surprising, because the post–World War II global governance system was designed by states, and its architects originally envisaged only a minor role for non-state actors. As noted in chapter 6, this began to change in the post–Cold War era, as the shift from "international" to "global" governance stressed the need for a greater role for non-state actors in the collective governance of the globe, which could no longer be left to states and their international bureaucracies alone (Brühl & Rittberger, 2002). In theory, incorporating civil society into international institutions would therefore improve their legitimacy and accountability by opening them up to a more representative array of actors, who would not only bring greater scrutiny to global policy agendas but also enhance their quality by bringing in new ideas and perspectives (Scholte, 2011).[2] This would also aid implementation, often by delivering global policy agendas that civil society actors had a hand in devising and legitimating (Verweij & Josling, 2003).

The UN was part of this process, most famously with the Panel of Eminent Persons on United Nations–Civil Society Relations under the leadership of Fernando Cardoso, which delivered a report to the secretary general in 2004 setting out a number of recommendations to enable greater engagement with civil society as "a necessity, not an option" (UN Panel of Eminent Persons on United Nations–Civil Society Relations, 2004, p. 9). Yet, despite this lofty rhetoric, the reality has been much less impressive, with civil society incorporated from a subordinate position and given little opportunity to meaningfully contribute to global debates, let alone to contest policy agendas (Anheier, 2018). The UN is not unique in this, as the overall trend for international organizations has been to facilitate participation of civil society as a way to boost legitimacy, while at the same time constraining contestation to ensure that capital-friendly policy agendas are not displaced (Chodor, 2020; Gerard, 2014). Nevertheless, if the UN crime policy agenda is to open up to new ideas and perspectives, and if the Third UN is to play a key role in delivering the SDGs (as prescribed by SDG 17), then civil society organizations must be afforded meaningful opportunities to participate in key decision-making processes. This is crucial not only for enhancing the deliberative democratic credentials of the international crime policy apparatus but also for ensuring that the interests of local actors (including grassroots organizations and social movements), who often lack formal recognition from the UN system and even their national governments, are represented in Vienna and New York.

However, an important note of caution is warranted. While there is undoubtedly a lively and active civil society sphere when it comes to issues relating to SDG 16+, it does not exist in a vacuum. Rather, just like UNODC, it is shaped by the interests and power of global capital and its sovereign protectors. Organizations like the Global Initiative, Transparency International, and the UNCAC Coalition all work within the confines of the liberal internationalist consensus. Thus, regardless of their aspirations, these civil society organizations (CSOs) face material and ideological constraints that limit their ability to advance a radical agenda that might seek to address the underlying structural causes of crime, inequality, or ecological devastation at a global level (Hindess, 2005). Many CSOs are therefore working to advance variations of the same agenda that is anchored in UNTOC and UNCAC, albeit without the diplomatic and institutional constraints that limit UNODC's autonomy. In this regard, some civil society actors, including the Global Initiative, have used research and advocacy to bring a political economy perspective into focus, including in relation to high-level corruption (see Mahadevan, 2019), but much of this work continues to focus on these problems in the Global South, because that is what donors will pay for.

Relatedly, we note that the sphere of global civil society is dominated by professionalized Northern NGOs, which do not necessarily represent the interests of those who are actually most impacted by criminal harms on the ground, especially in the South. Even those NGOs that do come from the South are often staffed by Western-trained local elites whose agendas and work may align more closely with the interest of Northern donors than local communities (Sénit & Biermann, 2021). Accordingly, if global crime governance is to be truly democratized, it needs to be opened up not only to Northern NGOs but also to popular social movements from the South, including indigenous and peasant groups, unions and informal workers movements, women's groups, or neighborhood associations. As Cox (1994) argued in the immediate aftermath of the Cold War, if the UN is to remain legitimate, it needs to embrace "bottom-up" multilateralism and act as an interlocutor between states and marginalized social forces in debates about alternative policy agendas. Admittedly, just like their Northern counterparts, nothing guarantees that these social forces will put forward any radical agendas. However, they do represent those communities most impacted by criminal harms (Currie, 2015), and which therefore have the most direct stake in development initiatives that would address them. This applies to marginalized communities in the Global South and those that exist in the North's South (Currie, 2017). Accordingly, democratizing global crime governance necessitates the creation of new deliberative forums that are authentic, inclusive, and consequential (Dryzek, 2009; Dryzek & Tanasoca, 2021). As the COVID-19 pandemic has demonstrated, holding these deliberations via virtual platforms may provide a simple and effective means of opening up global debates to a more diverse array of civil society actors who have previously lacked the financial resources to attend international conferences (Édes & Garrison, 2021). At the same time, there are those who argue that participation in virtual summits is not equivalent to attending in-person multilateral events, as diplomacy, networking, and lobbying typically take place beyond the formal proceedings (Naylor, 2020).

Reforming the governance structure of UNODC and enabling a diverse array of civil society voices to participate in deliberative processes may help to improve the authenticity and inclusivity of the agenda-setting process. The key challenge, however, is ensuring that an inclusive model of global crime governance that generates authentic (i.e., uncomfortable) debates about the causes and consequences of crime and corruption as *global* problems are ultimately consequential. The issue is that authentic dialogues inherently threaten global capital and its vested interest in maintaining an international crime policy agenda that promotes stability and order for the purpose of advancing economic growth. The simple fact that material power is overwhelmingly vested in the hands of those actors who are happy to maintain the status quo represents a significant obstacle to ensuring that a radical, or even a more progressive, international crime policy agenda will have any meaningful impact. Perhaps, then, the only option for transforming, or at least reorienting, these political economic structures toward a more socially just and sustainable agenda is to shift the focus of these deliberations altogether. Perhaps it is time to retire the "crime-development nexus" as a focal point of global crime governance.

TOWARD A HARM-SUSTAINABILITY NEXUS?

Reconfiguring the institutional and ideological architecture of global crime governance is essential for improving the quality of political debate, and for developing programs and projects that help address the structural causes of crime and corruption in a multidimensional and sustainable manner. At the same time, there are limits to what any democratic fora and enhanced multiscalar and polycentric governance networks can realistically accomplish if the transnational legal order remains wedded to the concepts of "crime" and "development." To this effect, Reiner (2016, p. 186) observes, the "modern legal conception of crime, distinguished from other forms of wrongdoing and troublemaking, emerged hand in hand with the development of capitalist nation-states." Addressing the structural causes and drivers of problems associated with crime and corruption, particularly their historical, transnational, and multi-sectoral dimensions, may therefore benefit from the adoption of a more critical and expansive framework for conceptualizing, labeling, and responding to those "forms of wrongdoing and troublemaking" (quoting Reiner, above) that threaten human and environmental security.

Critical criminologists have long acknowledged the conceptual limitations of "crime" and the politics of criminalization, so it's not particularly groundbreaking to note that "there is nothing intrinsic to any particular event or incident which permits it to be defined as a crime" (Hillyard & Tombs, 2004, p. 11). This is not to deny that activities/actors labeled "crimes"/"criminals" often cause harm to others; rather, it is an acknowledgment of the old cliché that not every action that is harmful is criminalized, and not every criminalized activity is necessarily harmful. Criminal codes are therefore the legally codified outcomes of social processes that reflect and reinforce the power inequalities characteristic of any given society (Quinney, 1974). Further to this point, a particular activity may be defined as a crime in law yet is seldom enforced in practice. To this effect, Maguire (2002, p. 322) writes, "whether people perceive a particular action or event as a crime, let alone whether they report it as such to anyone else (including police, or a survey interviewer), can vary according to their own knowledge, awareness, or feelings about crime, which may in turn be influenced by the general public 'mood' or the preoccupations of politicians and the media."

The social and political dynamics of criminalization are well documented at the international level (Andreas & Nadelmann, 2006), but to date, constructivist and critical perspectives have had little, if any, impact on the actual international crime policy agenda. There are several important reasons for this, but, most significantly, these perspectives are fundamentally at odds with the narrative that crime is a global problem that must be addressed through functional cooperation and the transnational legal ordering of criminal justice (Shaffer & Aaronson, 2020). Ignoring these perspectives is therefore convenient, arguably even essential, for maintaining a consensus-based international crime policy agenda, but this is highly problematic when it comes to addressing the underlying causes of issues that fall within UNODC's portfolio. Specifically, the concept of "crime" only provides a useful lens for examining or addressing harmful activities that are criminalized, visible (either through data or trends analyses), and whose perpetrators are identifiable *and* politically acceptable targets for labeling and sanctions. Thus, while enhancing the capabilities of civil society actors *may* under certain circumstances alleviate the criminological effects of structural violence in marginalized communities, improving the nature of functional cooperation alone offers little when it comes to addressing the ideological, institutional, and material drivers of structural violence, including inequality. For this reason, we argue that the international community must shift its focus from "crime" to "harm" if it actually wants to promote "just, peaceful and inclusive societies," as prescribed by SDG 16+.

This is not an original argument, and we note that scholars have long interrogated the concept of "crime" and advocated discursive shifts and the reformation of criminology as a field of study (e.g., Shearing, 1989). Most recently, self-described "zemiologists" have emphasized that the concept of crime—the criminal law, criminal justice institutions, and other regulatory systems used to promote social control—fundamentally serve the interests of corporate and political elites (Hillyard et al., 2004). These institutions not only fail to address the ideological, institutional, and material drivers of social harms that disproportionately impact marginalized populations but also often contribute to these social harms in various ways. For example, criminology as a field of research is said to reproduce and validate a myopic interest in addressing criminalized harms and in upholding the assumption that crime is "natural" (Canning & Tombs, 2021, p. 3). Governing institutions and regulatory systems, particularly those associated with neoliberal states, are also argued to function by locating responsibility for criminalized social harms on individuals or communities (again often marginalized) in order to control these populations and deflect attention away from political economic structures and harmful, unjust, or unethical policies.

The zemiological approach has been particularly influential among critical researchers who do work on what criminologists once referred to as "crimes of the powerful" (Pearce, 1976) because it supports "deeper," "multidimensional" analyses of the harms perpetrated or enabled by state and/or corporate actors that are argued to be greater in scale and impact than those associated with conventional categories of crime (Hillyard et al., 2002). Climate change has been an obvious and important focal point of this research, which seeks to account for the failures and deficiencies of governing actors and regulatory systems to identify, prevent, and respond to environmental harms in a meaningful way (Brisman & South, 2018; White, 2021). For this reason, it provides a useful starting point for addressing high-level corruption, which even proponents of the post–Washington Consensus have described as a key explanation for global inaction on climate change. These are obviously issues that fall beyond the portfolio of UNODC, but situating the international crime policy agenda in a broader global dialogue about "harm" would seemingly provide a useful starting point for developing the "multidimensional approaches" prescribed by the Kyoto Declaration. Even if an important coordinating node like UNODC lacks the mandate or capabilities to address these wider issues, it should at least be aware of these debates so it can work to ensure that its efforts to support the global governance of crime do not conflict with or undermine the global governance of harm.

This is undeniably a bold prescription for transforming an inherently conservative sphere of global governance, but there are reasons it may actually prove viable. For starters, reorienting the international crime policy agenda toward a harm-based agenda does not necessarily mean rejecting the concept of crime altogether or abandoning important normative instruments like UNTOC or UNCAC. Rather, locating the international community's ongoing efforts to address criminalized harms within a wider, multi-sectoral discourse that seeks to analyze and address the underlying causes of economic, environmental, and social harms may actually serve to enhance the ability of actors like UNODC and its civil society partners to support the wider aspirations of the 2030 Agenda. To those who argue that the concept of "harm" is too vague, broad, or ill-defined, we ask, "How is this any different to 'crime'?"

We would also stress that adopting a harm-based approach does not necessarily mean adopting a radical or abolitionist agenda, which, for obvious reasons, is unlikely to appeal to the vast majority of governments around the world. In fact, in recent decades a variety of criminologists and public health researchers with diverse agendas and ideological orientations have incorporated the broader concept of "harm" into their work. In many cases, the reasons for doing so reflect recognition of the aforementioned cliché that "crime" and "harm" are not synonymous, or that criminalization is itself harmful. Examples include drug policy researchers and practitioners who promote harm reduction (Marlatt, 1996), policing researchers who are interested in how societies work to improve their resilience in response to new and emerging "harm landscapes" (Berg & Shearing, 2018), and even "mainstream criminologists" who seek to compile crime-harm indices for developing targeted crime prevention strategies and improving the allocation of limited resources (Sherman, Neyroud & Neyroud, 2016). These diverse examples are admittedly rooted in Anglo-centric traditions and institutions, but we believe that locating the international crime policy agenda in a broader "harm"-based approach would provide greater scope for genuine, intercultural dialogues about the nature of "crime" and its causes to take place. Put simply, "harm" lacks the colonial baggage of "crime" and the "rule of law," so a harm-based discourse would not simply assume that the state or its governing institutions are part of the solution (Tauri, 2014; Agozino, 2014).

Finally, we argue that shifting the discursive focus from crime to harm is potentially advantageous insofar as it offers the international crime policy community greater scope to engage with wider debates about how "development that meets the needs of the present without compromising the ability of future generations to meet their own needs" (Brundtland Commission, 1987) might be achieved. We are not in a position to answer this question, but raising it is essential for advancing a more sophisticated global dialogue about the causes and consequences of harm, criminalized or otherwise. The historical construction of the crime-development nexus has arguably been a useful development from a global governance standpoint insofar as it has established recognition of the need for multidimensional approaches for addressing transnational problems that represent a threat to order and stability. At the same time, this discursive framework remains oriented toward reproducing a global capitalist system that exacerbates inequality and is harming our planet, and it offers little when it comes to addressing the ideological, institutional, or structural drivers of these issues. Shifting the focus from "crime and development" to "harm and sustainability" may therefore provide a useful starting point for improving global crime governance and supporting the UN's ongoing efforts to promote "systemwide coherence" and "deliver as one." If nothing else, putting this proposal on the table will stimulate some long overdue conversations that may contribute, at least in some small way, to a better global politics of harm.

Notes

INTRODUCTION

1. UN (2013).
2. Our emphasis on a Manichaean narrative/worldview is consistent with Bowling and Sheptycki's (2012) analysis of the subculture of global policing; it is also a core theme of the constructivist literature that theorizes the rise of transnational organised crime in the 1990s (see chapter 6).
3. The interviews were conducted between 2018 and 2021. Ethics approval was provided by the Monash University Human Research Ethics Committee and the Texas State University IRB.

CHAPTER ONE

1. The limitations of official statistics are widely acknowledged (see Addington, 2010).

CHAPTER TWO

1. For a useful overview of International Relations theory, see Burchill et al. (2017).
2. For an overview of realism, see Donnelly (2000).

CHAPTER THREE

1. Although the two movements were ideologically distinct.
2. The fact that the overall standard of living was also improving for the British working class during the Victorian Era as a consequence of imperialism must also be acknowledged (Hobsbawm, 1989).
3. For a detailed history of the 1961 UN Single Convention on Narcotic Drugs, see Collins (2021).
4. Colonized people, unlike the working classes in the metropole, were not viewed as a proximate threat to political and economic elites.
5. Although the same can be argued of their institutional counterparts in the Global North.
6. Similarly, the Hague Opium Convention of 1912 supplied a normative mandate in the sphere of drug control.
7. Pedersen (2015, p. 10) lists several areas where the League engaged in technical work and supported standards.
8. Noting that the Russian Revolution and US isolationist policies went against this liberal internationalist order.

CHAPTER FOUR

1. This section draws heavily on Murphy (2006) and Browne (2011). We have synthesized these institutional histories with structural and postcolonial histories of international development.
2. UNGA internal resolutions that relate to procedural and budgetary matters are binding, but those that relate to global policy issues and create obligations for states generally are not.
3. It served to reaffirm the sovereign authority of postcolonial governments.
4. The mandate also included trafficking in women and prostitution, thus highlighting continuity with the League's agenda; however, these issues were not a focus of social defense.
5. See the American Society of Criminology (n.d.). Information about Ferracuti and other members of the Secretariat was also provided by interview participants who worked with them.
6. All cited in the 1960 Secretariat report.
7. Despite their ideological differences, one participant suggested that the United States and Soviet delegates "got along wonderfully," although it is unclear whether this was a personal friendship or based on mutual recognition of the need for functional cooperation.

CHAPTER FIVE

1. Noting that the state typically orchestrated their economic development (Ong, 2006).
2. There was a chief, but the team was small and under-resourced.

CHAPTER SIX

1. Godson, who had previously been linked to the Heritage Foundation's involvement with the Iran-Contra scandal (Beamish, 1987), would also later become a vocal proponent of the "culture of lawfulness" agenda (Godson, 2000), which today features prominently in UNODC's Qatari-funded "Education for Justice" curriculum. It is beyond the scope of this book to explore these connections in forensic detail, but this may provide a fruitful avenue for future historical research on how neoconservative agendas have directly and indirectly shaped the construction of the crime-development nexus.
2. Although, as Sharman (2017) argues, there was strong support for the asset recovery provisions of UNCAC from developing countries, many of which were frustrated with the inability to retrieve assets stolen by their own corrupt officials and hidden in foreign, most often Northern, jurisdictions.
3. The Institute for International Economics (IIE) is one of the world's foremost Washington, DC, think tanks focusing on issues affecting the global economy and a strong advocate for neoliberalism and further economic integration.
4. See Foucault (1994).
5. By the early 1990s, researchers at the World Bank had already come to acknowledge that these policies were contributing to urban poverty (see Moser, Herbert & Makonnen, 1993).
6. The IADB would later reflect, for example: "It is key to increase the involvement of communities to strengthen both social capital and assist in developing innovative solutions to succeed in reducing and preventing violence" (Buvinić, Alda & Lamas, 2005, p. 22).
7. Perhaps most curiously, there is no reference to "human security" in the highly influential World Bank Report *Breaking the Conflict Trap*, authored by Paul Collier et al. (2003).

CHAPTER SEVEN

1. The UNCAC peer review mechanism only accounts for whether countries have adopted anti-corruption legislation in line with their treaty obligations. It does not provide an assessment of the nature or extent of corruption in different countries. Participation in the peer review process is voluntary, and the selection of peer reviewers and the content of their reports are highly political (Brunelle-Quraishi, 2011). As is

also evident with the UNTOC peer review mechanism, there is limited scope for civil society involvement (Tennant & Mahedevan, 2021).

2. Quoting former UNDP administrator Mark Malloch Brown, who reportedly led this drafting process (Tran, 2012).

3. See Findlay (1999).

4. The reputational damage with donors was evident even prior to the publication of the first report (see Burns, 2001a; Burns, 2001b).

5. Funded by the French government.

6. This characterization was provided by a former colleague.

CHAPTER EIGHT

1. Which once again embraced liberal internationalism under President Obama.

2. For a detailed overview of these processes, see Dodds, Donoghue, and Leiva Roesch (2016) and Kamau, Chasek, and O'Connor (2018).

3. See www.un.org/en/development/desa/policy/untaskteam_undf/them_tp.shtml.

4. See http://vote.myworld2015.org.

5. Quoting a former UNODC executive.

6. Country statements available at https://sustainabledevelopment.un.org/owg8.html.

7. The argument is also supported by the findings of the Pandora Papers investigation, which were published in the weeks preceding completion of this book.

CONCLUSION

1. Most of the "old-timers" and long-serving staff we interviewed were admittedly quite critical and acknowledged the limitations of UNODC. They nevertheless maintained a commitment to the liberal internationalist project and believed that the work of this agency was by and large necessary and beneficial. More-junior staff, particularly those who lacked field experience, were typically less cognizant of these limitations, or at least less willing to openly discuss them.

2. For example, the Global Organized Crime Index, developed by the Global Initiative against Transnational Organized Crime in 2021, offers a useful reference point for initiating authentic conversations about the nature and impact of illicit markets in different parts of the world (Global Initiative, 2021). The Index is noteworthy because its scores and rankings evidence that these are *global* as opposed to Southern issues, and that levels of criminality and resilience vary between countries in both the Global South and the Global North.

References

Aaronson, E., & Shaffer, G. (2021). Defining Crimes in a Global Age: Criminalization as a Transnational Legal Process. *Law & Social Inquiry*, *46*(2), 455–86.
Abbott, K. W., & Snidal, D. (2002). Values and Interests: International Legalization in the Fight against Corruption. *The Journal of Legal Studies*, *31*(S1), 144–77.
Acharya, A. (2017). After Liberal Hegemony: The Advent of a Multiplex World Order. *Ethics & International Affairs*, *31*(3), 271–85.
Adekanye, J. (1995). Structural Adjustment, Democratization and Rising Ethnic Tensions in Africa. *Development and Change*, *26*(2), 355–74.
African Union (2008). Revised AU Plan of Action on Drug Control and Crime Prevention (2007–2012). CMDCCP/EXP/3(III). https://www.unodc.org/documents/about-unodc/AU%20plan%20of%20action.pdf.
Agozino, B. (2003) *Counter-colonial Criminology: A Critique of Imperialist Reason*. Pluto Press.
Agozino, B. (2004). Imperialism, Crime and Criminology: Towards the decolonisation of criminology. *Crime, Law and Social Change*, *41*(4), 343–58.
Agozino, B. (2018). The Withering Away of the Law: An Indigenous Perspective on the Decolonisation of the Criminal Justice System and Criminology. *Journal of Global Indigeneity*, *3*(1). https://ro.uow.edu.au/jgi/vol3/iss1/2.
Aitchison, A. (2013). Governing through Crime Internationally? Bosnia and Herzegovina. *British Journal of Politics and International Relations*, *15*(4), 548–65.
Alatas, S. H. (1974) The Captive Mind in Development Studies. *International Social Sciences Journal*, *XXVI*(4).
Albanese, J. (2018). Countering Transnational Crime and Corruption: The Urge to Action versus the Patience to Evaluate. *Justice Evaluation Journal*, *1*(1), 82–95.
Allen, F. (1981). *The Decline of the Rehabilitative Ideal*. Yale University Press.
Ambraseys, N., & Bilham, R. (2011). Corruption Kills. *Nature*, *469*(7329), 153–55.
American Society of Criminology (n.d.). *Franco Ferracuti Remembered*. https://www.youtube.com/watch?v=7sPSntuFHFo.

Amin, S. (1982). After the New International Economic Order: The Future of International Economic Relations. *Journal of Contemporary Asia*, *12*(4), 432–50.

Amin, S. (2006). The Millennium Development Goals: A Critique from the South. *Monthly Review*, 1 March. https://monthlyreview.org/2006/03/01/the-millennium-development-goals-a-critique-from-the-south/.

Amin, S. (2011). *Maldevelopment: Anatomy of a Global Failure*. Fahamu/Pambazuka.

Amin, S., Watson, D., & Girard, C. (2020) *Mapping Security in the Pacific: A Focus on Context, Gender, and Organisational Culture*. Routledge.

Anheier, H. K. (2018). The United Nations and Civil Society in Times of Change: Four Propositions. *Global Policy*, *9*(3), 291–300.

Ancel, M. (1965). *Social Defence: A Modern Approach to Criminal Problems*. Routledge & Kegan Paul.

Andreas, P. (2015). International Politics and the Illicit Global Economy. *Perspectives on Politics*, *13*(3), 782–88.

Andreas, P., & Greenhill, K. (2010). *Sex, Drugs, and Body Counts: The Politics of Numbers in Global Crime and Conflict*. Cornell University Press.

Andreas, P., & Nadelmann, E. (2006). *Policing the Globe: Criminalization and Crime Control in International Relations*. Oxford University Press.

Andreas, P., & Price, R. (2001). From War Fighting to Crime Fighting: Transforming the American National Security State. *International Studies Review*, *3*(3), 31–52.

Anghie, A. (2005). *Imperialism, Sovereignty, and the Making of International Law*. Cambridge University Press.

Annan, K. (1998). The Quiet Revolution. *Global Governance*, *4*(2), 123–38.

Annan, K. (2005). *In Larger Freedom: Towards Development, Security and Human Rights for All*, A/59/2005. United Nations. http://undocs.org/A/59/2005.

Annan, K. (1999) *The State of Crime and Criminal Justice Worldwide*. A/CONF.185/5. United Nations. https://www.unodc.org/documents/congress//Previous_Congresses/10th_Congress_2000/012_ACONF.187.5_The_State_of_Crime_and_Criminal_Justice_Worldwide.pdf

Annan, K. (2003). Statement of Kofi Annan to the 20 January Security Council ministerial meeting on terrorism. *United Nations Security Council*, New York, 20 January. https://www.un.org/sg/en/content/sg/speeches/2003-01-20/statement-kofi-annan-20-january-security-council-ministerial-meeting.

Annan, K. (2005). *In Larger Freedom: Towards Development, Security and Human Rights for All*, A/59/2005.United Nations. http://undocs.org/A/59/2005.

Annan, K. (2006) *Note by the Secretary General*, A/61/583. https://undocs.org/A/61/583.

Araud, G. (2010). Statement by the President of the Security Council. *6277th Meeting of the Security Council*, New York, 24 February. https://undocs.org/en/S/PRST/2010/4.

Arlacchi, P. (2000). Statement of Pino Arlacchi to the Third Committee of the General Assembly. *Third Committee of the General Assembly*, New York, 29 September. https://www.unodc.org/unodc/en/about-unodc/speeches/speech_2000-09-29_1.html.

Arthur, J., & Marenin, O. (1995). Explaining Crime in Developing Countries: The Need for a Case Study Approach. *Crime, Law & Social Change, 23*, 191–214.

Ayres, R. L. (1998). *Crime and Violence as Development Issues in Latin America and the Caribbean.* https://elibrary.worldbank.org/doi/abs/10.1596/0-8213-4163-4.

Barnett, M., & Finnemore, M. (1999), The Politics, Power and Pathologies of International Organizations. *International Organization, 53*(4), 699–732.

Barnett, M., & Finnemore, M. (2004). *Rules for the World: International Organizations in Global Politics.* Cornell University Press.

Bauman, Z. (2013). *Liquid Modernity.* John Wiley & Sons.

Baumer, E., & Wolff, K. (2014). The Breadth and Causes of Contemporary Cross-national Homicide Trends. *Crime and Justice, 43*, 231–87.

Beamish, R. (1987, July 15). Conservative Think Tank Funneled Money to North Associates. Associated Press. https://apnews.com/article/9022634f7b9fd7ff0d23f1924c5036fa.

Beetham, D. (1991) *The Legitimation of Power.* Macmillan International Higher Education.

Bennett, R. (1991). Development and Crime: A Cross-National, Time-Series Analysis of Competing Models. *The Sociological Quarterly, 32*(3), 343–63.

Bennett, R., & Lynch, J. (1996). Towards a Caribbean Criminology: Prospects and Problems. *Caribbean Journal of Criminology and Social Psychology, 1*(1), 8–37.

Berg, J., & Shearing, C. (2018). Governing-through-Harm and Public Goods Policing. *The ANNALS of the American Academy of Political and Social Science, 679*(1), 72–85.

Berg, J., & Shearing, C. (2020). Polycentric Security Governance and Sustainable Development in the Global South. In J. Blaustein et al. (eds.), *The Emerald Handbook of Crime, Justice and Sustainable Development* (pp. 153–73). Emerald.

Berger, M. (2004). After the Third World? History, Destiny and the Fate of Third Worldism. *Third World Quarterly, 25*(1), 9–39.

Bergling, P., & Jin, S. (2015). The New Black on the Development Catwalk: Incorporating Rule of Law into the Sustainable Development Goals. *Washington International Law Journal, 24*(3), 435–57.

Betts, A., & Pilath, A (2017). The politics of Causal Claims: The Case of Environmental Migration. *Journal of International Relations and Development, 20*, 782–804.

Bewley-Taylor, D. (2012). *International Drug Control: Consensus Fractured.* Cambridge University Press.

Bhambra, G. (2014). Postcolonial and Decolonial Dialogues. *Postcolonial Studies, 17*(2), 115–21.

Bieri, F. (2010). *From Blood Diamonds to the Kimberley Process: How NGOs Cleaned Up the Global Diamond Industry.* Routledge.

Bjørnskov, C. (2015). Does Economic Freedom Really Kill? On the Association Between "Neoliberal" Policies and Homicide Rates. *European Journal of Political Economy, 37*: 207–19.

Blaustein, J. (2015) *Speaking Truths to Power: Policy Ethnography and Police Reform in Bosnia and Herzegovina.* Oxford University Press.

Blaustein, J. (2016). Exporting Criminological Innovation Abroad: Discursive Representation, "Evidence-Based Crime Prevention" and the Post-Neoliberal Development Agenda in Latin America. *Theoretical Criminology*, *20*(2), 165–84.

Blaustein, J., Pino, N. W., Fitz-Gibbon, K., & White, R. (2018). Criminology and the UN Sustainable Development Goals: The Need for Support and Critique. *The British Journal of Criminology*, *58*(4), 767–86.

Bottoms, A., & Tankebe, J. (2012). Beyond Procedural Justice: A Dialogic Approach to Legitimacy in Criminal Justice. *Journal of Criminal Law and Criminology*, *102*(1), 119–70.

Bourguignon, F. (2000). Crime, Violence, and Inequitable Development. In B. Pleskovic & J. E. Stiglitz (eds.), *Annual World Bank Conference on Development Economics 1999* (pp. 199–224). World Bank.

Bowling, B. (2010). *Policing the Caribbean.* Oxford University Press.

Bowling, B. (2011). Transnational Criminology and the Globalization of Harm Production. In M. Bosworth & C. Hoyle (eds.), *What Is Criminology?* (pp. 362–77). Oxford University Press.

Bowling, B., & Sheptycki, J. (2012). *Global Policing.* SAGE.

Braithwaite, J. (1989). *Crime, Shame, and Reintegration.* Cambridge University Press.

Brisman, A., & South, N. (2018). Green Criminology, Zemiology, and Comparative and Inter-Relational Justice in the Anthropocene Era. In A. Boukli & J. Kotzé (eds.), *Zemiology: Reconnecting Crime and Social Harm* (pp. 203–21). Springer International Publishing.

Brogden, M. (1987). The Emergence of the Police—The Colonial Dimension. *The British Journal of Criminology*, *27*(1), 4–14.

Brown, M. (2014). *Penal Power and Colonial Rule.* Routledge.

Brown, E., & Cloke, J. (2004). Neoliberal Reform, Governance and Corruption in the South: Assessing the International Anti-Corruption Crusade. *Antipode*, *36*(2), 272–94.

Browne, S. (2006). *Aid and Influence: Do Donors Help or Hinder?* Routledge.

Browne, S. (2011). *United Nations Development Programme and System (UNDP).* Routledge.

Browne, S. (2017). *Sustainable Development Goals and UN Goal-Setting.* Routledge.

Browne, S., & Weiss, T. (2014). *Post-2015 UN Development: Making Change Happen?* Routledge.

Brühl, T., & Rittberger, V. (n.d.). From International to Global Governance: Actors, Collective Decision-Making and the United Nations in the World of the Twenty-First Century. In V. Rittberger (ed.), *Global Governance and the United Nations System* (pp. 1–47). United Nations University Press.

Brunelle-Quraishi, O. (2011). Assessing the Relevancy and Efficacy of the United Nations Convention Against Corruption: A Comparative Analysis. *Notre Dame Journal of International and Comparative Law*, *2*(1), 101–66.

Burchill, S., Linklater, A., & Devetak, R. (2017). *Theories of International Relations*, 5th edition. Red Globe Press.

Burns, J. (2001, January 20). Critics Round on UN Drug Agency's "Bold" Leader. *The Financial Times*, 6.
Burns, J. (2001, April 11). Dutch Halt Cash for UN Drug Agency. *The Financial Times*, 15.
Burris, S., Drahos, P., & Shearing, C. (2005). Nodal Governance. *Australian Journal of Legal Philosophy*, 30, 30–58.
Buvinić, M., Alda, E., & Lamas, J. (2005) Emphasizing Prevention in Citizen Security The Inter-American Development Bank's Contribution to Reducing Violence in Latin America and the Caribbean. Inter-American Development Bank. https://publications.iadb.org/publications/english/document/Emphasizing-Prevention-in-Citizen-Security-The-Inter-American-Development-Bank-Contribution-to-Reducing-Violence-in-Latin-America-and-the-Caribbean.pdf.
Buzan, B. (1997). Rethinking Security after the Cold War. *Cooperation and Conflict*, 32(1), 5–28.
Buzan, B., Wæver, O., & Wilde, J. de. (1998). *Security: A New Framework for Analysis*. Lynne Rienner Publishers.
Cain, M. (2000). Orientalism, Occidentalism and the Sociology of Crime. *British Journal of Criminology*, 40, 239–60.
Cammack, P. (2017). The UNDP, the World Bank and Human Development through the World Market. *Development Policy Review*, 35(1), 3–21.
Canals, J. (1960). Classicism, Positivism and Social Defense. *The Journal of Criminal Law, Criminology, and Police Science*, 50(6), 541–50.
Canning, V., & Tombs, S. (2021). *From Social Harm to Zemiology: A Critical Introduction*. Routledge.
Carrapiço, H. (2012). Transnational Organized Crime as a Security Concept. In F. Allum & S. Gilmour (eds.), *Routledge Handbook of Transnational Organized Crime* (pp. 19–35). Routledge.
Cardoso, F. H. (1972). Dependent Capitalist Development in Latin America. *New Left Review*, I/74, 83–95.
Carothers, T. (1998). The Rule of Law Revival. *Foreign Affairs*, 77(2), 95–106.
Carrington, K., Hogg, R., & Sozzo, M. (2016). Southern Criminology. *The British Journal of Criminology*, 56(1), 1–20.
Carrington, K., et al. (2021). Women-led Police Stations: Reimagining the Policing of Gender Violence in the Twenty-First Century. *Policing and Society*, 0(0), 1–21. https://doi.org/10.1080/10439463.2021.1956925.
Chambliss, W. (1975). The political Economy of Crime: A Comparative Study of Nigeria and the USA. In I. R. Taylor, P. Walton, & J. Young (eds.), *Critical Criminology*. Routledge.
Chamlin, M., & Cochran, J. (2004). An Excursus on the Population Size—Crime Relationship. *Western Criminology Review*, 5(2), 119–30.
Chamlin, M., & Cochran, J. (2005). Ascribed Economic Inequality and Homicide Among Modern Societies: Toward the Development of a Cross-National Theory. *Homicide Studies*, 9(1), 3–29.
Chamlin, M., & Cochran, J. (2006). Economic Inequality, Legitimacy, and Cross-National Homicide Rates. *Homicide Studies*, 10, 231–52.

Chandler, D. (2004). The Responsibility to Protect? Imposing the "Liberal Peace." *International Peacekeeping*, *11*(1), 59–81.

Chandler, D. (2006) *Empire in Denial: The Politics of State-Building*. Pluto Press.

Chandler, D. (2012). Resilience and Human Security: The Post-Interventionist Paradigm. *Security Dialogue*, *43*(3), 213–29.

Chandler, D. (2014) *Resilience: The Governance of Complexity*. Routledge.

Chang, Y. S., Kim, H. E., & Jeon, S. (2019). Do Larger Cities Experience Lower Crime Rates? A Scaling Analysis of 758 Cities in the U.S. *Sustainability*, *11*(11), 3111. https://doi.org/10.3390/su11113111.

Chodor, T. (2015). *Neoliberal Hegemony and the Pink Tide in Latin America: Breaking Up with TINA?* Palgrave Macmillan.

Chodor, T. (2020). The G20's Engagement with Civil Society: Participation without Contestation? *Globalizations*, *17*(6), 903–16.

Clark, H., Pascoe, B. L., & Fedotov, Y. (2011, September 7). *[Untitled letter to UN Resident Coordinators]*. https://www.unodc.org/documents/southeastasiaandpacific/2012/06/tocta/TOCTA_EAP_Overview_13_30_May_2012_ACPR.pdf.

Clark, R. (1994). *The United Nations Crime Prevention and Criminal Justice Program: Formulation of Standards and Efforts at their Implementation*. University of Philadelphia Press.

Clement, M. T., Pino, N. W., & Blaustein, J. (2019). Homicide Rates and the Multiple Dimensions of Urbanization: A Longitudinal, Cross-National Analysis. *Sustainability*, *11*(20), 5855. https://doi.org/10.3390/su11205855.

Clifford, W. (1979). *Echoes and Hopes: The United Nations Committee on Crime Prevention and Control*. Australian Institute for Criminology.

Clinard, M., & Abbott, D. (1973). *Crime in Developing Countries: A Comparative Perspective*. Wiley.

Cloward, R. & Ohlin, L. (1961). *Delinquency and Opportunity: A Study of Delinquent Gangs*. Routledge.

Cohen, A. (1955). *Delinquent Boys: The Culture of the Gang*. University of Chicago Press.

Cohen, S. (2002). *Folk Devils and Moral Panics: The Creation of the Mods and Rockers*. Psychology Press.

Cohen, S. (1998). Western Crime Control Models in the Third World: Benign or Malignant? In S. Cohen (ed.), *Against Criminology*. Routledge.

Collier, P., et al. (2003). *Breaking the Conflict Trap: Civil War and Development Policy*. World Bank.

Collins, J. (2021). *Legalizing the Drug Wars: A Regulatory History of UN Drug Control*. Cambridge University Press.

Colvin, G. (1986). Report on the Seventh United Nations Congress on the Prevention of Crime and the Treatment of Offenders. *Crime and Social Justice*, *25*, 55–61.

Connell, R. (2020). *Southern Theory: The Global Dynamics of Knowledge in Social Science*. Routledge.

Cottrell, M. P. (2017). *The League of Nations: Enduring Legacies of the First Experiment at World Organization*. Routledge.

Cousens, E. (2014, February 7). *[Untitled Statement]*. Eighth Session of the SDG Open Working Group, New York. https://sustainabledevelopment.un.org/content/documents/6693us16.pdf.

Costa, A. M. (2002, August 30). *Address to World Summit on Sustainable Development*. World Summit on Sustainable Development, Johannesburg. https://www.unodc.org/unodc/en/about-unodc/speeches/speech_2002-08-30_1.html.

Costa, A. M. (2008, April 14). *Rule of Law: A (missing) Millennium Development that Can Help Reach the Other MDGs*. 17th Session of the United Nations Commission on Crime Prevention and Criminal Justice, Vienna. https://www.unodc.org/unodc/en/about-unodc/speeches/2008-04-14.html.

Costa, A. M. (2010, February 24). *Organized Crime Is a Threat to Security: Case Studies and Policy Options*. UN Security Council, New York.

Cox, R. W. (1969). The Executive Head: An Essay on Leadership in International Organization. *International Organization, 23*(2), 205–30.

Cox, R. W. (1980). The Crisis of World Order and the Problem of International Organization in the 1980s. *International Journal, 35*(2), 370–95.

Cox, R. W. (1983). Gramsci, Hegemony and International Relations: An Essay in Method. *Millennium: Journal of International Studies, 12*(2), 162–75.

Cox, R. W. (1987). *Production, Power, and World Order*. Columbia University Press.

Cox, R. W. (1994). The Crisis in World Order and the Challenge to International Organization. *Cooperation and Conflict, 29*(2), 99–113.

Cox, R. W. (2002). *The Political Economy of a Plural World: Critical Reflections on Power, Morals and Civilization*. Routledge.

Crawford, A. (1999). *The Local Governance of Crime: Appeals to Community and Partnerships*. Oxford University Press.

Cruz, J. M. (2011). Criminal Violence and Democratization in Central America: The Survival of the Violent State. *Latin American Politics and Society, 53*(4), 1–33.

Cruz, J. M., & Vorobyeva, Y. (2021). State Presence, Armed Actors, and Criminal Violence in Central America. *The Sociological Quarterly, 0*(0), 1–20. https://doi.org/10.1080/00380253.2021.1940349.

C-SPAN. (1993, August 13). *International Organized Crime*. https://www.c-span.org/video/?48634-1/international-organized-crime.

Currie, E. (1997). Market, Crime, and Community: Toward a Mid-Range Theory of Post-Industrial Violence. *Theoretical Criminology, 1*(2), 147–72.

Currie, E. (2015) *The Roots of Danger: Violent Crime in Global Perspective*. Oxford University Press.

Currie, E. (2017). Confronting the North's South: On Race and Violence in the United States. *International Journal for Crime, Justice and Social Democracy, 6*(1), 23–34.

Davis, D. E. (2014). Modernist Planning and the Foundations of Urban Violence in Latin America. *Built Environment, 40*(3), 376–93.

Davis, M. (2017). *Planet of Slums*. Verso.

de Boer, J. & Gottschacher, M. (2019) Introduction. In J. E. Salahub et al. (eds.), *Reducing Urban Violence in the Global South: Towards Safe and Inclusive Cities* (pp. 1–14). Routledge.

Deflem, M. (2002). *Policing World Society: Historical Foundations of International Police Cooperation.* Oxford University Press.

de Goede, M. (2009). Governing Finance in the War on Terror. In H. Friman (ed.), *Crime and the Global Political Economy* (pp. 103–18). Lynne Rienner Publishers.

Devlin, R. (2014). *Debt and Crisis in Latin America: The Supply Side of the Story.* Princeton University Press.

DiCristina, B. (2016). Durkheim's Theory of Anomie and Crime: A Clarification and Elaboration. *Australian & New Zealand Journal of Criminology, 49*(3), 311–31.

Dinkel, J. (2018). *The Non-Aligned Movement: Genesis, Organization and Politics (1927–1992).* BRILL.

Dod, S. (1986). Report on the Third Annual Latin American Critical Criminology Conference. *Crime and Social Justice, 25,* 62–66.

Dodds, F., Donoghue, A. D., & Leiva Roesch, J. (2016). *Negotiating the Sustainable Development Goals: A Transformational Agenda for an Insecure World.* Taylor & Francis Group.

Donnelly, J. (2000). *Realism and International Relations.* Cambridge University Press.

Douglas, J. (2013, November 14). *Regional Programme for Southeast Asia (2014–2017) Official Launch.* https://www.unodc.org/documents/southeastasiaandpacific//2013/11/rp-launch/2013.11.10_RP_Launch_IS_01.pdf.

Douglas, J. (2018, November 15). *Parts of Asia Are Slipping into the Hands of Organized Crime.* CNN. Retrieved September 10, 2021, from https://www.cnn.com/2018/11/14/opinions/asia-organized-crime-intl/index.html.

Dryzek, J. S. (2009). Democratization as Deliberative Capacity Building. *Comparative Political Studies, 42*(11), 1379–1402.

Dryzek, J. S., & Tanasoca, A. (2021). *Democratizing Global Justice: Deliberating Global Goals.* Cambridge University Press.

Duffield, M. (2007). *Development, Security and Unending War: Governing the World of Peoples.* Polity.

Durkheim, E. (1893/1964). *The Division of Labor in Society.* Free Press.

EBRD. (1990). *Basic Documents of the European Bank for Reconstruction and Development.* https://www.ebrd.com/news/publications/institutional-documents/basic-documents-of-the-ebrd.html.

ECOSOC. (1948). *Prevention of Crime and Treatment of Offenders, 155 (VII).* https://undocs.org/en/E/RES/155(VII).

ECOSOC. (1957). *Recommendations of the First United Nations Congress on the Prevention of Crime and the Treatment of Offenders, 663 (XXIV).* https://www.unodc.org/documents/commissions/CCPCJ/Crime_Resolutions/1950-1959/1957/ECOSOC_Resolution-663-XXIV.pdf.

ECOSOC. (1965). *Organizational Arrangements for the United Nations Social Defence Programme, 1086 (XXXIX) B.* https://www.un.org/en/development/desa/policy/cdp/cdp_res_dec/e_1965_1089.pdf.

ECOSOC. (1971). *Criminality and Social Change, 1584.* https://www.unodc.org/documents/commissions/CCPCJ/Crime_Resolutions/1970-1979/1971/ECOSOC_Resolution-1584-L.pdf.

Édes, B., & Garrison, J. (2021). *COVID-19 Has Boosted Civil Society Participation in International Meetings Despite Technical Glitches*. ORF. https://www.orfonline.org/expert-speak/covid-19-has-boosted-civil-society-participation-in-international-meetings-despite-technical-glitches/.

Edwards, A., & Gill, P. (2002). The Politics of "Transnational Organized Crime": Discourse, Reflexivity and the Narration of "Threat." *British Journal of Politics and International Relations*, 4(2), 245–70.

Edwards, A., & Hughes, G. (2009). The Preventive Turn and the Promotion of Safer Communities in England and Wales: Political Inventiveness and Governmental Instabilities. In A. Crawford (ed.), *Crime Prevention Policies in Comparative Perspective* (pp. 62–85). Willan.

Efrat, A. (2012). *Governing Guns, Preventing Plunder: International Cooperation Against Illicit Trade*. Oxford University Press.

Eliasson, J. (2013, September 26). *Deputy Secretary-General's Remarks*. Global Dialogue on Rule of Law and Post-2015 Development Agenda, UNGA. https://www.un.org/sg/en/content/dsg/statement/2013-09-26/deputy-secretary-generals-remarks-opening-high-level-session-global.

Ellison, G., & Pino, N. W. (2012). *Globalization, Police Reform and Development: Doing It the Western Way?* Springer.

Escobar, A. (2011). *Encountering Development: The Making and Unmaking of the Third World*. Princeton University Press.

Farber, M. A. (1985, October 18). U.S.-Italian Teamwork Bringing Organized-Crime Chiefs to Trial. *New York Times*. https://www.nytimes.com/1985/10/18/world/us-italian-teamwork-bringing-organized-crime-chiefs-to-trial.html.

Fattah, E. A. (1992). The United Nations Declaration of Basic Principles of Justice for Victims of Crime and Abuse of Power: A Constructive Critique. In E. A. Fattah (ed.), *Towards a Critical Victimology* (pp. 401–24). Palgrave Macmillan.

Fehling, M., Nelson, B. D., & Venkatapuram, S. (2013). Limitations of the Millennium Development Goals: A Literature Review. *Global Public Health*, 8(10), 1109–22.

Ferracuti, F. (1963). The Role of Social Defence in the United Nations. *Revista Juridica de la Universidad de Puerto Rico*, 32(4), 683–88.

Findlay, M. (1999). *The Globalisation of Crime: Understanding Transitional Relationships in Context*. Cambridge University Press.

Findlay, M. (2008). *Governing through Globalised Crime: Futures for International Criminal Justice*. Routledge.

Finnemore, M., & Sikkink, K. (1998). International Norm Dynamics and Political Change. *International Organization*, 52(4), 887–917.

Fitz-Gibbon, K., & Walklate, S. (2020). Eliminating all forms of violence against all women and girls: Some criminological reflections on the challenges of measuring success and gauging progress. In J. Blaustein, et al. (eds.), *The Emerald Handbook of Crime, Justice and Sustainable Development* (pp. 315–32). Emerald.

Foucault, M. (1994). Governmentality. In J. Faubion (ed.), *Michel Foucault: Power: The Essential Works 3* (pp. 201–22). Allen Lane.

Frank, A. G. (1966). *The Development of Underdevelopment*. New England Free Press.

Friman, R. (2010). Numbers and Certification: Assessing Foreign Compliance in Combating Narcotics and Human Trafficking. In P. Andreas & K. Greenhill (eds.), *Sex, Drugs, and Body Counts: The Politics of Numbers in Global Crime and Conflict* (pp. 75–109). Cornell University Press.

Fukuda-Parr, S. (2003). The Human Development Paradigm: Operationalizing Sen's Ideas on Capabilities. *Feminist Economics*, *9*(2–3), 301–17.

Gall, C. (2003, September 5). U.N. Aide Says Afghan Drug Trade Pays for Terrorist Attacks. *New York Times*. https://www.nytimes.com/2003/09/05/world/un-aide-says-afghan-drug-trade-pays-for-terrorist-attacks.html.

Garland, D. (2002). *The Culture of Control: Crime and Social Order in Contemporary Society*. Oxford University Press.

Garland, D. (2014). What is a "history of the present"? On Foucault's genealogies and their critical preconditions. *Punishment & Society*, *16*(4), 365–84.

Gerard, K. (2014). *ASEAN's Engagement of Civil Society: Regulating Dissent*. Palgrave Macmillan UK.

Global Initiative Against Transnational Organized Crime. (2021). Global Organized Crime Index 2021. https://ocindex.net/assets/downloads/global-ocindex-report.pdf.

Glynn, P., Kobrin, S. J., & Naím, M. (1997). The Globalization of Corruption. In K. A. Elliott (ed.), *Corruption and the Global Economy* (pp. 7–27). Institute for International Economics.

Godson, R. (2000). Guide to Developing a Culture of Lawfulness. *Trends in Organized Crime*, *5*(3), 91–102.

Goffman, E. (1973). *The Presentation of Self in Everyday Life*. Overlook Press.

Gould, D. J., & Amaro-Reyes, J. A. (1983). *The Effects of Corruption on Administrative Performance: Illustrations from Developing Countries*. World Bank.

Gouldner, A. W. (1970). *Coming Crisis of Western Sociology*. Heinemann.

Gramsci, A. (1971). *Selections from the Prison Notebooks of Antonio Gramsci*. Lawrence and Wishart.

Grygier, T. (1951). Soviet Views on Western Crime and Criminology. *The British Journal of Delinquency*, *1*(4), 283–92.

Gutterman, E. (2019). Banning Bribes Abroad: US Enforcement of the Foreign Corrupt Practices Act and Its Impact on the Global Governance of Corruption. *European Political Science*, *18*(2), 205–16.

Gutterman, E., & Lohaus, M. (2018). What Is the "Anti-corruption" Norm in Global Politics? Norm Robustness and Contestation in the Transnational Governance of Corruption. In I. Kubbe & A. Engelbert (eds.), *Corruption and Norms: Why Informal Rules Matter*, 1st edition (pp. 241–68). Palgrave Macmillan.

Gwatkin, D. R. (2005). How much would poor people gain from faster progress towards the Millennium Development Goals for health? *The Lancet*, *365*(9461), 813–17.

Haas, P. (1992). Epistemic Communities and International Policy Coordination. *International Organization*, *46*(1), 1–35.

Hall, S., et al. (1978). *Policing the Crisis: Mugging, the State and Law and Order.* Macmillan.

Halliday, T. C., & Shaffer, G. (2015). *Transnational Legal Orders.* Cambridge University Press.

Hallwood, P., & Sinclair, S. (2016). *Oil, Debt and Development: OPEC in the Third World.* Routledge.

Hameiri, S., & Jones, L. (2015). *Governing Borderless Threats: Non-Traditional Security and the Politics of State Transformation.* Cambridge University Press.

Hardyns, W., & Pauwels, L. (2017). The Chicago School and Criminology. In R. Triplett (ed.), *The Handbook of the History and Philosophy of Criminology* (pp. 123–39). John Wiley & Sons.

Harvey, D. (1989). *The Condition of Postmodernity: An Enquiry into the Origins of Cultural Change.* Blackwell.

Harvey, D. (2006). *A Brief History of Neoliberalism.* Oxford University Press.

Hayes, M. D. (1989). *The U.S. and Latin America: A Lost Decade?* Inter-American Development Bank.

Heiss, L., Ellsberg, M., & Gottmoeller, M. (2002). A Global Overview of Gender-Based Violence. *International Journal of Gynaecology & Obstetrics, 78*(S1), S5–S14.

Held, D., et al. (1999). *Global Transformations: Politics, Economics and Culture.* Stanford University Press.

Heine, J., & Thakur, R. (2011). *The Dark Side of Globalization.* United Nations University Press. https://collections.unu.edu/eserv/UNU:2507/ebrary9789280811940.pdf.

Helleiner, E.(1999). State Power and the Regulation of Illicit Activity in Global Finance. in H. Friman & P. Andreas (eds.), *The Illicit Global Economy and State Power.* (pp. 53–90). Rowman & Littlefield.

Hettne, B. (1995). *Development Theory and the Three Worlds: Towards an International Political Economy of Development.* Longman.

Hickel, J. (2017). *The Divide: A Brief Guide to Global Inequality and its Solutions.* Random House.

High-Level Panel of Eminent Persons on the Post-2015 Development Agenda. (2013). *A New Global Partnership: Eradicate Poverty and Transform Economies through Sustainable Development.* United Nations Publications. https://www.un.org/sg/sites/www.un.org.sg/files/files/HLP_P2015_Report.pdf.

Hignett, K. (2012). Transnational Organized Crime and the Global Village. In F. Allum & S. Gilmour (eds.), *Routledge Handbook of Transnational Organized Crime* (pp. 281–93). Routledge.

Hilgers, T., & Macdonald, L. (2017). *Violence in Latin America and the Caribbean: Subnational Structures, Institutions, and Clientelistic Networks.* Cambridge University Press.

Hills, A. (2014). What Is Policeness? On Being Police in Somalia. *The British Journal of Criminology. 54*(5), 765–83.

Hillyard, P., et al. (2004). *Beyond Criminology: Taking Harm Seriously.* Pluto Press.

Hindess, B. (2005). Investigating International Anti-corruption. *Third World Quarterly, 26*(8), 1389–98.

Hobsbawm, E. (1962). *The Age of Revolution: Europe, 1789–1848*. Abacus.
Hobsbawm, E. (1989). *The Age Of Empire: 1875–1914*. Abacus.
Hobsbawm, E. (1994). *Age of Extremes: The Short Twentieth Century 1914–1991*. Abacus.
Hollway, W., & Jefferson, T. (1997). The Risk Society in an Age of Anxiety: Situating Fear of Crime. *The British Journal of Sociology, 48*(2), 255–66.
Hope, J. R., & Skinner, S. K. (1986, April 21). Opinion | The Crime Commission's Value. *New York Times*. https://www.nytimes.com/1986/04/21/opinion/the-crime-commission-s-value.html.
Hope, K. R. (1997). *Structural Adjustment, Reconstruction and Development in Africa*. Routledge.
Howard, G., Newman, G., & Pridemore, W. (2000). Theory, Method, and Data in Comparative Criminology. In US Department of Justice (ed.), *Measurement and Analysis of Crime and Justice* (pp. 139–211). US Department of Justice.
Hübschle, A. M. (2017). The social economy of rhino poaching: Of economic freedom fighters, professional hunters and marginalized local people. *Current Sociology, 65*(3), 427–47.
Huggins, M. (1983). A World of Crime: Review of Shelley, Crime and Modernization. *Crime and Social Justice, 19*, 102–6.
Huggins, M. (1985). *From Slavery to Vagrancy in Brazil: Crime and Social Control in the Third World*. Rutgers University Press.
Hutchinson, S., & O'Malley, P. (2007). Crime-Terror Nexus: Thinking on Some of the Links between Terrorism and Criminality. *Studies in Conflict & Terrorism, 30*(12), 1095–1107.
Huhn, S., & Warnecker-Berger, H. (2017). The Enigma of Violent Realities in Central America: Towards a Historical Perspective. In S. Huhn & H. Warnecker-Berger (eds.), *Politics and History of Violence and Crime in Central America* (pp. 1–21). Palgrave Macmillan.
Hülsse, R. (2007). Creating Demand for Global Governance: The Making of a Global Money-Laundering Problem. *Global Society, 21*(2), 155–78.
Illich, I. (1974). *Limits to Medicine: Medical Nemesis: The Expropriation of Health*. M. Boyars.
Inter-American Development Bank. (2012). *Citizen Security: Conceptual Framework and Empirical Evidence*. Inter-American Development Bank. https://publications.iadb.org/en/citizen-security-conceptual-framework-and-empirical-evidence.
International Crime Victim Survey (n.d.). *About the ICVS, International Crime Victims Survey (ICVS)*. https://wp.unil.ch/icvs/.
Iturralde, M. (2019). Neoliberalism and its impact on Latin American crime control fields. *Theoretical Criminology, 23*(4), 471–90.
Iturralde, M. (2020) The Emperor's New Clothes: A Critical Reading of the Sustainable Development Goals to Curb Crime and Violence in Latin America. In J. Blaustein et al. (eds.), *The Emerald Handbook of Crime, Justice and Sustainable Development* (pp. 175–96). Emerald.
Jacobs, J. B. (2007). *Mobsters, Unions, and Feds: The Mafia and the American Labor Movement*. NYU Press.

Jäger, J. (2002). International Police Co-operation and the Associations for the Fight Against White Slavery. *Paedagogica Historica, 38*(2–3), 565–79.

Jakobi, A. (2013). *Common Goods and Evils? The Formation of Global Crime Governance*. Oxford University Press.

Jakobi, A. P. (2020). *Crime, Security and Global Politics: An Introduction to Global Crime Governance*. Red Globe Press.

James, J. (2006). Misguided investments in meeting millennium Development Goals: A reconsideration using ends-based targets. *Third World Quarterly, 27*(3), 443–58.

Jenkins, D., & Leroy, J. (eds.). (2021). *Histories of Racial Capitalism*. Columbia University Press.

Jensen, R. (2001). The United States, International Policing and the War against Anarchist Terrorism, 1900–1914. *Terrorism and Political Violence, 13*(1), 15–46.

Jensen, R. (2009). The International Campaign Against Anarchist Terrorism, 1880–1930s. *Terrorism and Political Violence, 21*(1), 89–109.

Jensen, R. (2014). The Pre-1914 Anarchist "Lone Wolf" Terrorist and Governmental Responses. *Terrorism and Political Violence, 26*(1), 86–94.

Jerven, M. (2013). *Poor Numbers: How We Are Misled by African Development Statistics and What to Do About it*. Cornell University Press.

Jesperson, S. (2016). *Rethinking the Security-Development Nexus: Organised Crime in Post-Conflict States*. Routledge.

Jojarth, C. (2009). *Crime, War, and Global Trafficking: Designing International Cooperation*. Cambridge University Press.

Jolly, R., Emmerij, L., & Weiss, T. G. (2009). *UN Ideas That Changed the World*. Indiana University Press.

Jones, T. A. (1984). *Crime and Modernization: The Impact of Industrialization and Urbanization on Crime* by Louise I. Shelley. Southern Illinois University Press, 1981, and *Readings in Comparative Criminology*. L. Shelley (ed.). Southern Illinois University Press, 1981. *Social Forces, 62*(4), 1117–19.

Joshi, D., & O'Dell, R. (2013). Global governance and development ideology: The United Nations and the World Bank on the left-right spectrum. *Global Governance, 19*(2), 249–76.

Joutsen, M. (2018). The Globalized Reach of US Crime Policy. In P. Reichel & R. Randa (eds.), *Transnational Crime and Global Security* (pp. 317–36). Prager.

Kaldor, M. (1998) *New and Old Wars*. Blackwell.

Kamau, M., Chasek, P., & O'Connor, D. (2018). *Transforming Multilateral Diplomacy: The Inside Story of the Sustainable Development Goals*. Routledge.

Kantrow, L. (2014, June 16). *[Untitled Statement]*. 12th Session of the SDG Open Working Group, New York. https://sustainabledevelopment.un.org/content/documents/10329Business%20and%20Industry.pdf.

Karstedt, S. (2018). Is 'Big Picture Criminology' Policy Relevant?: Comparative Criminology, Evidence-Based Policies and the Scale of Our Discipline. *Criminology in Europe, 17*(3), 4–11.

Kaiser, P. (1996). Structural Adjustment and the Fragile Nation: the Demise of Social Unity in Tanzania. *The Journal of Modern African Studies, 34*(2), 227–37.

Kelly, R. J., & Levy, S. A. (2012). The Endangered Empire: American Responses to Transnational Organized Crime. In F. Allum & S. Gilmour (eds.), *Routledge Handbook of Transnational Organized Crime* (pp. 443–54). Routledge.

Kenen, P. B. (1990). Organizing Debt Relief: The Need for a New Institution. *Journal of Economic Perspectives, 4*(1), 7–18.

Kennedy, J. F. (1963, September 20). *Address Before the 18th General Assembly of the United Nations.* https://avalon.law.yale.edu/20th_century/truman.asp.

Kennedy, N. (2015, January 16). *[Untitled statement].* Stakeholder Preparatory Forum for the Post-2015 Development Agenda Negotiations, New York. https://sdgs.un.org/sites/default/files/statements/12267Norine%20Kennedy%20post%202015%20stocktaking%20forum%20business%20discussant%20tps%20011915.pdf.

Keohane, R. (1984). *After Hegemony: Cooperation and Discord in the World Political Economy.* Princeton University Press.

Kerry, J. (1997). *The New War: The Web of Crime That Threatens America's Security.* Simon & Schuster.

Khalifa, A. (1960). *Prevention of Types of Criminality Resulting from Social Changes and Accompanying Economic Development in Less Developed Countries: Part 2* (A/CONF.17/3; pp. 50–94). United Nations Department of Economic and Social Affairs. https://www.unodc.org/documents/congress//Previous_Congresses/2nd_Congress_1960/013_ACONF.17.3_Prevention_of_Types_of_Criminality_Resulting_from_Social_Changes.pdf.

Kick, E., & LaFree, G. (1985). Development and the social context of murder and theft. *Comparative Social Research, 8,* 37–58.

Knepper, P. (2009). *The Invention of International Crime: A Global Issue in the Making, 1881–1914.* Palgrave Macmillan.

Knepper, P. (2011). *International Crime in the 20th Century: The League of Nations Era, 1919–1939.* Palgrave Macmillan.

Koeppel, M. D. H., Rhineberger-Dunn, G. M., & Mack, K. Y. (2015). Cross-national homicide: A review of the current literature. *International Journal of Comparative and Applied Criminal Justice, 39*(1), 47–85.

Konadu-Agyemang, K. (2018). *IMF and World Bank Sponsored Structural Adjustment Programs in Africa: Ghana's Experience, 1983–1999.* Routledge.

Krasner, S. (ed.). (1983). *International Regimes.* Cornell University Press.

Krause, K. (2014). Violence, Insecurity, and Crime in Development Thought. In B. Currie-Alder et al. (eds.), *International Development: Ideas, Experience, and Prospects.* (pp. 379–94). Oxford University Press.

Krever, T. (2011). The Legal Turn in Late Development Theory: The Rule of Law and the World Bank's Development Model. *Harvard International Law Journal, 52*(1), 287–319.

Krueger, A. O. (1974). The Political Economy of the Rent-Seeking Society. *American Economic Review, 64*(3), 291–303.

Krugman, P. (1998, 7 September). Saving Asia: It's Time to Get Radical Fortune. https://money.cnn.com/magazines/fortune/fortune_archive/1998/09/07/247884/index.htm.

Kruijit, D. (2012). New Patterns of Violence in Latin America. In M. Nilsson & J. Gustafsson (eds.), *Latin American Responses to Globalization in the 21st Century* (pp. 171–87). Palgrave Macmillan.

LaFree, G. (1999). A Summary and Review of Cross-National Comparative Studies of Homicide. In M. Dwayne Smith & M. A. Zahn (eds.), *Homicide: A Sourcebook of Social Research* (pp. 124–45). SAGE.

LaFree, G., Curtis, K., & McDowall, D. (2015). How Effective Are Our 'Better Angels?': Assessing Country-level Declines in Homicide since 1950. *European Journal of Criminology, 12*, 482–504.

Larmour, P. (2005). *Civilizing Techniques: Transparency International and the Spread of Anti-corruption*. https://openresearch-repository.anu.edu.au/handle/10440/1158.

League of Nations. (1920). *The Covenant of the League of Nations*. https://libraryresources.unog.ch/ld.php?content_id=32971179.

League of Nations. (1934). *Enquiry into the Question of Children in Moral and Social Danger*. https://biblio-archive.unog.ch/Dateien/CouncilMSD/C-285-M-123-1934-IV_EN.pdf.

Leff, N. (1964). Economic Development through Corruption. *American Behavioural Scientist, 8*, 8–14.

Levchak, P. (2016). The relationship between urbanisation and cross-national homicide rates: Robustness across multiple estimation methods. *International Journal of Comparative and Applied Criminal Justice, 40*(3), 225–43.

Levy, C. (2004). Anarchism, Internationalism and Nationalism in Europe, 1860–1939. *Australian Journal of Politics & History, 50*(3), 330–42.

Liu, J. (2004). Social Transition and Crime in China: An Economic Motivation Thesis. *Australian & New Zealand Journal of Criminology, 37*(1), 122–38.

Littoz-Monnet, A. (2017). Production and uses of expertise by international bureaucracies. In A. Littoz-Monnet (ed.), *The Politics of Expertise in International Organizations: How International Bureaucracies Produce and Mobilize Knowledge* (pp. 1–18). Routledge.

Loader, I. (2006). Fall of the "Platonic Guardians": Liberalism, Criminology and Political Responses to Crime in England and Wales. *British Journal of Criminology, 46*(4), 561–86.

López-Rey, M. (1954). International Co-Operation by the United Nations in the Prevention of Crime and the Treatment of Offenders. *The British Journal of Delinquency, 5*(2), 125–37.

López-Rey, M. (1957). The First UN Congress on the Prevention of Crime and the Treatment of Offenders. *Journal of Criminal Law and Criminology, 47*(5), 526–38.

López-Rey, M. (1985). *A Guide to United Nations Criminal Policy*. Gower.

Love, J. L. (1980). Raúl Prebisch and the Origins of the Doctrine of Unequal Exchange. *Latin American Research Review, 15*(3), 45–72.

Lynch, M. (2017). Marx, Engels, Marxist/Radical Criminology, and the Explanation of Crime. In R. Triplett (ed.), *The Handbook of the History and Philosophy of Criminology*. (pp. 84–101). Wiley.

Maguire, M., Morgan, R., & Reiner, R. (eds.). (2002). Crime statistics: The "data explosion" and its implications. In *The Oxford handbook of criminology* (pp. 322–75). Oxford University Press.

Mahadevan, P. (2019). *Sand Mafias in India: Disorganised crime in a growing economy* (p. 27). Global Initiative Against Transnational Organized Crime. https://globalinitiative.net/wp-content/uploads/2019/07/Sand-Mining-in-India-Report-17Jul1045-Web.pdf.

Major Group: Business and Industry. (2014). *Business and Industry Proposed Revisions by Focus Area.* https://sustainabledevelopment.un.org/content/documents/10489business.pdf.

Mansfield, D. (1999). Alternative development: The modern thrust of supply-side policy. *Bulletin on Narcotics, LI*(1 & 2).

Marlatt, G. A. (1996). Harm reduction: Come as you are. *Addictive Behaviors, 21*(6), 779–88.

Martins, C. E. (2020). *Dependency, Neoliberalism and Globalization in Latin America.* Haymarket Books.

Mauro, P. (1995). Corruption and Growth. *The Quarterly Journal of Economics, 110*(3), 681–712.

Martínez, Ó. (2017). *A History of Violence: Living and Dying in Central America.* Verso Books.

Mauro, P. (1995). Corruption and Growth. *The Quarterly Journal of Economics, 110*(3), 681–712.

McNamara, R. (1971, October 28). *Address to the U.N. Economic and Social Council.* https://openknowledge.worldbank.org/handle/10986/33158.

McLean, C., et al. (2019). Exploring the Relationship between Neoliberalism and Homicide: A Cross-National Perspective. *International Journal of Sociology, 49*, 53–76.

McLeod, A. M. (2010). Exporting US Criminal Justice. *Yale Law & Policy Review, 29*(1), 83–164.

McMullin, J. (2009). Organised Criminal Groups and Conflict: The Nature and Consequences of Interdependence. *Civil Wars, 11*(1), 75–102.

Melossi, D., Sozzo, M., & Sparks, R. (2011). *Travels of the Criminal Question: Cultural Embeddedness and Diffusion.* Bloomsbury Publishing.

Merton, R. (1938). Social Structure and Anomie. *American Sociological Review, 3*(5): 672–82.

Messick, R. E. (1999). Judicial Reform and Economic Development: A Survey of the Issues. *The World Bank Research Observer, 14*(1), 117–36.

Messner, S. F. (1986). Modernization, Structural Characteristics, and Societal Rates of Crime: An Application of Blau's Macrosociological Theory. *The Sociological Quarterly, 17*(1), 27–41.

Miller, C. (2005). The Social Section and Advisory Committee on Social Questions of the League of Nations. In P. Weindling (ed.), *International Health Organisations and Movements, 1918–1939* (pp. 154–75). Oxford University Press.

Mittelman, J. H., & Johnston, R. (2011). The Globalization of Organized Crime, the Courtesan State, and the Corruption of Civil Society. In J. H. Mittelman (ed.),

Contesting Global Order: Development, Global Governance, and Globalization (pp. 116–35). Routledge.

Moosavi, L. (2019). Decolonising Criminology: Syed Hussein Alatas on Crimes of the Powerful. *Critical Criminology, 27*(2), 229–42.

Moosavi, L. (2020). The decolonial bandwagon and the dangers of intellectual decolonisation. *International Review of Sociology, 30*(2), 332–54.

Morgan, K. (2000). *Slavery, Atlantic Trade and the British Economy, 1660–1800*. Cambridge University Press.

Moser, C., & Holland, J. (1997). *Urban Poverty and Violence in Jamaica*. World Bank. https://elibrary.worldbank.org/doi/abs/10.1596/0-8213-3870-6.

Muggah, R. (2017). The Rise of Citizen Security in Latin America and the Caribbean. *International Development Policy*, (9), 291–322.

Murniningtyas, E. (2014, February 7). *Conflict Prevention, Post-conflict Peacebuilding and the Promotion of Durable Peace, Rule of Law and Governance*. Eighth Session of the SDG Open Working Group, New York. https://sustainabledevelopment.un.org/content/documents/6340indonesia3.pdf.

Murphy, C. (1994). *International Organization and Industrial Change: Global Governance Since 1850*. Polity Press.

Murphy, C. (2006). *The United Nations Development Programme: A Better Way?* Cambridge University Press.

Murphy, M. N. (2011). Somali Piracy. *The RUSI Journal, 156*(6), 4–11.

Nadelmann, E. (1990). Global Prohibition Regimes: The Evolution of Norms in International Society. *International Organization, 44*(4), 479–526.

Naik, A. (2013). Can the UN Adjust to the Changing Funding Landscape? *Future United. Nations Development System*. Retrieved November 6, 2018, from https://futureun.org/media/archive1/briefings/Briefing-2-FINAL.pdf.

Naylor, R. T. (1995). From Cold War to Crime War: The Search for a New "National Security" Threat. *Transnational Organized Crime, 1*(4), 37–56.

Naylor, T. (2020). All That's Lost: The Hollowing of Summit Diplomacy in a Socially Distanced World. *The Hague Journal of Diplomacy, 15*(4), 583–98.

Neopolitan, J. (1997). *Cross-National Crime: A Research Review and Sourcebook*. Greenwood Press.

Newsweek. (1993, 12 December). Global Mafia. *Newsweek*. https://www.newsweek.com/global-mafia-190816.

Nivette, A. (2011). Cross-National Predictors of Crime: A Meta-Analysis. *Homicide Studies, 15*(2), 103–31.

Nye, J. (2003). *The Paradox of American Power: Why the World's Only Superpower Can't Go It Alone*. Oxford University Press.

OECD. (1996). *OECD Symposium on Corruption and Good Governance*. Organisation for Economic Cooperation and Development.

O'Malley, P. (1992). Risk, power and crime prevention. *Economy and Society, 21*(3), 252–75.

O'Malley, P. (2012). *Risk, Uncertainty and Government*. Routledge.

O'Malley, P. (2018). Neoliberalism, Crime and Criminal Justice. In D. Cahill et al. (eds.), *The SAGE Handbook of Neoliberalism* (pp. 284–94). SAGE.

Ong, A. (2006). *Neoliberalism as Exception: Mutations in Citizenship and Sovereignty*. Duke University Press.
Osborne, D., & Gaebler, T. (1993). *Reinventing Government: How the Entrepreneurial Spirit Is Transforming the Public Sector*. Plume.
Paris, R. (2001). Human Security: Paradigm Shift or Hot Air? *International Security*, 26(2), 87–102.
Pearce, F. (1976). *Crimes of the Powerful: Marxism, Crime, and Deviance*. Pluto Press.
Panakal, J. J. (1960). *Prevention of Types of Criminality Resulting from Social Changes and Accompanying Economic Development in Less Developed Countries: Part 1* (A/CONF.17/3; pp. 2–49). United Nations Department of Economic and Social Affairs. https://www.unodc.org/documents/congress//Previous_Congresses/2nd _Congress_1960/013_ACONF.17.3_Prevention_of_Types_of_Criminality _Resulting_from_Social_Changes.pdf.
Panel of Eminent Persons on United Nations–Civil Society Relations. (2004). *We the peoples: Civil society, the United Nations and global governance* (A/58/817). United Nations. https://archive.globalpolicy.org/images/pdfs/0611report.pdf.
Pare, P., & Felson, R. (2014). Income Inequality, Poverty, and Crime Across Nations. *British Journal of Sociology*, 65(3), 434–58.
Park, R. (1921). *Introduction to the Science of Sociology*. University of Chicago Press.
Park, R., Burgess, E., & MacKenzie, R. (1925). *The City*. University of Chicago Press.
Payer, C. (1982). *World Bank: A Critical Analysis*. NYU Press.
Pedersen, S. (2007). Back to the League of Nations. *The American Historical Review*, 112(4), 1091–1117.
Pedersen, S. (2015). *The Guardians: The League of Nations and the Crisis of Empire*. Oxford University Press.
Perlman, J. (2010). *Favela: Four Decades of Living on the Edge in Rio De Janeiro*. Oxford University Press.
Permanent Subcommittee on Investigations. (2012). *U.S. Vulnerabilities to Money Laundering, Drugs, and Terrorist Financing: HSBC Case History*. United States Senate. https://www.hsgac.senate.gov/imo/media/doc/PSI%20REPORT -HSBC%20CASE%20HISTORY%20(9.6)2.pdf.
Polzer, T. (2001). *Corruption: Deconstructing the World Bank Discourse* (No. 01–18). London School of Economics DESTIN. https://www.files.ethz.ch/isn/138135 /WP18.pdf.
Prashad, V. (2007). *The Darker Nations: A People's History of the Third World*. The New Press.
Prashad, V. (2014). *The Poorer Nations: A Possible History of the Global South* (p. 316). Verso Books.
Pratt, J. (2007). *Penal Populism*. Routledge.
President's Commission on Law Enforcement and Administration of Justice. (1967). *The Challenge of Crime in a Free Society: A Report by the President's Commission on Law Enforcement and Administration of Justice*. (p. 664). US Government Printing Office. http://www.jstor.org/stable/2091056?origin=crossref.

President's Commission on Organized Crime. (1986). *The Impact: Organized crime today: Report to the President and the Attorney General*. United States Government Printing.

Pridemore, W. A. (2011). Poverty Matters: A Reassessment of the Inequality-Homicide Relationship in Cross-national Studies. *British Journal of Criminology, 51*, 739–72.

Quijano, A. (2007). Coloniality and Modernity/Rationality. *Cultural Studies, 21*(2–3), 168–78.

Rahman, M. (2014, February 7). *[Untitled Statement]*. Eighth Session of the SDG Open Working Group, New York. https://sustainabledevelopment.un.org/content/documents/6430bangladesh2.pdf.

Raine, L., & Cilluffo, F. (ed.). (1994). *Global Organized Crime: The New Empire of Evil*. Center for Strategic & International Studies.

Rapoport, D. (2004). The Four Waves of Modern Terrorism. In A. Cronin & J. Lodes (eds.), *Attacking Terrorism: Elements of a Grand Strategy* (pp. 46–73). Georgetown University Press.

Reagan, R. (1986, January 12). Declaring War on Organized Crime. *New York Times*. https://www.nytimes.com/1986/01/12/magazine/declaring-war-on-organized-crime.html.

Redo, S. (2012). *Blue Criminology: The Power of United Nations Ideas to Counter Crime Globally: A Monographic Study*. HEUNI.

Redo, S., & Platzer, M. (2013). The United Nations' Role in Crime Control and Prevention. In P. Reichel & J. Albanese (eds.), *Handbook of Transnational Crime and Justice*, 2nd edition (pp. 283–302). SAGE.

Reiner, R. (2016). *Crime, The Mystery of the Common-Sense Concept*, 1st edition. Polity.

Reitano, T. (2018). Organised Crime as a Threat to Sustainable Development: Understanding the Evidence. In V. Comolli (ed.), *Organised Crime and Illicit Trade: How to Respond to This Strategic Challenge in Old and New Domains* (pp. 23–36). Palgrave Macmillan.

Rio+20. (2012). *The Future We Want*. United Nations. https://sustainabledevelopment.un.org/content/documents/733FutureWeWant.pdf.

Rist, G. (2014). *The History of Development: From Western Origins to Global Faith*, 4th edition. Zed Books.

Robinson, C. D., & Scaglion, R. (1987). The Origin and Evolution of the Police Function in Society: Notes toward a Theory. *Law & Society Review, 21*(1), 109–53.

Rodney, W. (1972). *How Europe Underdeveloped Africa*. Bogle-L'Ouverture.

Rogers, J. (1989). Theories of Crime and Development: An Historical Perspective. *The Journal of Development Studies, 25*, 314–28.

Rogers, M., & Pridemore, W. (2018). Do National Homicide Rates Follow Supranational Trends? *Journal of Research in Crime and Delinquency, 55*(6), 691–727.

Romaniuk, P. (2018). Crime and Criminal Justice. In T. Weiss & S. Daws (eds.), *The Oxford Handbook on the United Nations* (pp. 515–27). Oxford University Press. https://doi.org/10.1093/oxfordhb/9780198803164.013.28.

Rose, C. (2015). *International Anti-Corruption Norms: Their Creation and Influence on Domestic Legal Systems*. Oxford University Press.

Rose-Ackerman, S. (1978). *Corruption: A Study in Political Economy*. Academic Press.

Rosenthal, G. (2018). Economic and Social Council. In T. Weiss & S. Daws (eds.), *The Oxford Handbook on the United Nations* (pp. 166–75). Oxford University Press.

Rostow, W. W. (1960). *The Stages of Economic Growth: A Non-Communist Manifesto*. Cambridge University Press.

Ruggie, J. G. (1982). International Regimes, Transactions, and Change: Embedded Liberalism in the Postwar Economic Order. *International Organization*, 36(2), 379–415.

Ruggie, J. (1992). Multilateralism: The Anatomy of an Institution. *International Organization*, 46(3), 561–98.

Sachs, J. D. (2012). From Millennium Development Goals to Sustainable Development Goals. *The Lancet*, 379(9832), 2206–11.

Sahasranaman, A., & Bettencourt, L. (2019). Urban geography and scaling of contemporary Indian cities. *Journal of the Royal Society Interface*, 16(152), 1–12.

Salahub, J., & Zaaroura, M. D. (2018). Conclusion. In J. E. Salahub et al. (eds.), *Reducing Urban Violence in the Global South: Towards Safe and Inclusive Cities* (pp. 221–36). Routledge.

Salahub, J., Gottsbacher, M., & de Boer, J. (2018). *Social Theories of Urban Violence in the Global South: Towards Safe and Inclusive Cities*. Routledge.

Sanchez, M. (2006). Insecurity and Violence as a New Power Relation in Latin America. *The Annals of the American Academy of Political and Social Sciences*, 606, 178–95.

Scholte, J. A. (2011). *Building Global Democracy?: Civil Society and Accountable Global Governance*. Cambridge University Press.

Schneider, J., & Schneider, P. (2011). Civil Society and Transnational Organized Crime: The case of the Italian Antimafia Movement. In F. Allum & S. Gilmour (eds.), *Routledge Handbook of Transnational Organized Crime* (pp. 353–65). Routledge.

Sen, A. (1999). *Development as Freedom*. Oxford University Press.

Sen, S. (2004). Counter-Colonial Criminology: A Critique of Imperialist Reason (review). *Journal of Colonialism and Colonial History*, 5(1). doi: 10.1353/cch.2004.0040.

Sénit, C.-A., & Biermann, F. (2021.). In Whose Name Are You Speaking? The Marginalization of the Poor in Global Civil Society. *Global Policy*. Online First. https://doi.org/10.1111/1758-5899.12997.

Shaffer, G. C., & Aaronson, E. (eds.). (2020) *Transnational Legal Ordering of Criminal Justice*. Cambridge University Press.

Sharkey, P. (2018). *Uneasy Peace: The Great Crime Decline, the Renewal of City Life, and the Next War on Violence*. W.W. Norton.

Sharman, J. (2011). *The Money Laundry: Regulating Criminal Finance in the Global Economy*. Cornell University Press.

Sharman, J. C. (2017). *The Despot's Guide to Wealth Management: On the International Campaign against Grand Corruption*. Cornell University Press.

Shaw, C., & McKay, H. (1942). *Juvenile Delinquency and Urban Areas*, 1st edition. University of Chicago Press.

Shaw, C., & McKay, H. (1969). *Juvenile Delinquency and Urban Areas*, 2nd edition. University of Chicago Press.

Shaw, M. (2001). The Political Economy of Crime and Conflict in Sub Saharan Africa. *South African Journal of International Affairs, 8*(2), 57–69.

Shaw, M., et al. (2018 November 2). What to make of the new UNTOC review mechanism? Global Initiative Against Transnational Organized Crime. https://globalinitiative.net/untoc-review-mechanism/.

Shelley, L. (1981). *Crime and Modernization*. Southern Illinois University Press.

Shelley, L. (1995). Transnational Organized Crime: An Imminent Threat to the Nation-State? *Journal of International Affairs, 48*(2), 463–89.

Shelley, L. I. (1998). Organized Crime and Corruption in Ukraine: Impediments to the Development of a Free Market Economy. *Demokratizatsiya, 6*(4), 648–63.

Sheptycki, J. (1995). Transnational Policing and the Making of a Postmodern State. *The British Journal of Criminology, 35*(4), 613–35.

Sheptycki, J. (2003). Against Transnational Organized Crime. In M. E. Beare (ed.), *Critical Reflections on Transnational Organized Crime, Money Laundering, and Corruption* (pp. 88–119). University of Toronto Press.

Sheptycki, J. (2007). The Constabulary Ethic and Transnational Condition. In A. Goldsmith & J. Sheptycki (eds.), *Crafting Transnational Policing: Police Capacity-Building and Global Policing Reform* (pp. 31–71). Hart Publishing.

Sherman, L., Neyroud, P. W., & Neyroud, E. (2016). The Cambridge Crime Harm Index: Measuring Total Harm from Crime Based on Sentencing Guidelines. *Policing: A Journal of Policy and Practice, 10*(3), 171–83.

Simon, J. (2006). *Governing through Crime: How the War on Crime Transformed American Democracy and Created a Culture of Fear*. Oxford University Press.

Simmons, B., Lloyd, P., & Stewart, B. (2018). The Global Diffusion of Law: Transnational Crime and the Case of Human Trafficking. *International Organization, 72*(2), 249–81.

Soares, R. (2004). Development, Crime and Punishment: Accounting for the International Differences in Crime Rates. *Journal of Development Economics, 73*(1), 155–84.

Steinberg, J. (2016). How Well Does Theory Travel? David Garland in the Global South. *The Howard Journal of Crime and Justice, 55*(4), 514–31.

Sterling, C. (1994).*Thieves' World: The Threat of the New Global Network of Organized Crime*. Simon & Schuster.

Strayer, R. (2016). *Why Did the Soviet Union Collapse? Understanding Historical Change*. Routledge.

SAPRIN (2004). *Structural Adjustment: The Policy Roots of Economic Crisis, Poverty, and Inequality*. Zed Books.

Summers, L. H., & Pritchett, L. H. (1993). The Structural-Adjustment Debate. *The American Economic Review, 83*(2), 383–89.

Sumner, C. (1982) *Crime, Justice and Underdevelopment*. Heinemann.
Sutherland, E. (1939). *Principles of Criminology*, 3rd edition. Lippincott.
Syal, R. (2009, December 13). Drug money saved banks in global crisis, claims UN advisor. *The Observer*. http://www.theguardian.com/global/2009/dec/13/drug-money-banks-saved-un-cfief-claims.
Tauri, J. (2018). The Master's Tools Will Never Dismantle the Master's House: An Indigenous Critique of Criminology. *Journal of Global Indigeneity*, *3*(1). https://ro.uow.edu.au/jgi/vol3/iss1/6.
Taylor, I. (2003). Hegemony, Neoliberal "Good Governance" and the International Monetary Fund: A Gramscian Perspective. In M. Boas & D. McNeill (eds.), *Global Institutions and Development: Framing the World?* (pp. 124–36). Routledge.
Tennant, I. (2021). *Kyoto Declaration: States affirm their primacy in crime prevention and criminal justice amid downgraded role of civil society* [Global Initiative Against Transnational Organized Crime]. Retrieved September 16, 2021, from https://globalinitiative.net/analysis/kyoto-declaration/.
Tennant, I., & Mahadevan, P. (2021). The Implementation Review Mechanism of the UN Convention Against Transnational Organized Crime (UNTOC): What Role for Civil Society? *Brill Research Perspectives in Transnational Crime*, *3*(2–3), 39–54.
Thant, U. (1964). *Assessment of arrangements for carrying out United Nations responsibilities in the field of the prevention of crime and the treatment of offenders: Note / by the Secretary-General*. United Nations. https://digitallibrary.un.org/record/669808?ln=en.
Tran, M. (2012, November 16). Mark Malloch-Brown: Developing the MDGs was a bit like nuclear fusion. *The Guardian*. http://www.theguardian.com/global-development/2012/nov/16/mark-malloch-brown-mdgs-nuclear.
Transnational Institute. (2005, November 17). *UNDCP Overview*. https://www.tni.org/es/node/12420.
Trent, C., & Pridemore, W. (2012). A Review of the Cross-National Empirical Literature on Social Structure and Homicide. In M. Liem & W. Pridemore (eds.), *Handbook of European Homicide Research: Patterns, Explanations, and Country Studies*. (pp. 111–35). Springer.
Trubek, D. M. (2006). The "Rule of Law" in Development Assistance: Past, Present and Future. In D. M. Trubek & A. Santos (eds.), *The New Law and Economic Development: A Critical Appraisal* (pp. 74–94). Cambridge University Press.
Trubek, D. M., & Santos, A. (2006). The Third Moment in Law and Development Theory and the Emergence of a New Critical Practice. In D. M. Trubek & A. Santos (eds.), *The New Law and Economic Development: A Critical Appraisal* (pp. 1–18). Cambridge University Press.
True, J. (2012). *The Political Economy of Violence Against Women*. Oxford University Press.
Tuttle, J., McCall, P., & Land, K. C. (2018). Latent Trajectories of Cross-National Homicide Trends: Structural Characteristics of Underlying Groups. *Homicide Studies*, *22*(4), 343–69.
United Nations. (1945). *United Nations Charter*. https://www.un.org/en/about-us/un-charter/full-text.

United Nations. (1995). Transnational Crime and Disrupting Development and Peace. https://www.unodc.org/documents/congress//Previous_Congresses/9th_Congress_1995/034_Backgrounder_Transnational_Crime_Disrupting_Development_and_Peace.pdf.

United Nations. (2005). Definition of "Urban." https://unstats.un.org/unsd/demographic/sconcerns/densurb/Defintion_of%20Urban.pdf.

United Nations. (2010). *The Millennium Development Goals Report.* New York: United Nations. Accessed 23 August 2021 at https://www.un.org/millenniumgoals/pdf/MDG%20Report%202010%20En%20r15%20-low%20res%2020100615%20-.pdf.

United Nations. (2012). UN Secretary-General appoints High-Level Panel on Post-2015 Development Agenda. United Nations. https://www.un.org/sg/sites/www.un.org.sg/files/documents/management/PRpost2015.pdf.

United Nations. (2013a). *The International Drug Control Conventions.* United Nations.

United Nations. (2013b). *A Million Voices: The World We Want.* New York. https://www.undp.org/publications/million-voices-world-we-want.

United Nations. (2015). Doha Declaration on Integrating Crime Prevention and Criminal Justice into the Wider United Nations Agenda to Address Social and Economic Challenges and to Promote the Rule of Law at the National and International Levels, and Public Participation. United Nations. https://www.unodc.org/documents/congress/Declaration/V1504151_English.pdf.

UN DESA. (1956). *The First United Nations Congress on the Prevention of Crime and Treatment of Offenders.* https://www.unodc.org/documents/congress//Previous_Congresses/1st_Congress_1955/114_ACONF.6.1_First_United_Nations_Congress_on_the_Prevention_of_Crime_and_the_Treatment_of_Offenders.pdf.

UN DESA. (1960). *Second United Nations Congress on the Prevention of Crime and the Treatment of Offenders.* https://www.unodc.org/documents/congress//Previous_Congresses/2nd_Congress_1960/023_ACONF.17.20_Second_United_Nations_Congress_on_the_Prevention_of_Crime_and_the_Treatment_of_Offenders.pdf.

UN DESA. (1966). *Third United Nations Congress on the Prevention of Crime and the Treatment of Offenders [Secretariat Report].* https://www.unodc.org/documents/congress//Previous_Congresses/3rd_Congress_1965/007_ACONF.26.7_Third_United_Nations_Congress_on_the_Prevention_of_Crime_and_Treatment_of_Offenders.pdf.

UN DPI. (1953). *Yearbook of the United Nations, 1953.* United Nations. https://digitallibrary.un.org/record/860246?ln=en.

UN DPI. (2010). Fact Sheet: UN Summit on the Millennium Development Goals. https://www.un.org/millenniumgoals/pdf/mdg_summit_factsheet.pdf.

UNDG. (2014). *People's Voices—Issue Brief to the SDG Open Working Group.* https://sustainabledevelopment.un.org/content/documents/3145UNDG-PeoplesVoicesIssueBrief-30JAN14.pdf.

UNDP. (1990). *Human Development Report 1990.* Oxford University Press. http://hdr.undp.org/sites/default/files/reports/219/hdr_1990_en_complete_nostats.pdf.

UNDP. (1994). *Human Development Report 1994*. Oxford University Press. http://hdr.undp.org/sites/default/files/reports/255/hdr_1994_en_complete_nostats.pdf.

UNDP. (1999). *Human Development Report 1999: Globalization with a Human Face*. Oxford University Press. http://hdr.undp.org/en/content/human-development-report-1999.

UNDP. (2013). *Issue Brief: Integrating the Rule of Law in the Post 2015 Development Agenda*. United Nations. http://www.undp.org/content/undp/en/home/librarypage/democraticgovernance/dg-publications/governance-and-the-post-2015-development-framework/.

UNGA. (1950). *Transfer of functions of the International Penal and Penitentiary Commission, 415 (V)*. https://www.unodc.org/documents/commissions/CCPCJ/Crime_Resolutions/1950-1959/1950/General_Assembly_A-RES-415-V.pdf.

UNGA. (1974). *Declaration on the Establishment of a New International Economic Order, A/RES/3201 (S-VI)*. https://digitallibrary.un.org/record/218450?ln=en.

UNGA. (2000). *United Nations Millennium Declaration, 55/2*. https://www.ohchr.org/EN/ProfessionalInterest/Pages/Millennium.aspx.

UNGA. (2001). *United Nations Convention Against Transnational Organized Crime, A/RES/55/25*. https://treaties.un.org/pages/viewdetails.aspx?src=ind&mtdsg_no=xviii-12&chapter=18&lang=en.

UNGA. (2003) *United Nations Convention against Corruption, A/RES/58/422*. https://treaties.un.org/pages/viewdetails.aspx?src=ind&mtdsg_no=xviii-14&chapter=18&lang=en.

UNGA. (2006). *The rule of law at the national and international levels, A/RES/61/39*. https://undocs.org/en/A/RES/61/39.

UNGA. (2009). *Implementation of Agenda 21, the Programme for the Further Implementation of Agenda 21 and the outcomes of the World Summit on Sustainable Development, A/RES/64/236*. https://undocs.org/en/A/RES/64/236.

UNGA. (2012). *Declaration of the High-level Meeting of the General Assembly on the Rule of Law at the National and International Levels, A/RES/67/1*. https://www.un.org/ruleoflaw/files/37839_A-RES-67-1.pdf.

UNGA. (2015). *Transforming Our World: The 2030 Agenda for Sustainable Development, A/RES/70/1*. https://www.un.org/ga/search/view_doc.asp?symbol=A/RES/70/1&Lang=E.

UNIS. (2015 April 15). The Nexus between Crime and Development. YouTube. https://www.youtube.com/watch?v=OhqPktXCr2c.

UNODC. (n.d.) *Education for Justice, The Doha Declaration: Promoting a Culture of Lawfulness*. https://www.unodc.org/e4j/.

UNODC. (2003). *The Opium Economy in Afghanistan*. United Nations. https://www.unodc.org/pdf/publications/afg_opium_economy_www.pdf.

UNODC. (2005). *Crime and Development in Africa*. United Nations. https://www.unodc.org/pdf/African_report.pdf.

UNODC. (2007). *Crime and Development in Central America*. United Nations. https://www.unodc.org/documents/data-and-analysis/Central-america-study-en.pdf.

UNODC. (2009a). *Transnational Trafficking and the Rule of Law in West Africa: A Threat Assessment.* United Nations. https://www.unodc.org/nigeria/en/transnational-trafficking-and-the-rule-of-law-in-west-africa_-a-threat-assessment.html.

UNODC. (2009b) *UNODC Executive Director to address Security Council on West Africa.* https://www.unodc.org/unodc/en/frontpage/2009/July/unodc-executive-director-to-address-un-security-council-on-west-africa.html.

UNODC. (2010). *The globalization of crime—A transnational organized crime threat assessment.* https://www.unodc.org/unodc/en/data-and-analysis/tocta-2010.html.

UNODC. (2011). *Regional Programme on Drug Control, Crime Prevention and Criminal Justice Reform in the Arab States 2011–2015.* https://www.unodc.org/documents/middleeastandnorthafrica//Regional-Programme-doc/RPArabStates.pdf.

UNODC. (2012a). *Transnational Organized Crime In Central America and the Caribbean: A Threat Assessment.* https://www.unodc.org/documents/data-and-analysis/Studies/TOC_Central_America_and_the_Caribbean_Exsum_english.pdf.

UNODC. (2012b) *Opiate Flows through Northern Afghanistan and Central Asia: A Threat Assessment.* https://www.unodc.org/documents/data-and-analysis/Studies/Afghanistan_northern_route_2012_web.pdf.

UNODC. (2013a). *Transnational Organized Crime in East Asia and the Pacific.* https://www.unodc.org/documents/data-and-analysis/Studies/TOCTA_EAP_web.pdf.

UNODC. (2013b). *Transnational Organized Crime in West Africa: A Threat Assessment.* https://www.unodc.org/toc/en/reports/TOCTAWestAfrica.html.

UNODC. (2013c). *Accounting for Security and Justice in the Post-2015 Development Agenda.* https://www.unodc.org/documents/mexicoandcentralamerica/publications/Agenda2030/2030UNODC_-_Accounting_for_Security_and_Justice_in_the_Post-2015_Development_Agenda.pdf.

UNODC. (2019). *Global Study on Homicide.* https://www.unodc.org/documents/data-and-analysis/gsh/Booklet1.pdf.

UN OIOS. (2001a). *Report on the inspection of programme management and administrative practices in the Office for Drug Control and Crime Prevention, A/56/83.* https://oios.un.org/resources/reports/a56_83.htm.

UN OIOS. (2001b). *Report of the Office of Internal Oversight Services on the investigation into allegations of misconduct and mismanagement of the "boat project" at the United Nations Office for Drug Control and Crime Prevention, A/56/689.* https://digitallibrary.un.org/record/455144?ln=en#record-files-collapse-header.

UN Panel of Eminent Persons on United Nations–Civil Society Relations. (2004). Transmittal letter dated 7 June 2004, UNGA. https://digitallibrary.un.org/record/523950?ln=en.

UN Secretariat. (1960). *Prevention of Types of Criminality Resulting from Social Changes and Accompanying Economic Development in Less Developed Countries, A/CONF.17/4.* https://www.unodc.org/documents/congress//Previous_Congresses/2nd_Congress_1960/014_ACONF.17.4_Prevention_of_Types_of_Criminality_Resulting_from_Social_Changes.pdf.

UN Secretariat. (1970). *Social Defence Policies in Relation to Development Planning.* https://www.unodc.org/documents/congress//Previous_Congresses/4th _Congress_1970/006_ACONF.43.1_Social_Defense_Policies_in_Relation_to _Development_Planning.pdf.

UN Secretariat. (1971). *Fourth United Nations Congress on the Prevention of Crime and the Treatment of Offenders, A/CONF.43/5.* https://www.unodc.org/documents /congress//Previous_Congresses/4th_Congress_1970/010_ACONF.43.5_Fourth _United_Nations_Congress_on_the_Prevention_of_Crime_and_the_Treatment _of_Offenders.pdf.

UN Secretariat. (1975). *Social Defence Planning in Relation to Development, A/ CONF.43/1.* https://www.unodc.org/documents/congress//Previous_Congresses /4th_Congress_1970/006_ACONF.43.1_Social_Defense_Policies_in_Relation _to_Development_Planning.pdf.

UN Secretariat. (1976). *Fifth United Nations Congress on the Prevention of Crime and the Treatment of Offenders, A/CONF.56/10.* https://www.unodc.org/docu ments/congress//Previous_Congresses/5th_Congress_1975/025_ACONF.56.10 _Fifth_United_Nations_Congress_on_the_Prevention_of_Crime_and_the_Treat ment_of_Offenders.pdf.

UN Secretariat. (1980). *Crime and the Abuse of Power: Offences and Offenders Beyond the Reach of the Law? A/CONF.87/6.* https://www.unodc.org/documents /congress//Previous_Congresses/6th_Congress_1980/007_ACONF.87.6_Crime _and_the_Abuse_of_Power_-_Offenses_and_Offenders_Beyond_the_Reach_of _Law.pdf.

UN Secretariat. (1985). *New Dimensions of Criminality and Crime Prevention in the Context of Development: Challenges for the Future, A/CONF.121/20.* https://www .unodc.org/documents/congress//Previous_Congresses/7th_Congress_1985/029 _ACONF.121.20_Working_Paper_New_Dimensions_of_Criminality_and _Crime_Prevention_in_the_Context_of_Development.pdf.

UN Secretariat. (1986). *Seventh United Nations Congress on the Prevention of Crime and the Treatment of Offenders, A/CONF.121/22/Rev.1.* https://www .unodc.org/documents/congress//Previous_Congresses/7th_Congress_1985/031 _ACONF.121.22.Rev.1_Report_Seventh_United_Nations_Congress_on_the _Prevention_of_Crime_and_the_Treatment_of_Offenders.pdf.

UN Secretariat. (1991). *Eighth United Nations Congress on the Prevention of Crime and the Treatment of Offenders, A/CONF.144/28/Rev.1.* https://www .unodc.org/documents/congress//Previous_Congresses/8th_Congress_1990/028 _ACONF.144.28.Rev.1_Report_Eighth_United_Nations_Congress_on_the _Prevention_of_Crime_and_the_Treatment_of_Offenders.pdf.

UN Secretariat. (2000a). *Promoting the rule of law and strengthening the criminal justice system, A/CONF.187/1.* https://www.unodc.org/documents/congress//Previ ous_Congresses/10th_Congress_2000/006_ACONF.187.3_Promoting_the_Rule _of_Law_and_Strengthening_the_Criminal_Justice_System.pdf.

UN Secretariat. (2000b). *Discussion Guide. A/CONF.187/PM.* Accessed 1 August 2021 at https://www.unodc.org/documents/congress//Previous_Congresses/10th _Congress_2000/031_ACONF.187.PM.1_Discussion_Guide.pdf.

UN Secretariat. (2001). *Report of the Tenth United Nations Congress on the Prevention of Crime and the Treatment of Offenders, A/CONF.187/5.* https://www.unodc.org/documents/congress//Previous_Congresses/10th_Congress_2000/030_ACONF.187.15_Report_of_the_Tenth_United_Nations_Congress_on_the_Prevention_of_Crime_and_the_Treatment_of_Offenders.pdf.
UNSC. (2010). *Resolution 1918, S/RES/1918/2010.* https://digitallibrary.un.org/record/681282?ln=en.
UNSC. (2011) *656th Meeting, S/PV.6565.* https://undocs.org/S/PV.6565.
UN System Task Team on the Post-2015 UN Development Agenda. (2012). *Realizing the Future We Want for All.* United Nations. https://sustainabledevelopment.un.org/content/documents/614Post_2015_UNTTreport.pdf.
UN Task Force on Transnational Organized Crime and Drug Trafficking. (2012, 30 May). UN Task Force on Transnational Organized Crime and Drug Trafficking. Australasian Centre for Policing Research, Bangkok. https://www.unodc.org/documents/southeastasiaandpacific/2012/06/tocta/TOCTA_EAP_Overview_13_30_May_2012_ACPR.pdf.
US Senate Committee on Foreign Relations. (1989). *Drugs, law enforcement, and foreign policy: A report.* https://catalog.hathitrust.org/Record/007608866.
van Dijk, J. (2001). Does Crime Pay? On the Relationships Between Crime, Rule of Law and Economic Growth. *Forum on Crime and Society, 1*(1), 1–16.
van Dijk, J. (2007). *The World of Crime: Breaking the Silence on Problems of Security, Justice and Development Across the World.* SAGE.
van Dijk, J., Nieuwbeerta, P., & Joudo Larsen, J. (2021). Global Crime Patterns: An Analysis of Survey Data from 166 Countries Around the World, 2006–2019. *Journal of Quantitative Criminology.* https://doi.org/10.1007/s10940-021-09501-0.
Verweij, M., & Josling, T. E. (2003). Special Issue: Deliberately Democratizing Multilateral Organization. *Governance, 16*(1), 1–21.
Vito, G. F. (1983). The Politics of Crime Control: Implications of Reagan Administration Pronouncements on Crime. *Journal of Contemporary Criminal Justice, 2*(2), 1–7.
Vlassis, D.(2002). The UN Convention Against Transnational Organized Crime. In M. Berdal & M. Serrano (eds.), *Transnational Organized Crime and International Security: Business As Usual?* (pp. 83–94). Lynne Rienner Publishers.
Weber, L., et al. (2021). *Place, Race and Politics: The Anatomy of a Law and Order Crisis.* Emerald.
Wacquant, L. (2009). *Punishing the Poor: The Neoliberal Government of Social Insecurity.* Duke University Press.
Walklate, S., & Fitz-Gibbon, K. (2018). Criminology and the Violence(s) of Northern Theorizing: A Critical Examination of Policy Transfer in Relation to Violence Against Women from the Global North to the Global South. In K. Carrington et al. (eds.), *The Palgrave Handbook of Criminology and the Global South* (pp. 847–66). Palgrave Macmillan.
Walters, R. (2001). Social Defence and International Reconstruction: Illustrating the Governance of Post-War Criminological Discourse. *Theoretical Criminology, 5*(2), 203–21.

Wang, H., & Rosenau, J. (2001). Transparency International and Corruption as an Issue of Global Governance. *Global Governance*, 7(1), 25–49.

Watson, D., et al. (2020). Problematising the Rule of Law Agenda in the SDG Context. In J. Blaustein et al. (eds.), *The Emerald Handbook of Crime, Justice and Sustainable Development* (pp. 131–52). Emerald.

Weatherburn, D., & Rahman, S. (2021). *The Vanishing Criminal: Causes of Decline in Australia's Crime Rate*. Melbourne University Publishing.

Wei, S.-J. (1997). *How Taxing Is Corruption on International Investors?* NBER Working Paper 6030. National Bureau of Economic Research.

Weiss, J., & Haldane, H. (2011). *Anthropology at the Front Lines of Gender-Based Violence*. Vanderbilt University Press.

Wendt, A. (1995). Constructing International Politics. *International Security*, 20(1), 71–81.

White, R. (2013). *Environmental Harm: An Eco-Justice Perspective*. Policy Press.

White, R. (2017). Carbon criminals, ecocide and climate justice. In C. Holley & C. Shearing (eds.), *Criminology and the Anthropocene*. Routledge.

White, R. (2021). Global Harms and the Natural Environment. In P. Davies, P. Leighton, & T. Wyatt (eds.), *The Palgrave Handbook of Social Harm* (pp. 89–114). Springer.

Whyte, D. (2014). Regimes of Permission and State-Corporate Crime. *State Crime Journal*, 3(2), 237–46.

Williams, P., & Baudin-O'Hayon, G. (2002). Global Governance, Transnational Organized Crime and Money Laundering. In D. Held & A. McGrew (eds.), *Governing Globalization: Power, Authority and Global Governance* (pp. 127–44). Polity.

Williams, J. W., & Beare, M. E. (2003). The Business of Bribery: Globalization, Economic Liberalization, and the "Problem" of Corruption. In M. E. Beare (ed.), *Critical Reflections on Transnational Organized Crime, Money Laundering, and Corruption* (pp. 88–119). University of Toronto Press.

Williamson, J. (1990). What Washington Means by Policy Reform. In J. Williamson (ed.), *Latin American Adjustment: How Much Has Happened* (pp. 7–20). Institute for International Economics.

Wilson, J. (2014). *Jeffrey Sachs: The Strange Case of Dr. Shock and Mr. Aid*. Verso Books.

Wilson, J. Q. (1975). *Thinking About Crime*. Basic Books.

Wolfensohn, J. D. (2005). *Voices for the World's Poor: Selected Speeches and Writings of World Bank President James D. Wolfensohn, 1995–2005*. The World Bank.

Wood, J., & Shearing, C. (2007). *Imagining Security*. Willan.

Woodiwiss, M. (2003a). Transnational Organised Crime: The Global Reach of an American Concept. In A. Edwards & P. Gill (eds.), *Transnational Organised Crime: Perspectives on Global Security* (pp. 13–27). Routledge.

Woodiwiss, M. (2003b). Transnational Organized Crime: The Strange Career of an American Concept. In M. E. Beare (ed.), *Critical Reflections on Transnational Organized Crime, Money Laundering, and Corruption* (pp. 3–34). University of Toronto Press.

Woodiwiss, M. (2012). The Past and Present of Transnational Organized Crime in America. In F. Allum & S. Gilmour (eds.), *Routledge Handbook of Transnational Organized Crime* (pp. 91–110). Routledge.

Woods, N. (2010). Global Governance after the Financial Crisis: A New Multilateralism or the Last Gasp of the Great Powers? *Global Policy, 1*(1), 51–63.

World Bank. (1983). *World Development Report 1983*. http://elibrary.worldbank.org/doi/book/10.1596/0-1952-0432-8.

World Bank. (1987). *World Development Report 1987*. Oxford University Press. https://openknowledge.worldbank.org/bitstream/handle/10986/5970/WDR%201987%20-%20English.pdf?sequence=1.

World Bank. (1990). *World Development Report 1990*. Oxford University Press. https://openknowledge.worldbank.org/bitstream/handle/10986/5973/WDR%201990%20-%20English.pdf?sequence=5&isAllowed=y.

World Bank. (1994). *Governance: The World Bank's Experience*. The World Bank.

World Bank. (1997a). *Helping Countries Combat Corruption: The Role of the World Bank*. The World Bank. http://www1.worldbank.org/publicsector/anticorrupt/corruptn/corrptn.pdf.

World Bank. (1997b). *World Development Report 1997: The State in a Changing World*. Oxford University Press. https://openknowledge.worldbank.org/handle/10986/5980.

World Bank. (1998). *East Asia: The Road to Recovery*. The World Bank. https://documents1.worldbank.org/curated/en/364021468770639382/pdf/multi-page.pdf.

World Bank. (2002). *World Development Report 2002: Building Institutions for Markets*. The World Bank.

World Bank. (2004). *Initiatives in Legal and Judicial Reform*. The World Bank.

World Bank. (2005). *World Development Report 2005: A Better Investment Climate for Everyone*. Oxford University Press. https://openknowledge.worldbank.org/handle/10986/5987.

World Bank. (2011). *World Development Report 2011: Conflict, Security, and Development*. Oxford University Press. https://openknowledge.worldbank.org/handle/10986/4389.

Wrage, S., & Wrage, A. (2005). Multinational Enterprises as "Moral Entrepreneurs" in a Global Prohibition Regime Against Corruption. *International Studies Perspectives, 6*, 316–24.

Zimring, F. E. (2008). *The Great American Crime Decline*. Oxford University Press.

Zinecker, H. (2017). How to Explain and How Not to Explain Contemporary Criminal Violence in Central America. In S. Huhn & H. Warnecker-Berger (eds.), *Politics and History of Violence and Crime in Central America* (pp. 23–63). Palgrave Macmillan.

Zvekic, U., & del Frate, A. (1995). *Criminal Victimization in the Developing World*. UNICRI. https://digitallibrary.un.org/record/198988?ln=en.

Index

Italicized page numbers indicate illustrations and figures. Endnotes are referenced with "n" followed by the endnote number.

Abbott, Daniel, 27–28, 31
abolitionism, 69–70
"Ad Hoc Advisory Committee of Experts" (UNGA), 93
Advisory Committee on the Traffic in Opium and Other Dangerous Drugs (League Secretariat), 77
advocacy networks, 57, 70–71
Afghanistan, 163–64, 165, 179, 180, 181
Africa:
 anti-corruption conventions on, 139; crime-development reports on, 27–28, 167–68; crisis decade impact on, 106; development goals implemented in, 172; drug control and crime prevention policies, 169; governance as economic development obstacle, 116, 119; maritime piracy, 177; neoliberal structural adjustment impact on, 125; organized crime in, 128, 180; private corporation activities in, 173; UNODC regional programs in, 180; urbanization and crime links, 98; victimization rate comparisons, 40
African Development Bank, 165

African slavery, 69–70, 72, 73
African Union Convention on Preventing and Combatting Corruption, 139
The Age of Extremes (Hobsbawm), 105
agricultural regulations, 70
Alatas, Syed Hussein, 46
alcohol, 38
Alliance for Progress, 87
Amin, Samir, 117
anarchism, 66–69
Ancel, Marc, 90
Annan, Kofi, 155, 158, 161, 184
anomie, 26, 62, 84, 97
anti-money laundering (AML), 52, 53, 54
Anti-Slavery Society, 70
Arab States, 180, 181, 182–83
Argentina, 190
Arlacchi, Pino, 153–54, 157, 158, 159, 163, 176
arms trade, 56, 168, 173
ASEAN (Association of Southeast Asian Nations), 181, 182
Asia:
 corruption and financial crisis, 139; crisis decades impact on, 105–6;

245

drug trafficking, 181–82; UNODC crime reports on, 179; UNODC regional programs in, 180, 181–82; victimization rate comparisons, 40
Asian Development Bank, 141, 163, 165
Asian Financial Crisis, 139
assassinations, 66, 67, 111
Association of Southeast Asian Nations (ASEAN), 181, 182
Australia, 45, 179–80, 181, 199
Austria, 67

Ban Ki-moon, 172, 177, 191
"Barriers to Adjustment and Growth in the World Economy" (World Bank), 118
Bolivia, 164, 190
Boutros-Ghali, Boutros, 129
Brazil, 42, 45, 190
Bretton Woods institutions, 86, 108
bribery, 53, 57, 128, 132–33, 137, 139
Britain, 67, 68, 69–70, 73
Bush, George H. W., 118
Bush, George W., 160, 199
business, 6, 69–73, 109–12, 116–17, 119, 192–95

Canada, 181, 189
capacity building, 146, 147, 148, 169, 181
capitalism:
 anarchism as response to, 66–69; benevolent imperialist policies supporting, 79–82; colonial administration and policing to protect, 73–75; commercial enterprise regulations, 69–74; corruption and crony, 139; corruption as threat to, 118; crisis decades and, 105; definition, 61; development and embedded liberalism as model for, 68; international crime and development of, 66; organized crime as threat to, 122; social relations of production of, 61; sovereign debt as threat to, 116; Soviet criminology theories on, 29, 99–100; sustainable development models, 3–4; UN development policies for support of, 84–85
Cardoso, Fernando, 112, 204
Cardoso Report, 194
Caribbean, 42, 147, 166, 170, 179, 180, 181
CCP (Centre for Crime Prevention), 13
CCPC (Committee on Crime Prevention and Control), 110–11, 133
CCPCJ (Commission on Crime Prevention and Criminal Justice), 13–14, 133–34, 171–72, 173, 176
Center for International Crime Prevention (CICP), 134, 153–54, 160, 161
Center for Strategic and International Studies, 130
Central America:
 crime research and reports on, 42, 44, 166, 169, 170, 179; regional programs in, 180, 181; US foreign policies on, 121
Centre for Crime Prevention (CCP), 13
Centre for International Crime Prevention (CHIC), 153
Chambliss, William, 28–29
CHIC (Centre for International Crime Prevention), 153
Chicago School of Sociology, 26, 28
children:
 developed countries and violence against, 189; exploitation of, 99; juvenile delinquency issues, 78–79, 92–93, 97; SDG targets on, 2; trafficking of, 71–72, 76, 77, 79
Child Welfare Committee (League Secretariat), 77, 79
China, 41, 86, 180, 181, 189
CICP (Center for International Crime Prevention), 134, 153–54, 160, 161
citizen security, 148–49, 170–71

Civil Society Coalition, 58
civil society organizations (CSOs), 57, 58, 63, 184, 186, 194, 204, 205
Clark, Helen, 178
Clifford, William, 103, 108, 110
Clinard, Marshall, 27–28, 31, 101–2
Clinton, Bill, 130, 132, 160, 199
CND (Commission on Narcotic Drugs), 14
Cohen, Albert, 27–28
colonialism, 43, 45–46, 73–75, 76, 79–82, 85, 86
Commission on Crime Prevention and Criminal Justice (CCPCJ), 13–14, 133–34, 171–72, 173, 176
Commission on Narcotic Drugs (CND), 14
Committee on Crime Prevention and Control (CCPC), 110–11, 133
Committee on Social Questions (League of Nations), 79
Committee on the Traffic in Women and Children (League of Nations), 77, 79
communication technology, 51, 66, 127, 173
communism, 27, 68, 131
Conflict, Security and Development (World Bank), 148–49
constructivism, 7, 8, 21, 50, 57–60, 207
corruption:
  bribery, 53, 57, 128, 132–33, 137, 139; global crime governance approaches to, 53, 57–58; global crime governance perception of, 9; globalization debates on, 53; governance as development obstacle due to, 115–19, 120–21; organized crime and, 127–28; as 1990s key issue, 126, 136–41; solutions to, 139; as sustainable growth obstacle, 1; terminology definition development, 135; Third World development and crisis of, 112; treaties on, 139; as UNODC issue, 12; US subcommittees on, 131

Corruption Action Plan Working Group, 138
Costa, Antonio Maria:
  colonialism issues, 180; crime-development nexus promotion, 160–67, 171–74; crime-development reports of, 167–68; personality descriptions, 159, 172–73; UNODC leadership, 159–60, 174, 176
counter-hegemony, 12, 22, 61, 63, 81
The Covenant of the League of Nations, 76
Cox, Robert:
  executive leadership influences, 108, 153, 176; global crime governance theories, 11, 50, 61–62, 198; hegemony, 63, 198; UN roles and policies, 205
CPCJB (Crime Prevention and Criminal Justice Branch), 111, 115, 152, 153
CPCJS (Crime Prevention and Criminal Justice Section), 110, 111
CPTED (crime prevention through environmental design), 170
crime, overview:
  as business, 109–12, 119; as governance strategy, 7–8; to harm, 206–10; historical view of, 6; as international concern, 66; as sustainable development obstacle, 1. See also *related topics*
Crime and Development in Africa (UNODC), 167–68
Crime and Development in Central America (UNODC), 169–70
Crime and Modernization (Shelley), 30–32
Crime and Violence as Development Issues in Latin America and the Caribbean (World Bank), 147
crime-conflict nexus, 5
crime-development nexus:
  construction and history of, 3–6, 94–98, 161–62; critical perspectives, 41–46; cross-national studies, 34–41;

debates on, 99–103; early foundations of, 25–34; historicizing, overview, 65–66; neoliberalist consequences, 32–34; public statements on, first, 158; study overview, 17–20; study structure and argument, 21–24; theoretical framework of, 7–8; UNODC agenda development, 160–74
Crime Prevention and Criminal Justice Branch (CPCJB), 111, 115, 152, 153
Crime Prevention and Criminal Justice Section (CPCJS), 110, 111
crime prevention through environmental design (CPTED), 170
criminal anthropology, 67
criminal justice:
colonialism influences on, 75; commissions and departments on, 13–14, 111, 115, 133–34, 152, 153, 171–72, 173, 176; constructivist global crime governance for, 58; global crime governance contributing to, 8–9; reform of, as UNODC issue, 12; as UN development priority, 8
CSOs (civil society organizations), 57, 58, 63, 184, 186, 194, 204, 205
Currie, Elliott, 34–35

Declaration of Basic Principles of Justice for Victims of Crime and Abuse of Power (CPCJB), 115
Declaration on the Establishment of a New International Economic Order (UNGA), 113
decolonization, 45–46, 74–75, 76, 79–82, 85, 86
Denmark, 181
dependency theory, 3, 31–32, 89, 99, 112, 167
deregulation, 32, 33, 117, 136, 137
development, overview:
criminology theories and impact on, 26–32; models of, 3–4; obstacles to,

1, 115–19; as UN foundational pillar, 84–89.
See also *related topics*
diamond industry, 52
differential association theory, 28
Dijk, Jan van, 40–41, 161–62, 163
Division of Public Safety (USAID), 87
divorce, 37
Doha Declaration, 5, 7, 183
Draper, William, 143
drug trafficking:
in Caribbean, 42; commercial regulations, 72, 76; crime policy agendas on, 120; as development obstacle, 121; money laundering and, 54; opium trade, 72, 76, 163–64, 179, 181; as transnational issue, 111; UN conventions on, 123; UNODC focus on, 13, 179, 181
Durkheim, Emile, 25, 26, 28–29, 84, 91

Economic and Social Council of United Nations. See ECOSOC
economic development:
corruption as threat to, 115–19, 120–21, 136; New International Economic Order, 112–15; organized crime as threat to, 122; shock therapies, 32–33, 118, 128; state as obstacle to, 115–19; UN focus on crime and, 94–98
Economic Freedom World Index, 36–37
ECOSOC (Economic and Social Council of United Nations):
crime-development link recognition, 99; funding challenges, 155; influences on, 87, 108; international crime acknowledged by, 110; roles of, 9, 85; social defense leadership role resolution, 101; social defense programs reporting to commissions of, 89; Third World delegates and influence on, 108
Ecuador, 190

education, 28, 32, 36, 87, 102, 138
efficiency, as development model, 3, 15, 83–84, 102, 108
E4J (Global Education 4 Justice Programme), 183, 199, 213n1
El Salvador, 32, 44
embedded liberalism, 68, 71, 78, 88, 105
entrepreneurial non-state actors (moral entrepreneurship), 7, 57–58, 70, 71–72
environmental issues, 1, 42–43
EPTA (Extended Program for Technical Assistance), 86
European Union, 165, 181, 199
Executive Opinion Survey (World Economic Forum), 161
Extended Program for Technical Assistance (EPTA), 86

family, 26, 27, 43, 71, 78
Fedotov, Yuri, 176, 178–79, 181
Ferracuti, Franco, 95–96
Financial Action Task Force (FATF), 52, 55, 135
Foreign Corrupt Practices Act (FCPA), 53, 57, 60, 132, 133
Forum on Crime and Society (journal), 161–62
France, 167, 180, 181
freedom:
as development model, 3–4, 5, 83, 108, 114, 142; human security issues of, 145, 148–49, 168
Freeh, Louis, 130
functionalism, 49, 51–54, 91, 127, 128, 129
The Future We Want (Rio+20 Conference), 186

G77, 189
GBA (Global Business Alliance), 193, 194–95
General Act of the Brussels Conference, 70

General Purpose Fund (UN), 15, 154–55
Germany, 67, 80, 179, 181
Gini index, 37
Global Business Alliance (GBA), 193, 194–95
global crime governance:
anti-anarchist policies, 67–69; commercial activity regulations, 69–73, 77; constructivist approaches to, 50, 57–60; definition, 8; functionalist approaches to, 49, 51–54; goals of, 9; influences on, 10–12; institutionalist approaches to, 50, 55–56; political economy focus for, 60–63; priorities of, 72–73; purpose of, 11; realist approaches to, 49, 54–55; significant developments and effects of, 8–9; theoretical framework of, overview, 49–51; transformation of, 203–6
Global Dialogue on Rule of Law and Post-2015 Development Agenda (UNDG), 187, 191
Global Education 4 Justice Programme (E4J), 183, 199, 213n1
Global Financial Crisis (GFC, 2008), 12, 173, 180, 184
Global Initiative against Transnational Organized Crime, 195, 205, 214n2
globalization:
challenges of, 125–26; corruption increase due to, 136–37; crime-development nexus impacted by economic, 6; definition, 51; global crime governance and importance of, 52; organized crime growth due to, 61, 126–36; research and reports on, 130, 173, 177, 213n2; 1990s focus, 125
The Globalization of Crime (UNODC), 173, 177
"Global Organized Crime" (Center for Strategic and International Studies), 130
Global Organized Crime Index, 214n2

GNP (Gross National Product), 3, 36, 38
Godson, Roy, 130
Golden Triangle, 181
good governance:
  challenges to, 156; as corruption solution, 139–41; as crime antidote, 172; criticism of, 190, 194; IFI support of, 23; as sustainable development requirement, 58, 163, 165, 166, 186, 193
governments and governance:
  challenges and threats to, 43, 130, 139; colonial administration and policing, 73–75; as economic development obstacle, 115–19, 120, 136, 147–48; human security and failure of, 145–46; organized crime growth due to ineffectiveness of, 127–28; state planning programs, 32, 84, 88, 102, 109–10.
  See also corruption; good governance
Gramsci, Antonio, 11, 50, 61, 67–68, 71
Great Depression, 68, 78, 79, 81
GRECO (Group of States Against Corruption), 139
Gross National Product (GNP), 3, 36, 38
growth, as development model:
  alternatives to, 142; concept overview, 3; ideologies influenced by, 115–16; shift from, 114; as Sustainable Development Goals agenda, 198; UN reorientation away from, 108; UN Secretariat model, 120
Guatemala, 44
Guterres, António, 202

Hammarskjöld, Dag, 94–95, 96
harm-sustainability nexus, 206–10
Helping Countries Combat Corruption: The Role of the World Bank (World Bank), 138

High-Level Panel of Eminent Persons on the Post-2015 Development Agenda (UN, 2013), 185, 186–87, 188, 189
Hoffman, Paul, 89, 108–9
homicide, 36, 37–38, 39, 40, 44
Honduras, 32, 44
human development:
  concept overview, 142–44; and human security nexus, 5, 126, 141–42, 144
Human Development Reports (UNDP), 143–44, 145, 168
human dignity, 114
human rights:
  development goals and, 168; security and protection of, 145–46; UN crime programs promotion of, 94, 107, 115, 183; as UN system pillar, 14, 94, 114, 142, 143
human security:
  concept overview, 144–47; and human development nexus, 5, 126, 141–42, 144; UN crime congresses addressing, 157; urban violence issues and citizen security models, 147–50, 170–71
human trafficking:
  African slave trade, 69–70; global crime governance on, 52; globalization and growth of, 127; of women and children, 71–72, 76, 77, 79

IADB (Inter-American Development Bank), 141, 148, 170, 179
ICVS (International Crime and Victims Survey), 40, 152, 161
IFIs. *See* international financial institutions; World Bank
IIE (Institute for International Economics), 136, 137
IMF (International Monetary Fund), 32, 116–17, 118, 165

imperialism:
    benevolent, 22, 75, 80–82; colonial administration and policing, 73–75; decolonization policies, 45–46, 74–75, 76, 79–82, 85, 86
Index of Economic Freedom, 36–37
individualism, 100, 105
industrialization:
    crime and destabilizing effects of, 26, 30, 66, 72, 91, 97, 98; imperialism stimulating, 73; socialist *vs.* capitalist comparisons, 29; Soviet rapid interwar period, 85, 88
In Larger Freedom (Annan), 184
Institute for International Economics (IIE), 136, 137
institutionalism, 50, 55–56
Inter-American Convention Against Corruption, 133, 139
Inter-American Development Bank (IADB), 141, 148, 170, 179
International Agreement for the Suppression of the White Slave Traffic, 71
International Anti-Anarchist Conference, 67
International Anti-Corruption Conference Council, 48
International Convention for the Suppression of White Slavery, 71
International Crime and Victims Survey (ICVS), 40, 152, 161
International Development Authority, 88
international financial institutions (IFIs):
    citizen security models of, 170; corruption as concern of, 136, 138–39; corruption solutions, 139–41; crime and economic sanctions, 132; crime-development agenda, 164–66; as crime-development nexus construction influence, 6; human/citizen security issues, 147–49; influences on, 12; law reform loans, 140–41; neoliberal economic agendas of, 32; sovereign debt crisis, 116–17, 118
"International Group of Experts on the Prevention of Crime and the Treatment of Offenders" (UNGA), 93–94
International Monetary Fund (IMF) IFI, 32, 116–17, 118, 165
International Opium Convention, 72
International Penal and Penitentiary Commission (IPCC), 93–94
"International Plan of Action" (CCPC), 110–11
International Relations (IR), 57, 65, 125, 131, 144, 151, 200
internet, 127, 173
IPCC (International Penal and Penitentiary Commission), 93–94
Italy, 67, 122–23, 129, 134, 153, 181

Jamaica, 147–48
Japan, 67, 73, 181
juvenile delinquency, 78–79, 92–93, 97

Kampala, Uganda, 27–28
Kennedy, John F., 87
Kerry, John, 131–32
Khalifa, A. M., 98
Kimberley Process, 52
Kyoto Declaration, 201, 203–4, 208

Latin America:
    citizen security models, 170–71; crime and violence reports, 147; criminology studies on, 42–44; crisis decade impact on, 106; governance as economic development obstacle, 116, 118, 119; liberalization agendas, 140; neoliberalist policies in, 125; neoliberal structural adjustment impact on, 125; victimization rate comparisons, 40
law and development movement, 87
law enforcement:

as crime-development nexus construction influence, 7; crime management roles of, 28–29, 31; crime prevention and investment in, 170, 177, 180; international cooperation, history of, 67; limitations of, 169. *See also* policing
lawfulness, culture of, 122, 162, 183, 199
law reform programs, 140–41
League of Nations:
   agendas of, 76–79, 92–93; crime as international problem addressed by, 110; historical perception of, 75; legacy of, 75–76; organizational structure, 77; origins, 76; penal and penitentiary commissions of, 93; policies of, 12, 22, 76, 78, 80–82; US involvement in, 27
League Secretariat, 12, 77, 90
liberal internationalism:
   decline of, 4, 146; doctrine descriptions, 146; global crime governance and, 9, 12, 67, 76, 80, 132, 145–46, 161; social defense, 91; US policies and, 160, 199
liberalism, embedded, 68, 71, 78, 88, 105. *See also* liberal internationalism; neoliberalism
loans, 116–17, 140–41
Lome Declaration, 168
López-Rey, Manuel, 92–93, 94

Major Group for Business and Industry, 193–94
Mandate System, 22, 76, 80–82
manufacturing, 66, 74, 105, 113
maritime piracy, 8, 177
Marshall Plan, 89
Marxist criminology, 28–29
McNamara, Robert, 117
Merton, Robert, 26, 27–28
Milan Plan of Action, 123

Millennium Declaration, 157–58, 184, 186
Millennium Development Goals (MDGs):
   assessments of, 168, 185–86; crime and corruption omission from, 136, 151, 156–57, 158, 184; crime-development nexus link to, 172; criticism of, 175, 186; function, 156; preconditions for, 171, 185; security-development nexus, 149–50
modernization:
   crime-development nexus and, 101–3; decolonization challenges, 74–75; development models for, 88, 142; social defense movement addressing, 84, 91; theories of, 24, 27, 62; as traditional family threat, 71
Modernization Theory, 24, 27, 62
money laundering, 8, 51, 52, 53, 54, 55, 123, 128, 173
moral entrepreneurship, 7, 57–58, 70, 71–72
multilateralism, 9, 66, 160, 184, 192, 199, 205
MY World Global Survey, 187, 188

naming and shaming, 57, 58
narcotics. *See* drug trafficking
National Strategy Information Center, 130
NATO (North Atlantic Treaty Organization), 145
Nazis, 85, 90
nébuleuse, 61
neocolonialism, 3, 5, 112, 170
neoliberalism:
   crime policy agenda influenced by, 119; crisis decades and rise of, 105, 106; cross-national studies on, 36–37, 43; development models favored by, 3, 115–16, 142; development principles, 117; early crime-development theories and

consequences of, 32–35; governance as development obstacle and, 115–19, 121–22; human development and, 143; human security and, 149–50; international backlash against, 184; rise of, 71, 116; as US agenda, 125
"New Dimensions of Criminality and Crime Prevention in the Context of Development" (UN Secretariat), 120
New International Economic Order (NIEO), 9, 63, 108, 112–17, 118, 121–23, 125
The New War (Kerry), 131
New Zealand, 179–80, 181
NGOs (non-governmental organizations), 10, 57, 139, 205
Nicaragua, 44
NIEO (New International Economic Order), 9, 63, 108, 112–17, 118, 121–23
nodes, 11, 17, 92, 97
Non-Aligned Movement, 9, 87, 108, 112, 189
"Non-Communist Manifesto" (Rostow), 88
non-governmental organizations (NGOs), 10, 57, 139, 205
non-state actors: abolitionism, 70, 71–72; anti-corruption and bribery lobbying, 57–58; as crime prevention partners, 148; influence of, 7, 49, 203; Latin American violence due to, 43. *See also* international financial institutions (IFIs)
North Atlantic Treaty Organization (NATO), 145
Norway, 181

Obama, Barack, 180, 189, 199
Occidentalism, 41
OECD. *See* Organisation for Economic Co-operation and Development
OIOS (United Nations Office of Internal Oversight Service), 159

Open Working Group (OWG), 185, 186, 187, 188, 191, 192–94
Opiate Flows through Northern Afghanistan and Central Asia (UNODC), 179
opium trade, 72, 76, 163–64, 179, 181
Organisation for Economic Co-operation and Development (OECD): Anti-Bribery Convention, 53, 54, 60, 133, 139; criticism of, 95; globalization impact on economy, 137; US involvement in, 133
organized crime, transnational: as capitalism threat, 122; character of, 53; congresses addressing, 114, 122–23, 129–30, 135–36; crime policy agendas on, 119, 120, 122–23, 129; crisis decades and Third World, 112; as development obstacle, 1; global crime governance perception of, 9; globalization and growth of, 51, 126–36; initiatives and commissions on, 122, 195, 205, 214n2; research and reports, 130, 179–80, 214n2; task forces on, 177, 178–79; terminology definition development, 135; as UNODC issue, 12, 179; US recognition as threat, 122. *See also* United Nations Convention against Transnational Organized Crime
Orientalism, 41
Orlando, Leoluca, 122
othering, 75
Ottoman Empire, 80
OWG (Open Working Group), 185, 186, 187, 188, 191, 192–94

Pakistan, 164
Panakal, J. J., 97–98
Panel of Eminent Persons on United Nations–Civil Society Relations (2004), 194, 204
Pascoe, Burton Lynn, 178
Pedersen, Susan, 76, 78, 80–81

penal culture, 106
Peru, 164
Pink Tide, 171
policing:
    anarchist violence prevention, 68; colonial administration and, 73–75; in developing countries, 45; gender-specific models of, 45; over-, 29, 31; transnational, 51–52. *See also* law enforcement
population density, 37–38
population structure, 37
post-interventionism, 146–47
poverty:
    conflict and, 188, 189; crime and assumptions about, 29; crime prevention and reduction of, 147, 157, 158, 161, 171; cross-national studies focusing on, 38, 42; as development obstacle, 33; governance failures contributing to, 121, 126; human development for reduction of, 149; modernist urban planning contributing to, 43; neoliberal policies linked to, 37, 119; post-Soviet, 128; rule of law for eradicating, 184; structural adjustment programs contributing to, 33, 43, 118; and urban violence studies, 147
power:
    abuses of, 114, 115; crime as strategy for, 7–8; global crime governance and influence of, 11–12, 54–55, 60
Prebisch, Raúl, 89, 112–13
President's Commission on Law Enforcement and the Administration of Justice, 102
President's Commission on Organized Crime, 122
Prevention of Types of Criminality Resulting from Social Changes and Accompanying Economic Development in Less Developed Countries (UN Secretariat), 96–97

privatization, 32, 33, 106, 117, 136, 138
Problems of Social Disorganization Linked with the Industrialization and Urbanization of Countries Undergoing Rapid Economic Development (United Nations), 97
prostitution, 71, 98, 110

Qatar, 183–84, 199, 213n1

racial ideologies, 75
Racketeer Influenced and Corrupt Organizations (RICO) Act, 135
Rappard, William, 80
RBM (results-based management), 155
Reagan, Ronald, 121, 122, 169
realism, 49, 54–55
Regional Transnational Organized Crime Threat Assessments (TOCTA), 179
religious movements, 70–71, 72
rent-seeking behaviors, 115, 117, 136
Report on the World Social Situation (UN), 97
results-based management (RBM), 155
Revised Plan of Action on Drug Control and Crime Preventions (African Union), 169
RICO (Racketeer Influenced and Corrupt Organizations) Act, 135
Rio+20 Conference, 185, 186
Rostow, Walt, 87, 88, 96, 112
rule of law:
    crime congresses promoting, 157; as development prerequisite, 165, 171, 172, 174, 177, 181, 184–85, 186; for good governance, 140–41; for human security, 147; political debate challenges, 183; as SDG target, 2; UNGA meetings and declarations on, 187
Rule of Law Unit, 190
Russia, 37, 128, 180, 181

Sachs, Jeffrey, 33
SAPs. *See* structural adjustment programs
Saudi Arabia, 183
Schulenburg, Michael von der, 159
SDGs. *See* Sustainable Development Goals; Sustainable Development Goal 16
securitization, 7–8, 49, 151, 189
security-development nexus, 5, 126, 141–50
self-determination, 80–82, 84
Sellin, Thorsten, 96
Sen, Amartya, 168
shaming, 57, 58
Shanghai Opium Commission, 72
Shelley, Louise, 30–32, 100
slavery, 69–70, 71, 73, 76, 77
Slavery Convention, 70
social bonds, 78
social defense:
  drug trafficking agendas, 76, 77; failure of, 103, 106–7; genealogy of, 90; juvenile delinquency agendas, 78–79; League of Nations programs, 76–79; universal assumptions of, 84; urbanization consequences addressed by, 62; white slavery agendas, 76, 77.
  See also Social Defense Section (United Nations)
social defense movement:
  development models favored by, 83–84; focus of, 91; ideology of, 90–91; influence of, 90; proponents of, 90
Social Defense Section (United Nations):
  crime advisory committees for, 93; crime-development nexus impact on, 101; development models favored by, 83, 102; economic development focus, 94–95; function of, 83–84, 90–91; funding challenges limiting role of, 92, 95, 101, 103, 107, 108;

governance approaches of, 91; influences on, 99; legal flexibility of, 91; norms and standards promotion, 94; reorientation of, 109–10; significance of, 92; status of, 103, 107; technical assistance integration plans, 103; uniqueness of, 92–93
Social Defense Trust Fund, 103, 107
social democracy, 105
social disorganization theory, 26, 27, 95–96
socialism, 29, 30, 67, 85, 127–28
social pressure, 57, 58, 97–98
sociological positivism, 25, 26–28, 29, 84, 100
South Korea (Republic of Korea), 98, 181
Soviet Union (USSR, Union of the Soviet Socialist Republics):
  capitalist development and hegemonic competition with, 85; collapse of, 125, 143–44; crime-development theories, 28–30, 99–100; criminology traditions, 100; crisis decades impact on, 105; industrialization of, 85, 88; social defense policies, 90; UN development policies and, 86–87
Spain, 68
Sri Lanka, 42
stagflation, 116
Stakeholder Preparatory Forum, 194
Standard Minimum Rules for the Treatment of Prisoners, 94
state planning programs, 32, 84, 88, 102, 109–10
states. *See* governments and governance
St Petersburg Anti-Anarchist Protocol, 67
strain theory, 26, 27–28
structural adjustment programs (SAPs):
  anti-corruption and, 118, 136; effects of, 33, 43, 115, 117, 118, 125, 126, 142, 147; policies replacing, 149, 170; purpose, 32, 115, 117

Subcommittee on Terrorism, Narcotics and International Relations, 131
subcultural theory, 27–28
Sumner, Colin, 31
sustainable development, 1, 3–4, 181. *See also* Sustainable Development Goals (SDGs); Sustainable Development Goal 16
Sustainable Development Goals (SDGs):
business and industry interests in, 192–95; crime, justice and security targets of, 2; influences on, 6, 56, 190–92; negotiations for, 184–87, 191; overview, 1, 175–76; United Nations focus on, 5.
See also Sustainable Development Goal 16
Sustainable Development Goal 16:
business and industry interests in, 192–95; crime-development nexus as element of, 5, 7, 197; importance of, 8; indicators of, 191; negotiations on, 184–85, 190, 191, 197; politics of, 188–90; targets of, 2
Sutherland, Edwin, 27–28
Sweden, 181

terrorism, 8, 12, 55, 66–69, 160
Thailand, 98, 164, 181, 182
Thant, U, 101
Third Annual Latin American Critical Criminology Conference, 121
Third World:
commercial loans to, 116; crime as business, 111–12; crisis decades impact on, 105; governance as economic development obstacle, 115–19; UN delegates from, 107–8; Western development models criticized by, 62, 112–13
Transnational Organized Crime in Central America and the Caribbean (UNODC), 179

Transnational Organized Crime in East Asia and the Pacific (UNODC), 179–80
Transnational Organized Crime in West Africa (UNODC), 180
Transnational Organized Crime Threat Assessments (TOCTA), 179
Transparency International (TI), 57–58, 60, 205
transportation technology, 51, 66–67, 127
Truman, Harry, 86
Turkey, 164, 179

Uganda, 27–28, 32, 101
UNCAC. *See* United Nations Convention Against Corruption
UNDCP (United Nations Drug Control Programme), 13, 134, 152, 160
UNDESA (United Nations Department of Economic and Social Affairs), 96, 99, 101, 102, 103
UNDP. *See* United Nations Development Programme
UNDPA (United Nations Department of Political Affairs), 95, 177–78
UNGA. *See* United Nations General Assembly
United Arab Emirates, 183
United Kingdom (UK), 167, 181
United Nations:
budget and funding, 15, 154–55; crime policy agenda, 94–103, 129, 139; crime reports, 96–97; decolonization and self-determination functions, 81–82; development system of, 84–89; early crime-development studies, 28; founding purpose, 83; influences on, 62; opium commissions, 72; policies of, 83, 88, 102; special funds for development investments, 88; technical assistance programs of, 86; US development work and, 87.

Index 257

See also *specific UN departments, conventions, programs, etc.*
United Nations Commission for Latin America, 112
United Nations Conference on Trade and Development, 112–13
United Nations Consultative Group on the Prevention of Crime and the Treatment of Offenders, 109
United Nations Convention Against Corruption (UNCAC): challenges of, 9–10, 14; corruption prevention agendas, 139; CPCJB budgets based on, 152; criminal activity terminology definitions of, 135; function of, 9; funding challenges, 155–56; global crime governance approaches using, 58; negotiation and adoption of, 8, 52, 134; US adoption of, 56
United Nations Convention against Illicit Traffic in Narcotic Drugs, 130
United Nations Convention against Transnational Organized Crime (UNTOC): challenges of, 9–10; criminal activity terminology definitions of, 135; criticism of, 135; function of, 9; funding challenges, 155–56; negotiation and adoption of, 8, 52, 55–56, 134, 154; resolution adoption conflicts, 15; terrorism and organized crime, 160; UN crime congresses addressing, 157; US adoption of, 56
United Nations Crime Congresses: 1955 (First), 94; 1960 (Second), 95, 96, 97, 99, 100–101; 1965 (Third), 101–3; 1970 (Fourth), 107, 109–10; 1975 (Fifth), 111; 1980 (Sixth), 114, 122–23; 1985 (Seventh), 114, 119–20, 122–23, 129–30; 1990 (Eighth), 123; 1995 (Ninth), 135–36; 2000 (Tenth), 157; 2015 (Thirteenth), 5, 183; 2021 (Fourteenth), 5, 203–4

United Nations Crime Prevention and Criminal Justice Branch (CPCJB), 111, 115, 152, 153
United Nations Crime Prevention and Criminal Justice Section (CPCJS), 110, 111
United Nations Department of Economic and Social Affairs (UNDESA), 96, 99, 101, 102, 103
United Nations Department of Political Affairs (UNDPA), 95, 177–78
United Nations Development Programme (UNDP): crisis decades and reorientation of, 108–9; development models favored by, 4, 83, 108, 142; funding challenges, 108; human development agenda, 142–44, 150; human security advocacy, 141–42, 144–47; permissive climate established by, 143; rule of law agenda, 187, 191; security-development nexus priorities, 5, 17, 126; task force participation, 177–78; task teams co-chaired by, 184; UNODC competition with, 178
United Nations Drug Control Programme (UNDCP), 13, 134, 152, 160
United Nations General Assembly (UNGA): budget administration, 154; crime-development link recognition, 99, 158; decolonized countries influence on policy agenda through, 87; funding challenges, 155; Millennium Declaration, 157–58, 184, 186; New International Economic Order declarations, 113; predecessor of, 77; rule of law, 184, 187; Sustainable Development Goals adopted by, 1; Third World delegates influence on, 108; transnational organized crime conventions, 134; UNODC governance challenges and, 14

United Nations Office for Drug Control and Crime Prevention (UN-ODCCP): creation of, 55; crime-development agenda, 156–59, 162–63; development goals of, 136, 151, 156–57, 158; formative years, 152–54; funding challenges, 154–56, 159; mismanagement scandals, 159; reputation repair and restructuring, 159–60

United Nations Office of Internal Oversight Service (OIOS), 159

United Nations Office on Drugs and Crime (UNODC): creation of, 13, 129, 160; crime and corruption agenda, 151–52, 158; crime-development agenda development, 160, 161–67, 197–98; crime-development research and reports, 6, 167–74; crime statements and reports, 6; development models of, 15; development programs competing with, 143; function and roles of, 15, 52, 55; funding, 15, 17, *152*, 167, 181; global crime governance influence of, 56; global crime governance reform, 200–206; governance challenges, 14–15; governance descriptions, 11, 14, 17, 126; human development advocacy, 144; issues addressed by, 13; leadership, 153, 159–60, 176, 202–3; limitations of, 199–200; mandates of, 13; maritime piracy agenda, 177; money laundering reports, 173; organizational structure, 13–14, *16;* organizational worldview, 14; organized crime task force participation, 177–79; regional programs of, 179–84; SDG negotiations, 185–86, 190–92; security-development nexus, 142; task team participation, 185; terrorism challenges, 160–61; threat assessment reports, 179–80;

UNDP competition with, 178; work portfolio and success of, 176–77

United Nations Peacebuilding Support Office (UN PBSO), 190

United Nations Program of Action on Small Arms and Light Weapons, 56

United Nations Secretariat: crime and abuse of power, 114; crime and development panel discussions using research of, 101–2; crime as obstacle to development, 120; crime-development nexus, 157; criminality reports of, 96–99; development models of, 120; function and roles of, 9, 12–13, 96; influences on, 120; predecessor of, 77; SDG negotiations and role of, 190–92; social defense resources, 103; transnational crime reports of, 111

United Nations Security Council (UNSC), 77, 145, 172, 176–77

United Nations Social Defense Research Institute (UNSDRI), 103

United Nations Summit on the MDGs, 185

United Nations System Task Force on Transnational Organized Crime and Drug Trafficking (UN Task Force), 177, 178–79

United Nations System Task Team, 185

United Nations Task Team, 185–86

United Nations Technical Support Team (UN TST), 185, 190, 191

United Nations Women, 203

United States: agendas of, 125; anti-anarchist policies, 68; crime-development theories, early, 26–27; decolonization movement, 79, 81, 82; development promotion and policies, 85, 86–87; drug regulations, 72; global crime governance and, 9, 11–12, 53–55, 56, 135; Global Financial Crisis

response, 180; homicide statistic comparisons, 189; League of Nations and, 27, 79; organized crime agenda, 122–23, 129–34; terrorism focus, 160; as UNODC donor, 179, 181
UNODC. *See* United Nations Office on Drugs and Crime
UN-ODCCP. *See* United Nations Office for Drug Control and Crime Prevention
UN PBSO (United Nations Peacebuilding Support Office), 190
UNSC (United Nations Security Council), 77, 145, 172, 176–77
UNSDRI (United Nations Social Defense Research Institute), 103
UN Task Force, 177, 178–79
UNTOC. *See* United Nations Convention against Transnational Organized Crime
UN TST (United Nations Technical Support Team), 185, 190, 191
urbanization, 26, 30, 37, 39–40, 96–98
Urbanization and Crime and Delinquency in Asia and the Far East (UN Secretariat), 97
Urban Poverty and Violence in Jamaica (World Bank), 147
US Agency for International Development (USAID), 87, 121, 140, 142
US Federal Reserve, 116
US Senate Committee on Foreign Relations, 131
USSR (Union of the Soviet Socialist Republics). *See* Soviet Union

Vienna Convention Against Illicit Traffic in Narcotics, 123
Vienna Declaration, 157–58
Vietnam, 181, 182
violence:
anarchist, 66–69; as development goal target, 2, 175, 188, 189; gender-based, 40, 44–45, 189; global

surveys on, 187; homicide, 36, 37–38, 39, 40, 44; neoliberal reforms contributing to, 33, 34, 43; state, as governance strategy, 68; studies on, 42–44; urban, and human security, 141, 147–50
Vitoria, Francisco de, 82

Waly, Ghada Fathi, 202
white slavery, 71–72, 76, 77
Wilson, James Q., 121
Wilson, Woodrow, 81, 82
Wolfensohn, James D., 138, 164
women:
gender-based violence against, 40, 44–45, 189; trafficking of, 71–72, 76, 77; urbanization destabilization and vulnerability of, 97–98; white slavery, 71–72, 76, 77
Woolsey, James, 130
World Bank:
Afghanistan's opium economy, 163; corruption agenda, 57, 136, 138, 139–40; crime and violence reports of, 147–48; as development obstacle, 116–18, 120; human/citizen security models, 148–49; law reform loans, 141; policies of, 12, 32, 88, 119, 132; political interference prohibitions, 136; rule of law, 140, 166. *See also* World Development Reports
World Development Reports (World Bank):
crime and corruption themes, 118, *137*, 147–48, 149; development obstacles, 117; poverty themes, 119; security-development themes, 149
World Economic Forum, 161
World Ministerial Conference on Organized Transnational Crime, 134
World Summit on Sustainable Development, 162–63

zemiologists, 208

About the Authors

Jarrett Blaustein is an associate professor in the School of Regulation and Global Governance at the Australian National University. His research explores the intersections between security governance and sustainable development and how security actors adapt to anthropogenic risks.

Tom Chodor is a lecturer in International Relations at Monash University in Australia. A political economist, his research examines neoliberal governance at domestic, regional, and global levels, and the ways in which civil society actors contribute to and contest policy agendas.

Nathan W. Pino is a professor of Sociology at Texas State University in the United States. His research examines the relationship between globalization, development, crime, and crime control, with a focus on police reform.

www.ingramcontent.com/pod-product-compliance
Lightning Source LLC
Chambersburg PA
CBHW021847300426
44115CB00005B/53